Philosophy in Schools

Edited by
Michael Hand
and
Carrie Winstanley

Continuum Studies in Research in Education

continuum

Continuum International Publishing Group

The Tower Building   80 Maiden Lane
11 York Road   Suite 704
London, SE1 7NX   New York, NY 10038

www.continuumbooks.com

© Michael Hand, Carrie Winstanley and Contributors 2008
This edition published 2009

British Library Cataloguing-in-Publication Data
A catalogue record for this book is available from the British Library.

ISBN: 9781441102652 (paperback)

Library of Congress Cataloging-in-Publication Data
A catalog record for this book is available from the Library of Congress.

Typeset by Newgen Imaging Systems Pvt Ltd, Chennai, India

Contents

Notes on Contributors

Dr Harry Brighouse is Professor of Philosophy and Affiliate Professor of Educational Policy Studies at the University of Wisconsin, Madison.

Dr James Conroy is Professor of Education and Dean of the Faculty of Education at the University of Glasgow.

Dr Robert Fisher is Professor of Education at Brunel University.

Lynn Glueck is Librarian of the Mendota Elementary Library in the Madison Metropolitan School District.

Dr Michael Hand is Reader of Philosophy of Education at the Institute of Education, University of London.

Dr Stephen Law is Senior Lecturer in Philosophy at Heythrop College, University of London, and Editor of the Royal Institute of Philosophy journal *Think*.

Dr Gareth Matthews is Professor of Philosophy at the University of Massachusetts, Amherst.

Dr Karin Murris is Visiting Professor at the University of Wales, Newport and Senior Lecturer in Philosophy of Education at the University of the Witwatersrand, Johannesburg.

Dr Richard Pring is Professor of Education at the University of Oxford.

Dr Harvey Siegel is Professor of Philosophy and Chair of the Department of Philosophy at the University of Miami.

Dr Judith Suissa is Senior Lecturer in Philosophy of Education at the Institute of Education, University of London.

Dr Carrie Winstanley is Principal Lecturer in Education at Roehampton University.

Foreword

A. C. Grayling

Dictionaries correctly, inspiringly, but unhelpfully, define 'philosophy' as 'love of wisdom', but a better definition would be 'reflective and critical enquiry'. Philosophy is of course a subject as well as a process, though a very comprehensive one: its two great questions might be said to be 'What is there?' and 'What matters in what there is?', which jointly and immediately invite the central range of more specific questions about knowledge, truth, reason, value, the mind and more, which constitute the core of the enterprise. Efforts to gain understanding in these matters requires the kind of thought that is distinctively philosophical: questioning, probing, critical, reflective, exacting, restless, accepting that there might be several answers or none, and therefore accepting the open texture of enquiry where there is rarely a simple solution to a problem, and hardly ever closure. Minds experienced in this kind of thinking are generally resistant to the quick fixes of ideology and dogma, and are healthily prone to examine, with a clear and when necessary sceptical eye, everything put before them.

Enquiry of this kind is obviously a highly exportable process; practice in it constitutes what is now called a 'transferable skill'. For this reason alone philosophy ought to be a central and continuous feature of the school curriculum from an early age, because (as some of the discussions in what follows show) it immediately potentiates students' work in other subject areas. There is a view that education should be as much if not more about teaching children how to get and evaluate information than about imparting pre-digested information to them – at least after they have the literacy, numeracy and framework knowledge that provides the necessary basis on which a training in thinking and research can build. Philosophy is par excellence what offers the evaluatory part of this desideratum.

And because philosophy is not only about critical reflection and the construction of good arguments, but also about substantive questions – in morality, in epistemology, in logic, and judicially in relation to the claims, assumptions and methodologies of all other more specific areas of enquiry in the natural and social sciences and humanities – the training in thinking brings with it a rich furnishing of insights and understanding in many fields besides. In a curriculum devoted to acquiring knowledge and technique, there has to be time for reflection on what it all means, what it is for, and why it matters, for almost any 'it', and this too is distinctively the province of philosophy.

I have talked about philosophy at primary schools and sixth forms both, and found exactly what one would antecedently expect: that young minds are naturally philosophical minds. Inviting a class of primary school children to discuss how they can claim to know that there really is a table here before them – that hoary old example – is a thrilling and instructive enterprise. The question seems to them, as indeed it is, a good one; and they are quick to appreciate the force of sceptical defeaters to the standard evidence adduced in favour of the claim, and the countervailing force of the standard evidence itself. This openness and readiness to engage with ideas that adult minds might resist on the grounds of obvious silliness (which often means: unobvious importance) is a fertile thing. In view of this, and of the instant exportability of the methods and insights of philosophy to almost everything else in the curriculum, the case for placing it at the curriculum's heart makes itself.

Students of philosophy gain a possession that enriches them as individuals and social beings for the rest of their lives; Aristotle said 'we educate ourselves so that we can make a noble use of our leisure'. But they gain even more than that, for there is the harsh reality of economics and the world of work to be considered, and here too a philosophical education proves its high worth. Our age is one in which people have to be flexible, adaptable, and well-equipped to meet and handle a constant stream of new ideas, techniques, technologies, complexities and problems. Contemporary economies may still have a use for people trained in a single practical skill, but this is rarer than it was and it is not the way of the future. A training in critical and reflective thought, a training in handling ideas, is of the essence in this new and demanding environment. Philosophy thus provides both for individual development and enrichment, and a bright set of apt intellectual tools for meeting the world's challenges.

This is a claim which the following essays powerfully support, and it is to be hoped that, as a result, this volume will establish beyond question the value of putting philosophy and its rich gift of insights and methods at the centre of schooling for children of all ages.

Introduction

Michael Hand and Carrie Winstanley

Over the last week or so we've been asking you for ideas about what subjects ought to be taught in schools but are not taught. Now, there have been many suggestions: basic conversation skills, that was one of them; how to change a plug; map-reading, could be useful for some; but the overwhelming winner – you may be surprised by this – was philosophy.

(John Humphrys, *Today*, BBC Radio 4, broadcast on 26/08/04)

Is it time to put philosophy in the school curriculum? The contributors to this volume believe it is. We are united in the conviction that exposure to philosophical ideas, questions and methods should be part of the basic educational entitlement of all children. In what follows we set out our reasons for this conviction. We examine and refute some familiar objections to the teaching of philosophy in schools: that it is a peculiarly difficult subject; that children are not cognitively equipped to cope with its distinctive demands; that philosophical thinking inclines children towards moral and religious relativism. And we advance a series of positive arguments for its inclusion in the school curriculum: that a grasp of epistemological principles and problems is part and parcel of what it is to be a critical thinker; that philosophical competence is an important attribute of citizens in democratic polities; that 'philosophical intelligence' is one of the basic intellectual capacities of human beings that schools have a responsibility to nurture; that the study of philosophy is peculiarly conducive to the development of such central virtues as autonomy, authenticity, imagination and wisdom. We address our arguments to teachers and curriculum planners in schools, to theorists, researchers and students in the field of education, and above all to the educational policy-makers and advisers responsible for designing and improving school curricula.

This introduction has two parts. In the first we briefly survey the extent of existing provision for philosophical education in schools. In the second we outline the structure of the book and the central arguments of each chapter.

Existing school philosophy programmes

For the purposes of this survey, we draw a loose distinction between *formal* philosophy programmes, by which we mean those that are part of prescribed national or local curricula or are subject to public examination, and *informal* philosophy programmes, by which we mean those that supplement prescribed curricula and are typically introduced into schools in an ad hoc fashion by individual teachers and headteachers.

Formal programmes

The UK Qualifications and Curriculum Authority (QCA), in conjunction with Eurydice at the National Foundation for Educational Research (NFER), maintains a comparative archive of curriculum and assessment frameworks in 20 more economically developed countries (www.inca.org.uk). The countries are Australia, Canada, England, France, Germany, Hungary, Ireland, Italy, Japan, Korea, the Netherlands, New Zealand, Northern Ireland, Scotland, Singapore, Spain, Sweden, Switzerland, the USA and Wales. At present, none of these countries includes philosophy in its prescribed curricula for the primary and lower secondary phases of schooling. The overwhelming majority of children in Europe, North America and Australasia have no statutory or otherwise established entitlement to encounter philosophy during the period of compulsory schooling.

At the upper secondary level – that is, the post-compulsory phase of schooling – the situation is a little better, particularly in continental Europe. In France, all students following one of the general Baccalaureat programmes study philosophy as a core compulsory subject. Similarly, in Spain, philosophy is a common core subject on each of the four types of Bachillerato course. In Italy, philosophy is studied by all students in both liceo classico and liceo scientifico, and in Hungary by all students following the National Core Curriculum. It is worth noting too that one of the three core units on the well-regarded International Baccalaureate (IB) is Theory of Knowledge, an interdisciplinary course with a strong epistemological focus.

Opportunities to study philosophy at upper secondary level in the English-speaking world are fewer and further between. Only a minority of US and Canadian high schools offer elective classes in philosophy. In Australia there have been recent moves in most states to make optional philosophy courses available to students in their final years of secondary education, but 'implementation is incomplete' and 'the programs are geared toward high academic achievers' (Millett, 2006). In the UK one public examination board now awards an Advanced Level General Certificate of Education in philosophy, but, again, the course is offered by a minority of secondary schools. In 2007 it was completed by 3,011 students nationwide. Another board awards an A Level GCE in critical thinking, which has substantial philosophical content and which in 2007 was completed by 2,009 students.

There are a few countries, outside the 20 in the QCA's comparative archive, that introduce philosophy into the school curriculum earlier than the upper secondary level. In Brazil, for example, philosophy is a compulsory curriculum subject in many secondary schools and some primary schools. In Turkey, all secondary school pupils follow a course in philosophy, history, religion and ethics. And in Norway a 2004 White Paper mooting the possibility of philosophy as a statutory school subject has led to philosophy lessons being trialled in primary and secondary schools across the country. These developments are promising, but at present they represent the exception rather than the rule.

Informal programmes

Fortunately, the range of subjects and activities children encounter in school is not restricted to (though it is heavily dominated by) the content of prescribed curricula and public examination syllabuses. Thanks in large part to the commitment, industry and effective international networking of key players in the Philosophy for Children (P4C) movement over the last forty years, philosophy is currently offered as a supplementary or extra-curricular activity in a remarkable number of schools around the world.

The father of the P4C movement is the philosopher Matthew Lipman, who, dismayed at the poor thinking of his undergraduate students, began in the late 1960s to write books designed to introduce philosophy to children and teenagers. In 1974 he established the Institute for the Advancement of Philosophy for Children (IAPC) at Montclair State University, to train teachers and develop resources and strategies for teaching philosophy in schools. The distinguishing features of the model of philosophical education advocated by the IAPC are (i) the use of philosophical stories as stimuli to philosophical discussion and (ii) the 'community of inquiry' pedagogy, which gives pupils responsibility for setting the agenda for discussion and casts the teacher in the role of facilitator rather than instructor.

Today the IAPC reports formal affiliations with some 75 P4C centres across the US and in 45 countries around the world (ICPIC, 2006a). It continues to play a key role in coordinating and sustaining the international P4C movement, but now shares this task with the International Council of Philosophical Inquiry with Children (ICPIC) and the European Foundation for the Advancement of Doing Philosophy with Children (SOPHIA). With the expansion of P4C has come some diversification of approach: distinctions are sometimes drawn between P4C proper and, for example, Philosophy with Children (PwC), or the Community of Philosophical Inquiry method (CoPI) (for a recent discussion of some of these distinctions, see McCall, 2007). However, P4C is still widely used as an umbrella term for these approaches, a practice justified by the notable similarities between them, their shared ancestry in the pioneering work of Matthew Lipman, and the willingness of their respective advocates to make common cause in the quest to bring philosophy to children.

The recent global surge of interest in the development of children's 'thinking skills' has brought P4C to a new level of public and professional awareness in a number of countries. In England, for example, the National Curriculum now explicitly includes a requirement to develop pupils' thinking skills, identified as 'information-processing skills', 'reasoning skills', 'enquiry skills', 'creative thinking skills' and 'evaluation skills' (DfES, 2004, pp. 22–3). The Department for Children, Schools and Families (DCSF) suggests that 'philosophical approaches' are one way of meeting this requirement and recommends a range of P4C resources and introductory texts (www.standards.dfes.gov.uk/thinkingskills).

It is difficult to find reliable figures on just how many schools are currently offering P4C programmes to pupils. Roger Sutcliffe estimates that some 2,000 primary schools and 200 secondary schools in England, Wales and Northern Ireland now have connections with P4C (ICPIC, 2006a), while Catherine McCall reports that 10,000 children are presently involved in P4C projects in Scotland (http://sophia.eu.org). In Austria, more than 4,000 teachers have received some training in P4C over the last 20 years, and Bulgaria has around 200 certified P4C teachers (ICPIC, 2006b). In Spain, it is thought that over 200 teachers and 10,000 children are engaged in P4C in schools (ICPIC, 2006a). Latin America has long been the part of the world with the most vigorous levels of P4C activity. In 1997, Matthew Lipman reported to the American Philosophical Association that 100,000 children a year were encountering P4C in Brazilian schools (Lipman, 1997), and Walter Kohan confirms that the Brazilian Centre for Philosophy for Children has trained thousands of teachers across the country (ICPIC, 2006a). In one state in Mexico, more than 400 schools have been teaching P4C continually for over 10 years (ICPIC, 2006a).

This is an impressive record, and is indicative of both a thirst for and an ability to cope with philosophical inquiry in schools. But it remains a drop in the ocean. Few schools, comparatively speaking, offer P4C at all, and among those that do there is huge variation in both frequency of sessions and numbers of pupils involved. Precisely because of its supplementary or extra-curricular status, P4C in schools tends to be under-resourced and a low priority for continuing professional development, to be the first casualty of curriculum overcrowding, and to be precariously dependent on the passion and commitment of one or two members of staff. If the educational benefits of philosophy are as significant as the contributors to this volume believe, it is not enough to rest content with the achievements of the P4C movement, formidable though they are: philosophy should be part of the educational entitlement of all children, and this requires its inclusion in prescribed school curricula.

Outline of the book

The contributors to the book are philosophers of education, mainstream philosophers with an interest in education and philosophy educators. The remit we set ourselves was to develop a series of robust philosophical arguments for the inclusion of philosophy in the school curriculum, paying attention to both the possibility and the desirability of teaching philosophy to children.

We do not speak with one voice. We disagree, in various ways, on what exactly philosophy is, on how it is best taught or facilitated in the classroom, and on the age at which children or young people should first encounter it. But we are all firmly committed to the view that philosophy should, in some form and for some portion of compulsory schooling, be part of the curriculum.

The book is divided into two parts, though there is a degree of arbitrariness in the distribution of chapters between them. The first part comprises those chapters we (as editors) consider to be primarily concerned with *meeting objections* to the teaching of philosophy in schools; the second those chapters we judge to be principally focused on *advancing positive arguments* for the inclusion of philosophy in the school curriculum. In fact many of the chapters address both concerns, and in some cases it was not easy to decide which was dominant. But we think the distinction is sufficiently instructive, and sufficiently reflected in the arguments of each chapter, to justify the element of arbitrariness.

Part I: Meeting the objections to philosophy in schools

The first three chapters focus on the familiar objection that philosophy is somehow too difficult for children and young people, that they are not cognitively equipped to cope with its distinctive methods or characteristic subject-matter. Michael Hand tries to show that philosophy does not make significantly greater cognitive demands on learners than other subjects routinely found on primary school curricula. He begins by identifying and challenging three misconceptions about philosophy – the 'no right answers', 'no progress' and 'canonical study' views – which he thinks may underpin the perception that philosophy is a peculiarly difficult subject. He then sets out a positive account of what philosophy is, loosely defining it as 'the study of concepts and conceptual schemes', the discipline that has for its subject-matter 'not the world itself but the concepts we use to make sense of it'. Hand recognizes that the methods by which philosophers conduct their conceptual investigations are many and varied, but argues that there is one well-established method – conceptual analysis – which is both central to the mainstream practice of philosophy and capable of being understood and applied by children. The chapter concludes with some examples of conceptual questions relevant to the lives and interests of children and suitable for investigation in the primary classroom.

Richard Pring is similarly concerned to show that philosophy is not as inaccessible as it is reputed to be, arguing that 'philosophy begins when one is systematically puzzled about what is meant by what is said'. Drawing on his experience of discussing moral dilemmas with secondary school pupils, he shows that young people are capable not only of clarifying and mapping contested moral concepts, but also of tracing different interpretations of moral concepts to their source in deeper disagreements about the nature of moral truth and justification. Such thinking, he says, is 'at least embryonically philosophical'. Pring goes on to suggest that Lawrence Kohlberg encountered (and stimulated) just this kind of embryonic philosophizing in children and young people in his extensive empirical research on moral reasoning.

Gareth Matthews locates the source of scepticism about whether children can cope with philosophy in Piagetian developmental psychology, according to which the concepts wielded by children are primitive and deficient, so presumably offer a poor return on the investment of philosophical effort. He claims that his own experiences of doing philosophy with children, over a period of some 25 years, have repeatedly falsified Piaget's 'deficit conception of childhood' and shown that children 'make comments, ask questions and engage in reasoning that professional philosophers can recognize as philosophical'. He proceeds to support this claim with accounts of recent philosophical inquiries with primary school children in the US and China on the demanding topics of time and happiness. Matthews concludes that we should replace the deficit conception of childhood with a 'mirror-image conception', which recognizes that children not only lack abilities adults typically possess, but also possess abilities adults typically lack, not the least of which is a lively interest in philosophical questions.

Stephen Law aims to refute two popular objections to the enterprise of teaching philosophy in schools. Both objections assume, correctly, that teaching philosophy involves encouraging children to think critically and independently about moral and religious questions. The first objection is that 'to encourage a thinking, questioning attitude on these topics is to promote relativism'; the second is that 'parents have a right to send their child to a school where their religious beliefs will not be subjected to critical scrutiny'. In response to the first objection, Law argues that critical thinking presupposes an interest in the truth and is thus antipathetic to relativism, that there are compelling rational arguments for the falsity of relativism, and that relativism is rooted in a retreat from, not an excess of, critical reasoning. His challenge to the second objection is to ask those who advance it whether they also favour the establishment of party political schools in which children are educated for uncritical acceptance of particular political creeds. Law goes on, in the second half of the chapter, to show that objections of these kinds to teaching philosophy in schools neglect or ignore the crucial distinction between 'educating within the logical space of reasons' and 'educating via the purely causal route'.

Part II: Making the case for philosophy in schools

Harry Brighouse focuses on the role of philosophical thinking in understanding, and forming reasoned opinions on, the sort of controversial issues that are now widely addressed in programmes of political, civic or citizenship education. He welcomes the recent surge of interest in citizenship education and the teaching of controversial issues: in democratic polities, responsibility for political decisions is shared by all citizens, so it is important that all citizens learn 'to deliberate in a more impartial and well-informed manner about issues at stake in public life'. And since these issues are fundamentally moral in character, deliberating well about them requires a facility with the methods of moral philosophy. The most useful of these, he thinks, is 'the method of reflective equilibrium', whereby we move back and forth between our moral principles and our judgements about particular cases, modifying each in the light of the other and thus ironing out contradictions and inconsistencies. This does not guarantee that we will get things right, but it entitles us to have 'increasing confidence in the truth of the outcomes'. Brighouse describes some of the moral philosophical categories and principles needed to think intelligently about controversial issues, and illustrates their application in assessing arguments for and against abortion and 'designer babies'.

Harvey Siegel declares himself sympathetic to general arguments for teaching young people philosophy per se, but focuses in his chapter on some specific reasons for initiating them into the sub-discipline of epistemology. He advances five such reasons: (i) fundamental epistemological questions about knowledge, truth and rationality are matters of basic interest to many young people; (ii) a grasp of epistemological principles is necessary for an understanding of what it is to think critically; (iii) a grasp of epistemological principles is necessary for an understanding of why it is desirable to think critically; (iv) critical thinkers ought to be aware of the contentious epistemological positions to which they are committed; and (v) to educate young people without teaching them some epistemology would constitute a failure to respect them as persons.

Like Siegel, Carrie Winstanley is interested in the relationship between philosophy and critical thinking. She develops two arguments for the view that 'philosophy might plausibly be thought to develop children's critical thinking more effectively than the traditional subjects of the school curriculum'. The first is that critical thinking stands in a peculiarly intimate relationship to the discipline of philosophy. While all subjects involve the application of critical thinking, only philosophy has 'the idea of what it is to think critically as one of its central foci'. The second argument is that, because philosophy is 'not dependent on a substantial empirical knowledge-base', class discussions are rarely derailed by ignorance of pertinent facts or closed down by their introduction. Because philosophical questions cannot be settled by appeal to a body of empirical knowledge, they focus attention more sharply than questions of other kinds on the coherence of arguments and the relevance of reasons – that is, on the quality of critical thinking.

Robert Fisher defends the existence of a basic capacity of mind or form of intelligence that he terms 'Philosophical Intelligence' (PI). He argues that schools have a responsibility to develop children's PI and that the ideal pedagogy for discharging this responsibility is philosophical dialogue in communities of enquiry. PI is an alternative designation for Howard Gardner's Existential Intelligence (EI), defined as the 'proclivity to pose and ponder questions about life, death and ultimate realities', and represents an improvement on EI because it 'ties Gardner's eighth intelligence to a long and well-defined academic tradition, to a rich literature and established procedures of enquiry'. To claim that PI is a basic human capacity is not to hold that young children can read and understand 'the great books of philosophy', or to deny that philosophizing comes more easily to some than to others; but it is to maintain that all children are capable of 'discursive or dialogic engagement with conceptual problems and questions of existential concern'. Fisher draws on his own empirical research to show how such engagement is facilitated by the community of enquiry approach to philosophical education.

Karin Murris argues that a particular approach to philosophy in schools – an approach she terms 'philosophy with picturebooks' – can transform power relationships in the classroom and create space for children to think autonomously and authentically. She regrets the current reliance of educational practice on 'the certainty of right and wrong answers', on 'adults' psychological need to be in control', and on 'the game of guess-the-answer-in-the-teacher's-head', pathologies which combine to disempower and alienate children in schools. Philosophy with picturebooks invites children to determine not only how questions are tackled but also what questions are asked: the picturebooks used as starting points for enquiry are chosen precisely for their eschewal of 'didactic purposes', for their 'multiple narratives, ambiguity and contradictions'. Murris draws on her work in schools with the picturebook *Frog in Love* to illustrate the authentic, unpredictable and conceptually demanding lines of enquiry philosophy with picturebooks can generate.

In their co-authored chapter, Lynn Glueck and Harry Brighouse build a case for philosophy in schools on the unavoidability of philosophical themes in children's literature. They argue that philosophical ideas and questions are prominent features of books beloved of children throughout the English-speaking world, and that to ignore or refuse to discuss these ideas and questions would be to 'staunch the intellectual curiosity of those to whom we read'. The point is illustrated with reference to the children's classics *Where the Wild Things Are, Charlotte's Web, Alice's Adventures in Wonderland* and *The Wizard of Oz*. Glueck and Brighouse also address some of the objections to philosophy in schools. Like Gareth Matthews, they see worries about children's capacity to cope with philosophy as having their roots in Piaget's stage development theory, and they draw on Matthews' previous work to show that such worries are unfounded. They have more sympathy with the objection that teaching children philosophy might do a certain kind of harm, acknowledging that activities 'not well-modelled in public life' are liable to be taught 'in ways that are either off-putting or deeply misleading for children'. But this, they urge, is a reason for thinking carefully about teacher education in this area, not for giving up on the idea.

Judith Suissa concentrates on secondary education and argues that philosophy is the only form of inquiry capable of answering to the preoccupation of adolescents 'with questions of meaning, with the struggle to see the 'big picture', and with 'why' questions about every aspect of life'. The kind of philosophy adolescents need, she thinks, is a Deweyan, pragmatist philosophy, concerned more with 'meaning' than with 'truth' and construed as 'an intelligent, critical response to questions of meaning thrown up by human and cultural experience'. Suissa is critical of school philosophy programmes that have as their principal focus either the development of general, transferable thinking skills or the examination of abstract and abstruse philosophical questions: neither kind of programme offers young people much assistance in grappling with the questions of meaning and purpose that press upon them. Philosophy should rather play a 'meta-meaning-seeking role' in the school curriculum, offering a space for reflection on the sort of questions that lie beneath and between school subjects and activities, questions about their point and place in human life and about the connections and distinctions between them.

Finally, James Conroy's case for teaching philosophy in schools rests on the obligation of educators to nurture in young people the qualities of wisdom and discernment. He argues that 'the cultivation of wisdom is a central aim of education', and that this is best achieved by initiating children into 'the rich heritage of great philosophical and literary works'. Such works are important not because they offer a range of 'possible vocabularies and cultural determinations of human being', in relation to which pupils can construct and individuate themselves, but rather because they embody genuine insights into the human condition. They tell us something about our nature, status, possibilities and responsibilities as persons. Conroy is sharply critical of approaches to philosophy teaching that focus merely on 'exercises in thought' and the development of 'metacognitive processes', which he sees as symptomatic of a contemporary obsession with the false gods of relevance and competence. If the justification for philosophical education lies in its power to cultivate wisdom, he insists, it must be concerned first and foremost with 'reading real books' and enabling children to 'begin the process of assessing their own reflections against those of the tradition'.

Part One

Meeting the Objections to Philosophy in Schools

Chapter One

Can Children be Taught Philosophy?

Michael Hand

In this chapter I shall defend the claim that children can be taught philosophy. I shall not defend the stronger claim that they *should* be so taught. To make the latter case, it would be necessary to show that philosophical inquiry is not only *possible* for children, but also confers on them some significant educational benefit. I think it does, but the task of articulating this benefit I leave in the capable hands of other contributors to the present volume. Nevertheless, to the extent that 'ought' implies 'can', the argument I shall present for the possibility of teaching philosophy to children may be construed as the first step towards a justification for doing so.

Opponents of the claim that children can be taught philosophy maintain that the subject is simply too difficult for them. Children are not cognitively equipped to cope with the distinctive methods or characteristic subject matter of philosophical inquiry. The problem with this position is not so much that it underestimates the cognitive abilities of children as that it overestimates the cognitive demands of philosophy. My strategy will be to show that philosophy does not make significantly greater cognitive demands on learners than other forms of inquiry routinely found on primary school curricula. To show this I will need to make a fairly close examination of the nature of philosophical inquiry.

As a prelude to my central argument, however, I should like to give brief consideration to the curious but currently fashionable idea that children are philosophers *by nature*, and therefore do not need to be *taught* philosophy but merely given periodic opportunities to engage in it.

Are children natural philosophers?

There is something of an irony in the fact that the most vocal advocates of primary school philosophy programmes are united behind the supposition that children are natural philosophers. For it is a supposition that renders such programmes more or less superfluous. If it is true that children have an innate or naturally acquired ability to ask and answer philosophical questions, there is plainly little need for philosophy lessons in school. All schools can offer such

naturally equipped children is a supervised environment in which to exercise
their philosophical skills; and one may well doubt that this is the most effective
use of either teachers' pedagogical expertise or children's time in school.

What are the grounds for the claim that children are philosophers by nature?
The evidence advanced by its supporters consists almost entirely of instances of
children spontaneously raising philosophical questions. Gareth Matthews, for
example, devotes much of his book *Philosophy and the Young Child* (1980) to
reporting and discussing such instances. Some of his examples are as follows:

> TIM (about six years), while busily engaged in licking a pot, asked, 'Papa,
> how can we be sure that everything is not a dream?' (p. 1)

> DAVID worries about whether an apple is alive. He decides that it is when it's
> on the ground but not when it has been brought into the house. (p. 6)

> JOHN (six years), reflecting on the fact that in addition to books, toys and
> clothes he has two arms, two legs and a head, and that these are *his* toys, *his*
> arms, *his* head and so on, asked, 'Which part of me is really me?' (p. 86)

It is certainly true that children sometimes ask such questions as these. What
seems less certain is that this fact warrants the inference that children have
natural philosophical ability.

In his forthright critique of the idea that 'the impulse to philosophise begins
in early childhood', John White contends that, in the mouths of children, questions
of the kind reported by Matthews are not *philosophical* questions at all (White,
1992). What makes a question philosophical, he argues, is not only its verbal
form but also the intention with which it is asked. And we have no reason to
suppose that Tim is driven by 'doubts of a categorial sort about the distinction
between appearance and reality' (p. 75), or that David is exercised by 'the possibility of survival after death or the ethics of abortion' (p. 76). It is more likely,
White thinks, that when children ask questions of this sort they are simply trying
to learn the correct use of English words:

> We all know that when children are learning new concepts they are often at
> first uncertain how they are to be applied. But the remarks they make and the
> questions they ask to reduce this uncertainty must be distinguished from phi-
> losophers' comments. Once again, different intentions are at work. Children
> want to know how to use the concept; philosophers, who have no trouble
> using it, are interested in mapping it from a higher-order perspective, and
> usually in the pursuit of larger theoretical inquiries. (White, 1992, p. 75)

David just wants to know whether it is good English to say of plucked apples that
they are alive; the philosopher, on the other hand, is assembling reminders
about ordinary usage with a view to mapping conceptual terrain or solving logical

problems. What appear to be philosophical questions raised by children, then, are really no more than requests for assistance in the process of language acquisition.

White's argument here is not entirely persuasive. While it is plausible to suppose that David genuinely does not know whether to describe plucked apples as alive or dead, it is rather less plausible to suppose that Tim is unsure how to use the word 'dream', or that John has difficulty with first person singular pronouns. By far the most natural explanation for the verbal behaviour exhibited by Tim and John is that they have stumbled across genuine philosophical problems. The anecdotal evidence amassed by Matthews and others *does* seem to show that children spontaneously raise philosophical questions: there is an undue scepticism in White's attempt to deny this.

But the claim with which we are here concerned is that children are philosophers by nature. And there is plainly more to being a philosopher than raising philosophical questions. Asking how we can be sure that everything is not a dream no more constitutes 'doing philosophy' than asking how far it is to the moon constitutes 'doing astronomy'. Children are continually asking questions about the past, about how things work, about right and wrong; but we do not say, on the strength of this, that they are natural historians, scientists and ethicists. To be competent in a form of inquiry is not just a matter of asking questions of a particular kind: it is a matter of *answering* questions of a particular kind *by means of appropriate methods of investigation*. And while all manner of questions come naturally to the minds of children, the methods of investigation required to answer them typically do not.

This is perhaps especially true in the domain of philosophy. A characteristic feature of philosophical questions is their intractability to those unfamiliar with the techniques of philosophical inquiry. It is easy enough to *ask* how we can be sure that everything is not a dream, or which parts of our bodies constitute ourselves, but not at all easy to see how these questions can be satisfactorily answered. The problem is not that the evidence required to settle them is particularly hard to come by, or collectable only with the aid of specialist equipment, but rather that gathering evidence does not seem to help here: the questions remain even when all the facts are known. In the absence of philosophical training, the natural response to such questions is to dismiss them as unanswerable.

If Matthews succeeds in showing that children naturally raise philosophical questions, his suggestion that they are able to make genuine progress with these questions is rather less well supported by the evidence. He reports that, after a few more licks of his pot, Tim decides that everything cannot be a dream because 'in a dream people wouldn't go around asking if it was a dream' (p. 23). This, according to Matthews, is 'a fine example of philosophical reasoning in a young child' (p. 27). But what exactly is philosophical about Tim's line of reasoning? His solution exhibits none of the careful attention to the concepts of dreaming, sleeping and being awake we should expect from a philosophical approach to the problem. On the contrary, it looks as though Tim has simply noticed that he has not yet had a dream in which people have asked whether they are dreaming, and falsely inferred that this question is never asked in dreams. A patently unjustified inductive inference hardly constitutes 'a fine example of philosophical reasoning'.

In my judgement, then, the claim that children are philosophers by nature must be rejected. Children may stumble now and again across questions of the sort that attract the attention of philosophers, but they are no more naturally able to find their way into those questions than philosophically untrained adults.

I turn now to my central task: that of showing that children can be taught to do philosophy. While philosophical inquiry does not come so naturally to children that it need not be taught, nor does it require so radical an extension of their thinking that it cannot be. The burden of my argument, it will be recalled, is that philosophy does not make significantly greater cognitive demands on learners than other disciplines commonly found on primary school curricula. In what follows I begin by examining some popular misconceptions about philosophy which may underpin the widely held view that it is a peculiarly difficult subject. I then set out a positive account of what philosophy is and how it is conducted. I conclude with some examples of the sort of philosophical questions which seem to me to be suitable for investigation in the primary school classroom.

Three misconceptions about philosophy

The first misconception I should like to consider is the 'no right answers' view of philosophy. According to this view, a philosophical question is, either characteristically or by definition, a question to which there is no right answer. And questions to which there are no right answers look to be about as difficult as questions get. If I believe that philosophical questions are unanswerable I shall probably be inclined to think that asking children to grapple with those questions not only places unreasonably heavy cognitive demands on them, but also lacks any discernible point.

Even more ironic than their support for the idea that children are philosophers by nature, then, is the support found among advocates of primary school philosophy programmes for the 'no right answers' view. Sara Stanley and Steve Bowkett, in their guide to developing philosophical thinking in the primary classroom, put the following words into the mouth of a character called Philosophy Bear: 'I am always thinking about questions such as: Why do I exist? What made the world? Why do people love each other or hate each other? The great thing about this sort of thinking is that I can never be wrong, because these sorts of questions have no right or wrong answers' (Stanley and Bowkett, 2004, p. 79). And Mandy Hextall, who teaches philosophy to four- and five-year-olds in Leicester, writes: 'It doesn't matter if they haven't got the correct letter formation or can't count up to ten because in philosophy there are no right or wrong answers' (Hextall, 2006, p. 8).

The problem with the 'no right answers' view is not just that it is false, nor just that it renders philosophical inquiry futile, although both of these things are true. It is, more basically, that the view is logically incoherent: it simply does not make sense to talk about questions with no right answers. The view implies that answerability is a contingent feature of questions, as if wondering whether a question has an answer were analogous to wondering whether a story has a moral or a song has a chorus. But in fact it is *necessarily* true that questions are answerable, in the same way (and for the same reason) as it is necessarily true that propositions are verifiable or falsifiable. An indicative sentence only succeeds in expressing a proposition if there is some way of determining whether that proposition is true or false; and an interrogative sentence only succeeds in expressing a question if there is a class of possible answers to that question and some way of determining which of those possible answers is the right one.

This point is usefully elaborated by Renford Bambrough in his book *Reason, Truth and God* (1969). With a view to demonstrating the incoherence of certain theological treatments of questions like 'Does God exist?', Bambrough spells out 'the logical relations between what might be called the epistemic concepts' (p. 47), a category which includes such concepts as 'question, proposition, contradiction, truth and falsehood, reason and knowledge' (p. 49). To grasp the relations between these concepts, he argues, is to grasp that 'not only all theological questions, but all questions whatsoever, have right answers' (p. 50):

> Wherever there is a question there must clearly be the possibility of judgements and propositions which are possible answers to that question. Nothing can be an intelligible question at all unless it is possible to say of some judgements and propositions that they are answers to it . . . A question may be understood as an invitation from the questioner to the auditor to say of a number of propositions, any one of which would be a possible, a *relevant* answer to the question, which are true and which are false . . . To understand a question is to have some idea of what would count as an answer to it, and some idea of the steps by which it could be established for any given answer whether that answer is or is not a correct answer to it. (Bambrough, 1969, pp. 47–49)

To insist that all questions are answerable is not to deny that philosophers have long taken an interest in indicative and interrogative sentences that *appear* to express propositions and questions, but in fact fail to do so, or do so in systematically misleading ways. The exposure of meaningless or incoherent 'questions' is an important and respectable philosophical task, as is the rewriting of questions whose grammatical and logical forms are incongruent. But work of this kind gives no succour to the 'no right answers' view of philosophy. Even if we were to allow (which, strictly speaking, we should not) that nonsensical interrogative sentences might be described as 'questions with no right answers', the crucial point is that *analysing* such 'questions' is not the same as *asking* them.

When a philosopher examines the meaningfulness of an interrogative sentence Q, the question she is asking is not the one putatively expressed by Q, but the one expressed by the sentence 'Is Q meaningful?'. And *this* question always makes sense, so always has a right answer.

A second misconception is the 'no progress' view of philosophy, according to which philosophers have failed to make progress on questions with which they have been grappling for hundreds, if not thousands, of years. This view is sometimes allied with the 'no right answers' view: if philosophical questions are unanswerable it is only to be expected that philosophers will have been frustrated in their efforts to answer them. But the two views need not go together. One may recognize that philosophical questions must in principle be answerable, yet still doubt that philosophers have, in practice, been able to make much headway with them. And if philosophy is too difficult for philosophers themselves, it is fairly obviously too difficult for children in primary schools.

One philosopher who has put some energy into correcting this misconception is Antony Flew. At the outset of his *Introduction to Western Philosophy* (1989), Flew tackles head on the question of what counts as progress in philosophy (pp. 18–34). As an example of a philosophical question upon which progress has been made, he takes a question raised in Plato's *Euthyphro*: 'What is holiness?', or, more precisely, 'Is the holy loved by the gods because it is holy, or is it holy because it is loved?'. The question is an important one (for theists, at least) because it bears directly on the praiseworthiness of the gods. It makes sense to say that we praise the gods because they love what is holy if, and only if, loving what is holy constitutes a significant moral achievement. But if holiness is *defined* as that which is loved by the gods, loving what is holy is scarcely a moral achievement for the gods, and therefore scarcely something by virtue of which they can be deemed praiseworthy.

In what sense does Flew want to say that philosophical progress has been made on this question? Precisely in the sense of establishing that one cannot consistently hold *both* that things are holy because loved by the gods *and* that the justification for praising the gods lies in their loving what is holy. Flew puts it thus:

> . . . it is the sort of point which, once well and truly made and developed, cannot properly be ignored. No one with any pretensions to philosophical competence now has any business in any of the areas to which it is relevant to argue without recognizing this kind of challenge, and trying to come to terms with it . . . Leibniz, as we have seen, was scandalised at any suggestion of an answer other than that God approves of what is good for the reason that it is good. Hobbes, on the other hand, unflinchingly accepts the implications of the opposite position. What they have in common is that both see that the challenge first put by Socrates in the *Euthyphro* is relevant, where it is, and both see that the opposite answers carry the implications which they do carry. (Flew, 1989, p. 33)

Note here that philosophical progress does *not* consist in showing that particular words (for example, 'holiness') must or must not be used to mark particular concepts (for example, being loved by the gods). The relationship between words and the concepts they mark is a purely conventional one and we are at liberty to change or ignore these conventions as we please (though we risk making it difficult for others to understand us when we do). Rather, progress consists in tracing the logical implications of possible uses. *If* we use the word 'holiness' to mark the concept of being loved by the gods, it follows that one important kind of justification for religious devotion is no longer open to us. To take another example, moral philosophical work on what it means to be good has certainly not shown that the word 'good' must be used in such-and-such a way; but it has identified a range of uses to which people may be putting the word in the context of their moral utterances, and spelled out in some detail the implications of each. Once the kind of progress philosophers seek to make is properly understood, doubts about the fruitfulness of their inquiries quickly evaporate.

A third misconception contributing to philosophy's reputation as a difficult subject is the 'canonical study' view of philosophy. On this view, regrettably reinforced by the structure of many undergraduate philosophy programmes, doing philosophy consists in studying a canon of revered philosophical texts. Philosophers are people who fill their days reading, thinking about and arguing with Plato's *Republic*, Aristotle's *Ethics*, Kant's *Critique* and Wittgenstein's *Tractatus*.

Notwithstanding the laudable efforts of Jostein Gaarder (1995) and his ilk to make the philosophical canon accessible to teenagers, it is clear enough that landmark philosophical texts do not belong in the reading corners of primary classrooms. The writings of Hume, Hegel, Russell and Rawls are manifestly too sophisticated, too technical, and presuppose too much prior knowledge and reflection, to be understood by young children. So those tempted by the 'canonical study' view will naturally be suspicious of calls for philosophy to be taught in primary schools.

But the falsity of this view of philosophy is easily demonstrated. For it carries the absurd implication that most of the texts in the philosophical canon fail to qualify as works of philosophy, since they are not themselves studies or critiques of canonical texts. And this makes it impossible to give an intelligible answer to the question of why philosophers study these texts rather than others. The truth, of course, is that philosophers study these texts rather than others because they *are* works of philosophy, and because these are the texts most likely to furnish them with useful ideas, promising lines of argument and models of good practice for their own philosophical endeavours. Studying the philosophical canon, in other words, is an invaluable aid to and resource for philosophical inquiry, but it is not philosophical inquiry itself.

Canonical study is, to be sure, a tried and tested method of teaching philosophy; but it is not the only method, and probably not the best one for philosophical beginners, even beginners of more advanced years. Another method is to initiate learners directly into the practice of philosophy by confronting them with philosophical questions and equipping them with the tools and techniques needed to answer them. We may develop for philosophy the kinds of hands-on, process-based pedagogical programmes we have developed for such disciplines as history and science, programmes focused on engaging learners in inquiries of their own rather than acquainting them with the outcomes of inquiries conducted by others. We are no more obliged to teach philosophy through great philosophical works than to teach history through classic historical studies, or science through groundbreaking scientific papers.

I conclude that the 'no right answers', 'no progress' and 'canonical study' views of philosophy are serious misconceptions and afford no basis for the idea that philosophy is a peculiarly difficult subject. So much, then, for what philosophy is not: let us now address directly the question of what it is.

What philosophy is

Rumours of the difficulty of saying what philosophy is have been much exaggerated. It is true that philosophy, like other disciplines, is resistant to easy definition. But, as with other disciplines, there are true and illuminating things we can say about its central concerns and procedures. Here is what the Oxford and Penguin *Dictionaries of Philosophy* have to say on the matter:

> In philosophy, the concepts with which we approach the world themselves become the topic of inquiry. A philosophy of a discipline such as history, physics, or law seeks not so much to solve historical, physical, or legal questions, as to study the concepts that structure such thinking, and to lay bare their foundations and presuppositions. (Blackburn, 2005, p. 276)

> . . . philosophical inquiry is a second-order inquiry which has for its subject-matter the concepts, theories and presuppositions present in various disciplines and in everyday life. (Mautner, 2005, p. 466)

Philosophy, then, may be loosely but fairly described as the study of concepts and conceptual schemes. Philosophers have traditionally paid particular attention to 'the most fundamental or general concepts and principles involved in thought, action and reality' (Mautner, 2005, p. 466), and to the conceptual schemes constitutive of major social practices and disciplines. But they have also investigated concepts that do not sit comfortably in either of these categories: one thinks, for example, of J. L. Austin's painstaking inquiries into the use of such adverbs as 'deliberately', 'voluntarily', 'carelessly' and 'inadvertently' (Austin, 1956), or of Gilbert Ryle's clarification of the differences between capacities, liabilities, tendencies and habits (Ryle, 1949, pp. 121–130). So while it is true that philosophers are more interested in some concepts than others, it is unhelpful to impose restrictions on the range of concepts that fall within their purview, and unwise to suppose that there are any concepts about which they can have nothing useful to say.

Because the subject-matter of philosophy is not the world itself but the concepts we use to make sense of it, it is sometimes characterized as *second-order inquiry*, or (more crudely) as *talk about talk*. R. S. Peters puts it thus:

> The distinctive feature of philosophical inquiries, which accounts for the spectatorial role of the philosopher, is their second-order character, their concern with forms of thought and argument expressed in Socrates' questions, 'What do you mean?' and 'How do you know?', and Kant's questions about what is presupposed in our forms of thought and awareness. In asking such questions about concepts and about the grounds of knowledge, philosophers ponder upon and probe into manifold activities and forms of thought in which they and others already engage. (Peters, 1966, p. 60)

Philosophy is certainly, in this sense, a second-order form of inquiry; but the description is one that is apt to be misunderstood. One misunderstanding takes the description to imply that philosophical inquiries are conducted on a higher intellectual plane than inquiries of other kinds, or require the adoption of a peculiarly sophisticated cognitive perspective. Something like this view seems to be implicit in John White's claim that 'starting them young' is an unpromising strategy for improving the philosophical thinking of undergraduates because of 'the higher-order nature of philosophy' (White, 1992, p. 88). White does not explain what he means by 'higher-order' here, but if, as seems likely, he is adverting to philosophy's second-order character, he has supplied no reason at all for thinking that it might be difficult to 'start them young'. Another misunderstanding is the supposition that philosophy, as second-order inquiry, is predicated on mastery of one or more first-order forms of inquiry. It is true that we must know something about the world before we can start to ask questions about the concepts with which we approach it, but everyday, commonsense knowledge is quite sufficient for this. There is no need for the kinds of specialist knowledge and expertise furnished by other disciplines. Advanced study of mammals, mountains or metaphors is not a precondition of fruitful inquiry into the meanings of the words 'mammal', 'mountain' and 'metaphor'. To recognize the second-order character of philosophy, then, is just to observe that the objects of philosophical investigation are concepts rather than things; it is not to suggest that philosophy requires either a change in cognitive gear or extensive knowledge in other areas.

The reasons philosophers have for studying concepts and conceptual schemes may be thought of as lying on a spectrum. At one pole is the idea, perhaps particularly associated with the later Wittgenstein, that the aim of studying conceptual schemes is simply to get clear about them, to produce 'perspicuous representations' of 'the actual use of language' by 'assembling reminders' and 'arranging what we have always known' (Wittgenstein, 1953, Sections 109, 122, 124, 127). It is to 'bring words back from their metaphysical to their everyday use', and thus to dispel the confusion that results from understanding 'running its head up against the limits of language' (Sections 115, 119). On this view, philosophy 'leaves everything as it is' (Section 124). A similarly conservative rationale for philosophical inquiry underpins P. F. Strawson's efforts to 'describe the actual structure of our thought about the world' (Strawson, 1959, p. 9). A crucial feature of this structure, Strawson argues, is that it comprises 'categories and concepts which, in their most fundamental character, change not at all', which are both 'the commonplaces of the least refined thinking' and 'the indispensable core of the conceptual equipment of the most sophisticated human beings' (Strawson, 1959, p. 10). At the other pole of the spectrum is the idea that most or many of our concepts and conceptual schemes are bound up with erroneous 'folk theories' about the world, and that philosophy, far from leaving things as they are, has the radical aim of dismantling and rebuilding conceptual schemes to better fit and facilitate our developing scientific understanding of reality. So Paul Churchland tries to show that there is 'something theory-like' about 'the prescientific, commonsense conceptual framework that all normally socialised humans deploy in order to comprehend, predict, explain, and manipulate the behaviour of humans and the higher animals' (Churchland, 1996, p. 3), that the theory in question is false, and that recent developments in computational neuroscience hold out the possibility of a better one. In between these two poles lie a range of intermediate views according to which philosophers are in the business of neither pure description nor wholesale reconstruction, but of making ad hoc improvements and adjustments to conceptual schemes as and when they are needed. Mary Midgley articulates such an intermediate view with the help of a nice analogy between philosophy and plumbing:

> Plumbing and philosophy are both activities that arise because elaborate cultures like ours have, beneath their surface, a fairly complex system which is usually unnoticed, but which sometimes goes wrong. In both cases, this can have serious consequences. Each system supplies vital needs for those who live above it . . . When trouble arises, specialized skill is needed if there is to be any hope of locating it and putting it right. (Midgley, 1992, p. 139)

For Midgley, the purpose of philosophical inquiry is not merely to remind us how our conceptual schemes work, but nor is it to rebuild them from scratch; it is to identify areas of life, practice or theory in which our conceptual schemes are not serving us well, to work out why, and to propose alterations that might solve the problem. 'Time and again in the past, when conceptual schemes have begun to work badly, someone has contrived to suggest a change that shifts the blockage, allowing thought to flow where it is needed' (ibid., p. 140).

How do philosophers go about their conceptual investigations? This brings us to the heart of the matter in hand. Whether or not philosophy is too difficult for young children will turn on what exactly is involved in the study of concepts and conceptual schemes. The first thing to say here is that, while I think it is easier than is often supposed to say what it is that philosophers do, I am less optimistic about the possibility of making useful generalizations about how they do it. Both the history of philosophy and contemporary philosophical practice reveal a plethora of methods and techniques of inquiry, not all of which are well understood or easily articulated. The second thing to say is that at least some philosophical methods are fairly obviously unsuitable for inclusion in primary school curricula. Consider, for example, the method of logical analysis, whereby semantic puzzles are solved by translating sentences from a natural language into a logical one. No doubt we could give children some sense of what bothered Russell about expressions like 'the present king of France is bald', but we could scarcely hope to give them a facility with the system of predicate logic he used to interpret those expressions.

But these points need not discourage us: the fact that some methods of philosophical inquiry exceed the normal cognitive capacities of children does not imply that they all do. The question is whether it is possible to identify a philosophical method that is (i) central to the mainstream practice of philosophy and (ii) capable of being understood and applied by children. I think the answer to this question is yes, and the method that fits the bill is *conceptual analysis*.

Conceptual analysis is the attempt to clarify concepts and their relations by attending to the ordinary uses of words. Operating on the assumption that 'the meaning of a word is its use in the language' (Wittgenstein, 1953, Section 43), conceptual analysts seek to describe the rules or criteria that govern our use of words and so constitute their meanings. They draw a sharp distinction between the *tacit* knowledge of linguistic rules shared by all competent language-users and the *explicit* knowledge of linguistic rules yielded by philosophical inquiry. Ryle puts it like this:

> Many people can talk sense with concepts but cannot talk sense about them; they know by practice how to operate with concepts, anyhow inside familiar fields, but they cannot state the logical regulations governing their use. They are like people who know their way about their own parish, but cannot construct or read a map of it, much less a map of the region or continent in which their parish lies. (Ryle, 1949, pp. 9–10)

Conceptual analysis, then, is the process of mapping the conceptual terrain with which our language acquaints us. Its purpose is 'to determine the logical cross-bearings of the concepts which we know quite well how to apply', or 'to rectify the logical geography of the knowledge which we already possess' (ibid., pp. 9–10).

Despite what their detractors sometimes claim, conceptual analysts do not assume a rigid uniformity in ordinary language use, nor do they deny the role of judicious stipulation in the achievement of conceptual clarity. The method obviously presupposes a degree of stability and commonality in the ways words are used (without which communication would surely be impossible), but few of its serious practitioners have expected the rules followed by ordinary language-users to fall naturally into neat sets of necessary and sufficient conditions. Even Austin, a philosopher as optimistic as any about the 'soundness' and 'subtlety' of the conceptual distinctions embodied in 'our common stock of words' (Austin, 1956, p. 182), was ready to concede that 'essential though it is as a preliminary to track down the detail of our ordinary uses of words, it seems that we shall in the end always be compelled to straighten them out to some extent' (Austin, 1952, p. 134).

A particularly helpful and accessible account of what it is that conceptual analysts actually do is to be found in a little book by John Wilson called *Thinking with Concepts* (1963). Wilson breaks the method of conceptual analysis down into eleven constituent techniques. These techniques, which are described in detail in the book, may be summarized as follows:

1. Isolating the conceptual aspects of a question from its empirical and normative aspects
2. Recognizing that words can mean different things to different people
3. Identifying cases that are definitely instances of a particular concept
4. Identifying cases that are definitely not instances of a particular concept
5. Examining related but distinct concepts
6. Considering cases on the borderline of a concept and asking what makes them borderline
7. Inventing or imagining cases that reveal limits on the range of application of a concept
8. Investigating the social context in which a question is asked
9. Investigating the underlying anxiety or concern that motivates a question
10. Considering the immediate practical consequences of using a word in a particular way
11. Considering the broader linguistic consequences of using a word in a particular way

Here, then, is the philosophical method I should like to propose for use in primary schools. How does it fare against our two criteria of centrality to philosophy and accessibility to children? To take the latter first, I contend that none of the eleven techniques identified by Wilson would make significantly greater cognitive demands on children than the standard techniques of mathematical, scientific and historical inquiry ordinarily taught in primary schools. Conceptual analysis, like any serious method of inquiry, is hard to do really well;

but it is easy to make a start on. It is a practice whose basic purposes and procedures can be made readily intelligible to children and in which one can meaningfully engage on the basis of relatively little knowledge of the world or experience of life.

On the question of its centrality to philosophy, opinion is clearly divided. Some philosophers see conceptual analysis as the be all and end all of philosophy; others reject it out of hand. But the most plausible view, I think, is that it is one method among others in the philosopher's repertoire. Frank Jackson has recently offered an account of the important contribution made by conceptual analysis to the larger enterprise of 'serious metaphysics' (Jackson, 1998). The serious metaphysician, on Jackson's view, is interested in getting at the 'basic ingredients' of reality, and in showing that all other 'putative features' of the world are either supervenient on these basic ingredients or illusory. The role of conceptual analysis is to establish supervenience by demonstrating that propositions about some putative feature of the world are entailed by propositions about basic ingredients. Strawson also defends the view that conceptual analysis is a necessary but insufficient component of metaphysical inquiry:

> Up to a point, the reliance upon a close examination of the actual use of words is the best, and indeed the only sure, way in philosophy. But the discriminations we make, and the connexions we establish, in this way, are not general enough and not far-reaching enough to meet the full metaphysical demand for understanding . . . The structure [the metaphysician] seeks does not readily display itself on the surface of language, but lies submerged. He must abandon his only sure guide when the guide cannot take him as far as he wishes to go. (Strawson, 1959, pp. 9–10)

Conceptual analysis is not the whole of philosophy; but it is an indispensable part of it, and one that is accessible to children. And it surely makes sense, when one is starting out in philosophy, to examine first the conceptual structures that appear 'on the surface of language', before diving down to explore those that 'lie submerged'.

Philosophy in the primary classroom

I have tried to show that there is nothing in the nature of philosophy that precludes our teaching it to children, and that it ought therefore to be recognized as a serious candidate for inclusion in primary school curricula. By way of conclusion, I should like to offer a couple of examples of the sort of conceptual questions that seem to me to be relevant to the lives and concerns of children and ripe for investigation in the primary classroom.

Example 1

Gareth spills paint on the floor at the end of an art lesson. Miss Brent doesn't see him do it and he doesn't own up. She decides to keep the whole class in over breaktime to clear up the mess. Dawn says, 'But Miss, it's not fair to punish everyone!'

Is Dawn right?

The first concept in need of analysis here is that of fairness. Children could be asked initially to discuss the difference between treating people fairly and treating them unfairly. Is it always fair to hold people responsible for their actions? And when, if ever, is it fair to hold people responsible for the actions of others? One interesting case, with obvious resonance for children, is the practice of holding parents responsible for the actions of their children. Another, more directly pertinent to Dawn's question, is the practice of regarding groups of people as communally responsible for the actions of individuals within them. If a group is entitled to share the credit for the achievements of its members, is it also obliged to share the costs of their mistakes? And which are the groups whose members bear these communal entitlements and obligations?

The second concept requiring attention is that of punishment. Is Dawn right to characterize the requirement to clear up the mess as a punishment? What is the difference between a punishment and an unpleasant or inconvenient task? Children could be invited to recall their experiences of being made to do things they didn't want to, and to think about which of these cases counted as punishments and why. If Miss Brent's decision to keep the class in is not a punishment, but just a way to get the mess cleared up, does it cease to be unfair? And if it is a punishment, are there cases where groups should be ready to bear not only the costs of their members' mistakes but the punishments for their members' crimes?

Example 2

Tim goes up to Miss Brent and complains that Gareth has stolen his pencil. Miss Brent asks Tim if he saw Gareth steal it. Tim replies, 'No, Miss, but Gareth lost his pencil this morning and now he's got one exactly like mine, so I know it was him.'

Does Tim know that Gareth stole his pencil?

Here again there are two concepts that stand in need of investigation: those of knowledge and theft. One way of broaching the concept of knowledge would be to ask children to consider when we talk about knowing things and when we talk about believing, thinking or suspecting things. When are we justified in saying that we know something? Is the evidence cited by Tim sufficient to justify his knowledge claim? If it is concluded that Tim's evidence is insufficient, new pieces of evidence could be introduced: suppose Dawn comes forward and reports that she saw Gareth take the pencil from Tim's pencil-case. Is Tim now entitled to say that he knows Gareth is guilty, or would he only be justified in this if he had seen the theft with his own eyes? Is seeing things with our own eyes always sufficient warrant for a knowledge claim? Do we really know anything?

To help them investigate the concept of theft, children could be asked to discuss what they would say if Gareth took the pencil but sincerely intended to put it back at the end of the day. Is borrowing without permission the same as stealing? Or what if Gareth did not take the pencil from Tim's pencil-case, but rather found it on the classroom floor? Is it theft to keep things other people have lost? If only some cases of keeping lost things are cases of theft, how do we decide which ones? A more demanding line of inquiry might be opened up by suggesting that the pencil in question is a 'school pencil' rather than one Tim has brought in from home. If the pencil actually belongs to the school rather than Tim, and Gareth is a member of the school community, does it still make sense to talk about theft in this context?

These examples are designed to show that primary school philosophy lessons need not be remote from the things that matter to children. Philosophically interesting concepts are deployed on a daily basis in the ordinary exchanges of classroom life, in the judgements made by and about children, in the questions they ask and the questions we put to them. Teaching the techniques of conceptual analysis in relation to such concepts demonstrates the relevance of philosophy to problems children genuinely face, and its power to contribute to their solutions.

Chapter Two

Philosophy and Moral Education

Richard Pring

Philosophical thinking involves, but is by no means confined to, seeking to clarify the concepts through which we view the physical, social and moral worlds we inhabit, especially where those concepts are contentious in the sense that there is disagreement over their exact meaning and application. This is particularly the case where moral discourse is concerned. Such conceptual clarification can take place at different levels of sophistication, and there is a continuum between the clarification of meaning with young people and that with students of philosophy who are drawing upon the debates and arguments of previous generations of philosophers. This chapter illustrates this in the context of moral argument, drawing particularly upon the work of Lawrence Kohlberg in the use of moral dilemmas.

Doing philosophy

First, however, it is necessary to expand a little on what it is to 'do philosophy'.

There are some who think it absurd to teach young people philosophy at school – it is too abstract and intellectually demanding. As in the education of Plato's guardian class, it should await the attainment of greater maturity, induced no doubt by the study of less demanding pursuits such as mathematics. But such a sceptical attitude depends upon two assumptions. The first is that philosophical thinking is far removed from ordinary or commonsense thinking. The second assumption is that the commonsense thinking of adults does not itself build on the iconic and enactive forms of thought developed in childhood, to use the terminology of Jerome Bruner (1960). Indeed these two assumptions, both erroneous, are closely linked.

Philosophy begins when one is systematically puzzled about what is meant by what is said and written. By using the word 'systematically', I am eliminating the failure to understand simply on the grounds that one is unacquainted with the meaning of a word (let us say, 'osmosis' in biology). Rather is it the case that the meaning of a word within a language embraces different usages which often go unrecognized, thereby leading to confusion in argument or to apparent agreement when really there is none.

An obvious example, for the purposes of this chapter, is the concept of education. On the surface every user of the English language knows what 'education' means, and can happily talk of their education or of the education system. But a little probing about the meaning of what is said is likely to reveal important differences in usage. It would, in certain contexts, be meaningful to say, 'I was educated at the Smith Academy, but, sadly, as a result, I was not educated'. There is both a descriptive meaning of 'educated' (the process of formal learning which constitutes the educational system) and an evaluative meaning (the acquisition through learning of certain qualities of person which are believed to be of worth). The one usage does inevitably trade off the other, and there is often an unrecognized shift from one to the other in the course of conversation. Moreover, the evaluative usage implies, though often unacknowledged, certain criteria of value, which themselves will not be universally agreed – such as the attainment of certain kinds of understanding, the acquisition of certain skills, the formation of certain dispositions and virtues. That lack of universal agreement inevitably leads to misunderstandings. The more philosophically minded will be sensitive to these differences of usage and to the implications of these differences. They will seek clarification: 'what exactly do you mean?' And in seeking clarification, so the 'logic of the language' will be exposed, as, for example, the logical interconnection between the use of 'education' and that of 'indoctrination', 'training', 'learning', 'understanding' and so on.

However, as is indicated in the above example, that 'clarification of meaning' and that 'mapping' of the interrelated concepts through which we organize and understand experience, do themselves push the questioner into the traditional areas of puzzlement with which philosophers have been concerned. What makes key concepts contestable in our understanding of the physical, social and moral worlds we inhabit are the perennial problems of ethics ('how do we resolve disputes about what is good, right or worthwhile?), of knowledge ('what justification have we for believing one thing rather than another?'), of the mind ('can the mind be trained in the same way as the body can be trained?'), and so on. Thus, in thinking about 'education' in the evaluative sense, one is inevitably drawn into ethical concerns over what constitutes a worthwhile form of life, into epistemological concerns over the organization of knowledge, and into concerns over the autonomy and responsibility of individual agents.

Hence, to teach young people to think philosophically is to nurture a sense of puzzlement, to encourage the search for clarification of meaning, to get them to realize the systematic nature of the confusion in the usage of key concepts, and to enable them to recognize the foundations of these misunderstandings in the traditional areas of philosophical enquiry. I shall illustrate this using some moral dilemmas that I have explored with students in the class-room, which exhibit the two aspects of philosophizing referred to above. First, by having their initial judgements challenged by the criticisms of others or the questions of the teacher, students are provoked into clarifying such morally loaded concepts as 'loyalty', 'promise-keeping', 'respect' and 'true to oneself'. Second, this clarification leads into deeper discussion about the meaning of moral principles and the nature of moral justification.

Blood Wedding

Frederico Garcia Lorca's play, *Blood Wedding*, can, at one level, be summarized quite simply. A young woman, isolated in a rather poor farmhouse in the bleak landscape of rural Spain, awaits with trepidation an arranged marriage to a young man from a distant village. It would seem to be better than her present existence. However, a former lover, now married to someone else, turns up immediately before the wedding, and, after the wedding ceremony, when the guests return to the farmhouse for the reception, elopes with the new bride. They are pursued by the understandably angry groom's family. The seducer and the groom are killed. The wife returns to her aggrieved and grieving mother-in-law – there is nowhere else to go – to whom she tries to explain and justify her coduct. But what conceivable justification could be given for eloping with another man on her wedding day, dishonouring the groom's family in such a heinous way, causing the deaths of two young men, widowing a young mother?

Put like this to a class of 16- and 17-year-olds, the answer is unanimous and firm. Such an action was abominable and inexcusable. There could be no argument for an affirmative answer to the seemingly straightforward question: 'Could the young bride be in any way justified in eloping with another married man on her wedding day?'

However, even at this stage, the answers to the question 'Why was she wrong in her action?' show interestingly different reasons: one should not break solemn promises; one should not cause so much hurt to other people; marriage is sacred and indissoluble; adultery is wrong; it was very unfair on the groom; and so on. The conclusion might be the same, but the reasoning is different, reflecting somewhat different meanings of 'marriage' or different significances attached to 'hurting others' or to 'loyalty' – indeed, different principles as a basis for action. And, in anticipation of further argument and analysis by the students themselves, the reasons or justifications can be shown to be of different logical types – put crudely, consequentialist on the one hand ('it was wrong because it led to so much unhappiness'), and, on the other, deontological ('it was wrong in itself irrespective of the consequences'). But these differences lie submerged until one examines the text.

The students are asked to attend particularly to this account which the young bride gives to the grieving mother:

Because I went with him. . . . I went with him. [*Full of anguish*] And you would have gone, too. I was a woman burning, covered in sores inside and out, and your son was a trickle of water which would give me children, land, health, but he was a dark river, full of branches, filling me with the murmur of its reeds, singing to me through clenched teeth. And I ran with your son, with your little boy of cold water, and the other one followed me with flocks of birds, so that I couldn't even walk, and my flesh filled with frost, the wounded flesh of a woman already withering, of a young girl burning. Listen to me, I didn't want to, I didn't want to, do you hear? I didn't want to. Your son was all I ever wished for, and I didn't betray him, but the other one sucked me in with the force of the sea, and nothing could ever have stopped me from going. . . . Not ever, not even if I had been old and all your son's children were holding me by the hair.

The subsequent discussion shows a little wavering in the judgement of some in the class – the beginnings of sympathy for the young bride who 'didn't want to'.

In explaining this greater sympathy, some point to the overwhelming and passionate feeling, the limits in such circumstances to personal freedom, the notion of 'moral struggle' – and the bravest in the class find their own homely examples. That struggle is graphically illustrated earlier in the play where the bride and her 'lover' are hiding from the chase in the forest. She pleads

With your teeth
With your hands, whichever way you can,
Cut the metal chain which you've placed
Around my neck
And which dragged me from my father's house.
And if you won't kill me,
As you would crush a baby viper, then put the knife into my hands,
These hands that took his orange blossom . . .
My head is full of grief
And fire, and my tongue run through
With sharpest glass.

The sympathy with the bride lies in the recognition, not simply of an overwhelming passion which she tried heroically to resist, but also of the cry to be 'authentic' – her 'real self' in a social context which seemed oppressive and suffocating. It is seen as a cry of the human spirit against the restrictive practices of a closed society – captured in earlier passages when the bride-to-be is cross-examined by the bridegroom's mother, and told what marriage means:

> It's a man and his children, and a thick wall to keep the rest of the world out.

And this fits well with the 'selling point' given by the bride's father:

> What can I say about mine? She's up at 3, with the morning star itself, to bake bread. Never speaks at all, unless spoken to first; as soft and gentle as wool, she embroiders all sorts of . . . embroidery. And she can cut a rope with her teeth.

The discussion which this play engenders, based on the text to which constant reference is made, raises issues of personal authenticity, the importance (absolute or relative?) of promise-keeping, the meaning and place in the hierarchy of moral reasons of the pursuit of 'happiness', the ties of social obligation particularly within the family, the nature and indissolubility of marriage bonds, the meaning of and limits to free will. The sensuous account of the relation between bride and lover, contrasted with that between bride and groom, 'springs from the deepest parts of their being', as David Johnston argues in his introduction to *Blood Wedding*. That relationship arises from the assertion of the individual will, an assertion which struggles against social conditions that tend to smother it – the suffocating conventions, the 'stone wall' around one's life, the denial of the thirst for freedom.

The discussion becomes quite animated as the students struggle to come to terms with the complexity of the moral situation. That struggle requires the articulation of reasons for the oft wavering conclusions reached, and those reasons are subjected to the criticism of others. It requires constant reference to the text which reveals the motives, dispositions, states of mind of the protagonists and the social conditions in which they live. And it requires reference to the conflicting ethical bases for making judgements. The students are pressed to justify their positions, to get them to clarify why the pursuit of happiness should be an overwhelming principle, or indeed what they take happiness to be. They are entering into philosophical discussion that, if the teacher is sufficiently knowledgeable, draws upon the various traditions of philosophical thinking and relevant literature. They come to see that the difficulties they have in resolving a moral dilemma, which in many respects tallies with the moral dilemmas in their own lives, have been the very stuff of philosophical argument since Socrates. Indeed, at an appropriate moment, the introduction of a Socratic dialogue (for example, from the Meno) enables them to perceive more clearly a method of thinking, of clarifying meaning, of questioning definitions through contrary examples, of identifying contestable concepts and of seeing the deeper implications of particular usages. Above all they come to see, possibly for the first time in an educational programme geared to correct conclusions, that some of the most important questions we are concerned with have no certain answers. There is always room for further questioning – and a questioning of the foundations upon which possible answers to the questions rest.

Loyalty

A class of 12-year-olds are told a story of two girls on a shopping trip. One girl takes the opportunity provided by a changing cubicle to dress up in the blouse she wants and to leave the shop undetected, as she thinks, by the shopkeeper, much to the disapproval of her companion. However, detected she is, though only after she has left the shop, leaving her horrified companion to be detained and cross-examined. In the cross-examination the companion is given a choice: either inform the shopkeeper of the name and address of her friend or be reported to the police. What should she do? Differences immediately appear in the class, reflecting different moral reasonings – some appealing to loyalty among friends to justify silence, others appealing to justice for the shopkeeper to justify giving the information, yet others weighing up the consequences for the companion if she does not tell.

The probing and the arguing which follow are initially about the conclusion, and the decision whether to tell or not to tell divides the class roughly in half. But soon the discussion turns to the reasons for the conclusion rather than the conclusion itself, and there is often to be found greater agreement among those who come to opposite conclusions than among those who arrive at the same conclusion. Some appeal to the Bible: you should not steal, you should not tell a lie. Others appeal to 'loyalty to friends' – the basis of social cohesion and well-being. But even loyalty is evaluated in different ways: as a good of intrinsic value or as an instrumental good for one's own ultimate safety. And so, once again, there is a mixture of consequentialist and deontological thinking, and both are affected by consideration of the facts or of the possible facts, or indeed of what facts are relevant, for relevance is itself determined by the moral principles one appeals to.

In some cases, the consequences are seen simply in terms of what suffering is likely to accrue to the companion. Would she get into trouble with her parents or with the police if she were not to tell, and would the pain of the punishment outweigh the pain of losing a friend or of social exclusion? The implicit principle (if that is what it might be called) is that one should pursue one's own good – although that might itself be refined by a consideration of the particular circumstances (for example, the fact that the friend had not taken into account the consequences to the companion).

Are these young students 'doing philosophy'? Certainly they are forced into clarifying meanings, into realizing that what we mean is not as straightforward as it first appears, into seeing the consequences of different usages of key words, and into examining explicitly the principles which are only implicit in their ordinary deliberations about right and wrong. They are developing their capacities to articulate their reasons, to attend to criticism, and to reconsider their conclusions in the light of counter-examples and critical comment.

Perhaps at so early an age, they are not able to grasp the subtleties of Bentham's principle of utility, or of G. E. Moore's intuitionism, or of Ayer's emotive theory of ethics, let alone navigate through these competing accounts of moral language and deliberation. But their reasoning is at least embryonically philosophical, not only in the content but also in the articulation of reasons and in the growing disposition to attend to, and to take seriously, the critical comments of others. To do philosophy requires certain virtues as well as certain intellectual abilities, and such virtues need to be carefully nurtured. As Bruner (1960) so persuasively argued, the abstractions and theoretical accounts of the scholar can be anticipated in an intellectually respectable way, albeit in a different 'mode of representation', in the early thinking of each child. And by engaging in such deliberations as the ones described above, so the young learner is enabled to go deeper into reasons and arguments, reaching gradually to the more systematic thinking which we identify with doing philosophy.

Moral reasoning

The most thorough research to date into the growth of moral reasoning was carried out by Lawrence Kohlberg and his team at Harvard (Kohlberg, 1981). Kohlberg, influenced by Piaget's theory of cognitive development, sought to measure moral development in relation to the capacity to make moral judgements.

Kohlberg takes moral judgements to be centrally concerned with what one ought to do where there is a choice of different actions, each one being open to question. To deliberate over such choices required an appeal to more general principles. For example, if, after due consideration, I decide that I ought to tell the truth, even though I am tempted not to do so because of the inconvenience it will bring to me, I am appealing to the principle 'One ought not to tell lies'. What makes it a principle is its general life-guiding nature. Furthermore, the principle is seen to impose an obligation. In the terms of Kant's *Critique of Practical Reason*, the principle has the logical form of a categorical, rather than prudential, imperative. It applies to anyone in similar conditions, unless exceptions are to be made because of circumstances – and this involves appealing to some other principle which takes account of those circumstances.

Kohlberg draws upon the philosophical work of Richard Hare (1964) and John Rawls (1972) in developing the concept of 'generalisable principles' as the basis of moral action. As one both acts on principle and 'legislates' for others to act likewise, thereby brooking no exception on the grounds of personal advantage or preference, so justice and fairness are the ultimate moral principles. On this view it is the form rather than the content of moral judgements that is the key to living a moral life. As Hare argues:

> I am convinced that if parents first, and their children, understand the formal character of morality and of the moral concept, there would be little need to bother, ultimately, about the content of our children's moral principles; for if the form is really and clearly understood, the content will look after itself. (Hare, 1973, p. 164)

There are of course philosophical objections to this account of morality. The main one concerns the rather limited understanding of being moral or acting morally. There is more to moral development than learning to reason in a principled manner about what one ought to do when faced with a dilemma. The virtuous person may not see the situation as problematic, but rather act appropriately as a result of having the proper dispositions. On this view, the development of virtues rather than the capacity to deliberate like a canon lawyer should be the aim of moral education.

That as it may be, one *is* frequently in a dilemma as to the most appropriate action to take, and even virtuous persons have to deliberate – to ponder the principles upon which they should act in complex situations where there is little consensus. Being 'fair' or acting in accordance with the principle of justice (that is, treating people in the same way unless relevant reasons can be given for making exceptions) is certainly one aspect of the moral life if not the only one. And it is this aspect of moral life which Kohlberg thinks most important, and the development of which in young people most interests him.

In his theory of moral development, Kohlberg identifies three developmental levels, each divided into two stages. The first level, called 'pre-conventional', is where the overriding reason for doing what is right lies in the pursuit of self-interest – fear of punishment, pursuit of reward, obtaining of pleasure. The second level, called 'conventional', is where the reasons for behaving correctly appeal not to self-interest but to the social rules and conventions which prevail in a social group – a family or church, or society as a whole. Such conventions are treated as objective and not to be seriously questioned. The third level, called 'post-conventional', is where people question the conventions in terms of more universal and universalizable principles (for example, in the appeal to human rights). Kohlberg argues that it is through the discussion of moral dilemmas, such as the ones discussed above, that young people reveal the level at which they are operating. But they also provide the context and means for the students to progress in their moral thinking – to progress to the level of post-conventional deliberation which is implicit in what we mean by moral thinking.

One of Kohlberg's moral dilemmas is the story of Heinz, a young man in Chicago. It is the 1930s, a time of recession, and Heinz is almost penniless. He sees the doctor visit the young woman, with whom he has only passing acquaintance, in the next apartment. Upon enquiry, he is informed that she has a form of cancer and that the only chance of recovery is a medicine, not yet patented, not yet trialled, but developed by a chemist in downtown Chicago. Heinz visits the chemist, tries to persuade him to sell the drug, but fails – the chemist wants first to patent it so that he will finally profit from his life's work. On returning to the doctor, Heinz tells him sadly of his failed mission. The doctor signals that there is therefore no hope. But Heinz replies that there is: he will steal the drug. The doctor exclaims in a horrified tone, 'In no way – stealing is wrong!' The dilemma, then: should Heinz steal the drug?

This dilemma tends to divide young people. Asked to defend their decisions, they appeal to a range of principles (stealing is wrong; the Bible says stealing is wrong; it is too risky; life is more important than property; the chemist has a right to the fruit of his life's work; and so on). Gradually, as alternative reasons are given and as their positions are criticized, they are forced to dig deeper to find the ultimate foundation of the principles they invoke.

Again, we might ask, is this philosophy? Kohlberg certainly draws extensively on philosophical work to frame his theory and shape his empirical studies of moral reasoning; but this does not show that moral reasoning is itself philosophical. Is it fair to say that the sort of wrestling with moral dilemmas Kohlberg encounters in young people, and sees as the key to their moral development, qualifies as philosophical inquiry?

I think it is. What systematic deliberation on Kohlbergian moral dilemmas reveals, at the most basic level, is the need to clarify what is meant by 'loyalty', 'promise-keeping', 'authenticity', etc. The disagreements to which the dilemmas give rise can only be resolved by attending to the usage of particular words, with all that that usage entails. And this in turn prompts reflection on the nature of moral judgements and a deep questioning of the foundations on which they rest. Young people deliberating on such dilemmas might not be reading the *Critique of Practical Reason*, but they are addressing the very questions with which Kant was concerned.

Chapter Three

Getting beyond the Deficit Conception of Childhood: Thinking Philosophically with Children

Gareth B. Matthews

Jean Piaget, who has been the most influential developmental psychologist of all time, sought to identify stages in which children develop cognitive structures to understand themselves and the world around them. Piaget's key idea was that cognitive development is not simply an accumulative process, as, for example, learning more facts would be. Rather, he argued, cognitive development is marked by the acquisition of new and more sophisticated concepts to replace the simpler and more primitive ones.

Piaget's findings seem to make the prospects for having deep conversations with young children rather dim. If a four-year-old or an eight-year-old is working with a concept of time, say, that is more primitive and less sophisticated than mine, any attempt by me to have a good conversation with that child about the nature of time will have little chance of success. There will be nothing I can say that will bring the child up to my level of cognitive sophistication. The experience of cognitive dissonance will eventually, no doubt, bring this child, now perhaps as an adolescent, to form a concept of time that will first make it possible for us to have a good philosophical exchange about the nature of time.

I shall call Piaget's conception of childhood a 'deficit conception of childhood'. The deficit Piaget thinks he can identify in the children he locates at stage 1 or 2 or 3 in their acquisition of some concept is not primarily a deficit in information. It is more profound than that. It is a deficit in cognitive structure. This deficit seems to have profound implications for the expectations parents and teachers can reasonably have when they have discussions with their children.

I have criticized Piaget's interpretation of his findings elsewhere (Matthews, 1980, 1994). I am not here interested in the details of Piaget's findings, but rather in the model of childhood it supports, the deficit conception of childhood. Many of us, including many with little or no knowledge of Piagetian psychology, share with Piaget the assumption that children are well thought of primarily as lacking certain competencies that they can expect to develop by the time they are adults. On this model, children, by having only incompletely developed cognitive capacities, are essentially incomplete human beings.

Of course, we all realize, if we ever stop to think about it, that children typically have gifts and talents that their elders lack, and that, presumably, they will also lack when they grow up. A good example of such a talent is language learning. Children, on the whole, are far better at language learning, including learning a second or third language, than adults are. They are also better at this than they will likely be as adults. Appreciation of the ability of children to learn languages has inspired some educators and school systems to initiate instruction in a second language at a very early age. But it hasn't had much effect on our tendency to think of children according to the deficit conception of childhood.

Children are also widely, if not universally, recognized to have gifts as artists that will likely not persist through adolescence into adulthood. But, again, the recognition of the artistic abilities of children has not seriously affected our thinking about what it is to be a child.

I want to suggest here that, if we were to recognize the ability of children to think about important issues in philosophy, we might well become less inclined to view children on the deficit model of childhood. But to recognize the ability of children to do philosophy it is important that we not hobble our efforts by preconceptions of what they are capable of. If we talk down to our children, we should not be surprised to find that their responses conform to our limited expectations of them.

Some years ago I collected anecdotal evidence that even very young children sometimes, without any special encouragement from their elders, make comments, ask questions, and engage in reasoning that professional philosophers can recognize as philosophical. In my book *Philosophy and the Young Child* (Matthews, 1980), I lay out some of the evidence I had collected.

In the two and a half decades since that book appeared, I have collected evidence about what happens when one deliberately introduces children to philosophical inquiry. In my book *Dialogues with Children* (Matthews, 1984), I tell about how I made up story beginnings and took them to my philosophy class in St. Mary's Music School in Edinburgh, Scotland. Each story beginning I made up ends with a philosophical question, or puzzle. The project for class discussion was to say how the story ought to go on. Saying how the story should go on required, in each case, dealing with the philosophical puzzle or question with which I had ended the story beginning.

I have continued to use that method for doing philosophy with children. But more recently I have anchored my story beginnings more closely in classical texts in philosophy. I turn now to a story of mine based on reasoning in Aristotle, Sextus Empiricus and Augustine. I actually had the Augustine passage in mind when I wrote the story, but since that passage is much longer than the version in Aristotle, I'll just use Aristotle's version. It is the most succinct statement of the puzzle that I know. 'That time does not exist at all,' Aristotle writes at the beginning of Chapter 10 of Book IV of his *Physics*,

> might be suspected from the following consideration. Some of it [that is, some of time] has been and is not, [whereas] some of it is to be and is not yet. But it would seem to be impossible that what is composed of things that don't exist should participate in being. (217b32–18a3)

The Augustine passage, in Book XI of his *Confessions*, relies on the same reasoning, but adds a puzzle about the disappearing present, and, in general, makes the puzzle much more dramatic and engaging.

I composed a story based on these texts for a demonstration class a few years ago in Oslo, Norway. Here is the story I came up with:

Time

Mother: Hi, Tor, how was school today?

Tor throws down his school pack and begins to take off his jacket.

Tor: Oh, all right, I guess. But we have this girl in my science class who thinks she knows everything. She was in Switzerland last year. I think her father is a big scientist or something. He was working in a lab there. Her name is Ingrid. Do you know what she said today?

Mother: I don't have a very good way to guess from what you've told me so far.

Tor: Well, the teacher, Mr. Knudsen, was saying something about space and time and this Ingrid, she raised her hand and said in this sickly-sweet know-it-all voice of hers, 'You know, Mr. Knudsen, there really is no such thing as time.'

Mother: What did Mr. Knudsen say to that?

Tor: Well, you know how he always likes to humor students, especially the smart ones, so he just smiled and said, 'What makes you say that, Ingrid?'

Mother: Did Ingrid have a good reply?

Tor: Well, she started off by saying, 'You know, Mr. Knudsen, if there really were such things as times, some of them would be long and others would be short.'

Mother: Did Mr. Knudsen agree to that?

Tor: Of course. But then this Ingrid said in her sassy way – I can't stand her – 'But you know, Mr. Knudsen, the past doesn't exist anymore. So there is nothing of the past to be either long or short. And the future doesn't exist yet. So the future isn't there to be long or short either.'

Mother: That sounds pretty interesting. Did Mr. Knudsen have a good reply?

Tor: Well, he said, 'What about the present, Ingrid? That exists, doesn't it?' And you know what Ingrid said to that?

Mother: No, son, tell me.

Tor: Well she said, 'You might think a whole day, or a whole hour, or at least a whole minute could be present. But really,' she went on, 'even though it's now, say, Thursday, some of Thursday is already past and some is future. So some of it doesn't exist any more and the rest doesn't exist yet.'

Mother: What did Ingrid say about the present minute? Surely none of the present minute is already past or still future.

Tor: Oh yeah, she had an answer for that, too, She said, 'So and so many seconds are already past and the rest are future. All that is really present is something like a knife-edge of time. That's not either long or short. It's just a knife-edge. So,' she concluded, 'since, if there were such a thing as time, there would have to be long times and short times, and no such things ever exist, there is no such thing as time.'

Mother: I can tell Ingrid is very smart. Did Mr. Knudsen have a good answer for her?

Tor: Well, he said we were all to go home and think about what Ingrid had said. Tomorrow we are each supposed to come up with the best response we can. I wish I could think of something that would blow her out of the water. She thinks she's so smart.

Mother: Well, you could go over and talk to Olaf's big sister. I think she has done a little philosophy at the University.

Tor: No, I want to figure this out for myself. I want to show that Ingrid isn't really the smartest kid in the class. She just thinks she is.

Before I left for Norway I tried the story out on a class of fifth-graders in Northampton, Massachusetts. What follows is a description of the Northampton class.

The discussion began in a rather uncertain way. Sydney, let's call him, commented that 'Ingrid was using philosophy.' That was actually a rather promising starting point. I wrote it on the poster board for later discussion.

Three of the next four comments, however, focused on the psychological dynamics of the story. Thus Julie pointed out, what is surely correct, that 'Tor wants to have a response to show that Ingrid wasn't right.' May added that 'Tor is jealous of Ingrid,' which is highly plausible. And Anthony expressed the very reasonable thought that 'The continuation of the story should show that Ingrid isn't as smart as she thinks she is.'

In the midst of these comments, Kristine raised her hand and, with a frown on her face, blurted out, 'I don't get it.' Since I was, at that point, following the Community of Inquiry methodology, I responded by writing on the board, 'I don't get it,' with her name afterward. Several kids giggled and Kristine blushed a bit as I wrote her exasperated comment down, but I tried to reassure her that that was a really good thing to say and that we would try to deal with it once we had all the initial comments on the board.

So far there had been two good goads to further discussion, Sydney's 'Ingrid was using philosophy' and Kristine's 'I don't get it.' The other comments had more to do with what is called 'reading comprehension.' Still, I wasn't completely disappointed, since I had myself built the element of jealousy into the story to help motivate the search for a good reply to what is, after all, a rather abstract, even abstruse, bit of philosophical reasoning. It was good to be assured that the kids had understood the psychological dynamics of the story.

There is a more general issue here. I write story beginnings like this one and ask the kids how the story should go on to try to present philosophical problems as problems they themselves can have. In this case the question is what Tor should say in response to Ingrid. It is important to the enterprise I want to foster that the kids don't say at the end, 'Now tell us what the answer is.' And, in fact, they never do that. They soon take these problems on as their own. They may or may not be able to handle them to their own satisfaction. But the aim is, if possible, for them to take ownership of the problems. The aim is most definitely not to get them to learn some famous solution to the problem under discussion. It is not even to get them to recapitulate the history of philosophy, though that is often what they do. It is rather to help them become self-reliant thinkers who have the ability to address difficult and fascinating philosophical issues and work out articulate and well-argued responses.

But I am jumping ahead of my story. The first five comments did not actually tackle the *philosophical* issue the story raises. At this point I wondered if I had made a mistake in bringing such a difficult bit of reasoning to these fifth-graders. As I have already mentioned, the argument I had incorporated in the story is found in its most famous form in St. Augustine's *Confessions*, Book XI. I might add that the solution Augustine offers is not one that very many people find satisfactory. Something quite like it appears much earlier in Book IV of Aristotle's *Physics*. Uncharacteristically, Aristotle seems to offer no solution to the problem at all. So why should I expect a group of fifth-graders with no previous training in philosophy to be able to figure out an interesting response to a problem Aristotle apparently was not able to solve and Augustine responded to only in a fashion many people find disappointing?

Well, naïve or not, my faith was rewarded. Orson screwed up his face, twisted his body a bit and raised his hand. 'If the past doesn't exist,' he said carefully, weighing each word, 'I . . . couldn't . . . have . . . started . . . this . . . sentence.' My heart jumped with excitement. While the others were talking, Orson had clearly been working away in his own mind at a response to

Ingrid's argument. And his response was an excellent one. Other kids immediately jumped on it and expanded it. Jason said, 'If the past didn't exist, nothing would exist now.'

Orson's idea, in its full generality, is this: If the past doesn't exist, then there is nothing that could have brought anything that now exists into being – this sentence I am uttering, the people who are now talking about this philosophical question, the world around us, anything at all that now exists! I don't recall running across an attempt to establish the reality of the past exactly like Orson's anywhere in the history of philosophy. It was a stunning move.

In the discussion that followed, several kids tried to think about the specific kind of reality that the past has. Jason was particularly persistent in this effort. 'The past *sort of* exists,' he said at one point, 'because we [can] experience it'. He may have had Augustine's idea that the past exists in our memory. On the other hand, his idea seemed to be more that the past exists in a way that makes it possible for us to know things about it.

Later on, Jason wanted to add something about the 'sort of' existence that the past has. His idea at this point seemed to be that the past is settled, determinate, always one way or the other. It couldn't have the definite character it has, he seemed to be saying, if it didn't exist at all. His notion that the past is one way or another and we can't change it echoes the traditional notion, to be found in Aristotle, that the past has a kind of necessity; it is the necessity of the settled and unchangeable.

Talk about whether the past could be changed introduced the issue of time travel. Several kids had ideas about time travel, and whether, if you went back in time, you could actually change something that had happened in the past, rather than simply being an ineffectual observer.

Talk about the kind of existence the past has also introduced a question about the kind of existence the future has. Several kids seemed prepared to accept Ingrid's claim in the story, that the future simply has no existence at all. But some seemed to want to assign some existence to it as well. A summary way of putting their point would be this: The future 'sort of exists', too, because the same thing that *is now present, was future.*

I should also mention that Kristine, who first blurted out, 'I don't get it,' came to take an animated part in the discussion. It seems to have been important to the discussion as it developed that she had been fearless enough to say at the beginning that she didn't understand the problem. But eventually she certainly did get it and she made an important contribution to the class response.

We eventually returned to Sydney's comment that Ingrid was using philosophy. I asked the kids how they knew that what Ingrid was doing was using philosophy. Someone who had paid close attention to the story pointed out that the Mother in the story had suggested that Tor go over to someone who had studied philosophy at the University to get his problem solved. That observation was certainly a textually astute comment.

I think it was Sydney who picked up on his own comment and explained rather impressively that what Ingrid was doing was using philosophy because it was giving reasons for something, not just making an unsupported statement. There were then two or three rather eloquent comments from Sydney about how it wasn't enough just to have an opinion about something; one needs to be able to give reasons.

One of the last comments was very simple, yet, in its own way, also very profound. A kid who hadn't participated much in the discussion, let's call him Robert, said, eyeing the clock, 'There's a time when school gets out; so time exists.' Robert was making a point very much like one G. E. Moore was famous for in the last century. J. M. E. McTaggart, like Ingrid, had argued that time is unreal. Moore replied that he knew he had had breakfast that morning, so time must exist. Moore went on to say that he had much more certain knowledge that he had had breakfast that morning than he could possibly have that McTaggart's rather complicated argument for the unreality of time is sound.

I found the discussion I had with those fifth-graders as exciting as any philosophical discussion I can remember having recently with anyone, whether college students, graduate students or professors. The way in which the rather uncertain response to Ingrid's challenge at the beginning of our discussion turned into an exciting development of ideas was amazing. And the most gratifying thing of all is that no one ever said, 'Now tell us the answer.' I'm glad they didn't say that for two reasons. The first is that, as I have already said, I wanted these kids to accept Ingrid's problem as their own. And the second is that what they said in that discussion was actually more interesting than anything I would have been able to prepare for them if I had been asked to give a little lecture on the reality of time.

If I had been working with the deficit conception of childhood, I would hardly have been inspired to discuss an argument for the non-existence of time with fifth-graders. But I came to those schoolchildren with the hope that they could help me think about an old argument that I still find somewhat perplexing myself. They rewarded me by helping me get a little clearer about how I want to respond to that argument.

I turn now to another topic, happiness. What is happiness? Who among us can say? Certainly many philosophers have tried to explain what happiness is. But none of them has come up with an answer that satisfies all the others.

Yet there is a way in which each of us knows perfectly well what happiness is. As Aristotle puts the point, happiness (*eudaimonia*) is that of which the following two things are true: (1) virtually everyone wants it (*Nicomachean Ethics* 1.4), and (2) no one wants it for the sake of something else, but all want it for its own sake (*Nicomachean Ethics* 1.7). A dramatic way of putting the second point is to say that it is absurd to ask *why* we want to be happy.

To dwell for a moment on the second point, suppose you tell me that you want to buy a new dress or suit. I may sensibly ask you why you want to buy a new dress or suit. You might tell me that the old one is now out of fashion. I might then ask you why you want to wear something fashionable. You might say that you want to look good at work, or at a party, and to do that you need to be wearing something fashionable. But if, somewhere along the line, you answer that you just want a new dress or suit to make you happy, it would be absurd or nonsensical for me to ask, 'And why do you want to be happy?'

So these two characteristics of happiness – that virtually everyone wants it and that is absurd or nonsensical to ask *why* one wants it – provide what we can call a 'formal' characterization' of what happiness is. But they do not really give us any help in determining the *content* of the concept of happiness. This is what philosophers have disagreed about, and, indeed, continue to disagree about even today.

We might pause for a moment to note that our situation with respect to happiness is quite like that with respect to many other philosophically interesting concepts. Take the concept of a cause, or the concept of time. In a way we all know what a cause is and we all know what time is. If you tell me that the cause of the water boiling is that it has been heated to 100° Celsius I will understand you. And if you ask me what time it is now, I will understand what sort of answer will satisfy you. But there is also a way in which we are probably unclear about what time is, and what a cause is. The way in which we do not understand what time or causality is, is that we very likely do not have an analysis of the concept of time, or of the concept of causality, that will satisfy a tough-minded philosopher. Even if we think we have a pretty good analysis, there may be problems in explaining it, or defending it against objections. Thus, for example, if I follow Aristotle and say that time is the measure of motion with respect to before and after, I may not know what to say about whether everything in the universe could be completely still for a period of time, so that there would be no motion to measure time. What could time be then?

Happiness is like time and causality and most of the other philosophically interesting concepts. When we try to go beyond what I am calling the 'formal' features of happiness, we may well find ourselves unable to say in any satisfactory way what happiness is. And yet it is important that we reflect on happiness and try to come up with at least a moderately satisfactory understanding of what it is. It is important to do this for several reasons. For one thing, since the pursuit of happiness is the overall aim that motivates our lives, it is good for us to be as clear as we can about what, for us, happiness consists in. Moreover, since the pursuit of happiness is also the overall aim of other people around us, reflection on what *they* seem to understand as happiness will help us understand them better.

Plato, in his dialogue, *Gorgias*, has Socrates compare the various desires and appetites we have to jars – in fact, to *empty* jars, or at least *somewhat* empty jars, in the case of appetites and desires that have not been satisfied, and to *full* jars in the case of those that have been satisfied. The self-controlled person, Socrates suggests to his conversation partner, Callicles, has full jars, whereas the undisciplined person has leaky jars, which constantly need filling up. Socrates thinks that the person with full jars, being a contented person, is the happier one, whereas Callicles disagrees. 'The one who has filled himself up has no pleasure anymore,' Callicles says (494a). By contrast, according to him, the person who has lots of appetites that constantly need to be satisfied will be the happy person.

Socrates decides to put the 'leaky-jar' thesis of Callicles to the test. 'Tell me,' he says, 'whether a man who has an itch and scratches it and can scratch it to his heart's content, can be happy.' (*Gorgias* 494c). Socrates's idea seems to be that scratching an itch is like trying to fill a leaky jar. Scratching the itch will not make the itch go away. Instead, the itch will go on itching. Thus, even if one gains pleasure from the scratching, scratching does nothing to relieve the itching.

Callicles finds Socrates's example disgusting, which it certainly is. But Socrates persists. Under pressure from Socrates to answer the question, Callicles finally agrees that a person who takes great pleasure in scratching himself, and scratches himself to his heart's content, will be perfectly happy.

Callicles could have protested that, according to what he had said before, to be perfectly happy one would have to have many different empty jars, or at least many partly empty jars, that is, many different unsatisfied desires. But he doesn't say that. Instead, he lets Socrates make him think about the case in which someone is so preoccupied with the pleasure of scratching that, at the moment anyway, he doesn't want anything else besides that pleasure. Callicles reluctantly concedes that such a person would be happy.

This passage in Plato inspired me to write the following story:

Perfect happiness

'What happened in school today, Tony?' asked Tony's mother as she served him his helping of spaghetti and meatballs. The Allen family was seated around the dinner table for their evening meal.

'Actually, there was something kind of cool,' replied Tony. 'This new kid in the class, I think his name is Roy, he cracked everybody up by something he said.'

'What did he say?' asked Tony's sister, Heather.

'Well, you see,' explained Tony, 'our teacher, Ms. Hernandez, was talking about this story in which some kid said that she wanted to be totally happy. Ms. Hernandez asked us if we could think of a time when we were perfectly happy.'

'That's an interesting question,' put in Tony's father.

'Yeah, well, what this kid, Roy, said was that if he had an insect bite on his seat, you know, on his rear end, and it itched like crazy and he could scratch it as hard as he wanted to, he would be perfectly happy.'

'That's pretty gross,' said Heather, making an ugly face.

'Yeah, it was pretty gross all right,' Tony agreed, 'but it cracked everybody up. Kids laughed so loud you couldn't hear Ms. Hernandez trying to get us to shut up.'

'That was a disgusting thing to say,' said Tony's mother disapprovingly.

'Yeah,' agreed Heather, 'it was a yucky thing to say, but, you know, it's right! If scratching a very itchy insect bite gives you so much pleasure that, at that moment, you don't want anything else, then you're perfectly happy'.

'I wouldn't call that perfect happiness,' protested Tony.

'Why not?' insisted Heather; 'perfect happiness is just enjoying something, it doesn't matter what it is – scratching an insect bite, stuffing yourself with chocolate cake, whatever – enjoying it so much that you don't at that time want anything else. Do you have some other explanation of what perfect happiness is?'

Tony decided to change the subject. He wished he hadn't told his family about what Roy had said in school. He didn't think Heather was right about what perfect happiness is, but he didn't know how to prove she was wrong. She was always winning arguments. He hated that.

Still, Tony was puzzled about what happiness is, and especially about what perfect happiness is. Is it just enjoying something so much that the thought of everything else is blanked out? Somehow that didn't seem right to him. But what could he say about total happiness that he could defend against Heather?

I have used this story to discuss total or perfect happiness with groups of children in various parts of the world. Recently I used it with fifth-graders in Shanghai, China. I had hoped to have a discussion with about 20 Chinese children. But my host in Shanghai misunderstood my request. He thought I wanted to give a formal lecture to the fifth-graders in that school. There were, in fact, four fifth-grade classes in that elementary school, each with 50 pupils. When my interpreter and I arrived at the school, we learned that I would be presenting my story to all 200 Chinese fifth-graders in a very large auditorium, in fact, in one that seats exactly 200 children.

I have to say that I do not recommend conducting a philosophical discussion with 200 school children. Still, those Chinese children were immediately drawn to the issue I wanted them to discuss with me. The best way for us to have a discussion, it seemed, was for me to ask them to raise their hands, if they had a comment to make, and I would call on some of them. In fact, I asked eight children to come up to the microphone and express their thoughts on whether scratching an insect bite and enjoying it so much that, at the moment, one does not want anything else, is perfect happiness. After those eight children had expressed their opinions on this subject, I asked the group as a whole to vote on which of the eight opinions they wanted to discuss further. The one they chose was this: *Perfect happiness is being able to do whatever you want.*

Interestingly, this notion of perfect happiness is quite close to that of Callicles in Plato's dialogue. Callicles just adds the proviso that one should have lots of desires. But for him, as for this Chinese child, perfect happiness is the pleasure of satisfying all one's desires.

Next I asked for volunteers to respond to this idea that perfect happiness is simply being able to do whatever you want to do. Two of the responses I got were especially noteworthy. One child came up with an example that was at least as vulgar and disgusting as the example Socrates puts to Callicles. 'When you have to go to the toilet very badly,' he said, 'you can be sitting there enjoying the pleasure of relieving yourself so much that at that moment you don't want anything else.' He added with emphasis: 'But that is not perfect happiness.'

This child's example has the same structure as the example Socrates chose. Here again we have a bodily pleasure that may be quite intense. But that pleasure, like the pleasure of scratching, is only what we might call a 'lower' pleasure. Jeremy Bentham, the originator of utilitarianism, developed a calculus for measuring pleasures and comparing their value. For Bentham an intense pleasure counts for more than a mild pleasure and a longer-lasting pleasure counts for more than one of short duration. But Bentham refused to allow that there might be higher pleasures – say intellectual or aesthetic pleasures – that count for more than lower pleasures. So the toilet experience might, in principle, count for as much as the pleasure of enjoying a late quartet of Beethoven or a Shakespearean sonnet.

John Stuart Mill accepted much of Bentham's theory. But, unlike Bentham, Mill insisted on distinguishing higher and lower pleasures. In a famous phrase he maintained that it would be better to be Socrates dissatisfied than a pig satisfied. The defenders of Bentham countered that, if some pleasures were higher than others, and so more valuable than others, there would be something good besides just having pleasure, which they denied.

The other memorable comment I got in that Shanghai elementary school came from a child who pointed out that some of our pleasures may come from doing something that hurts others. Perhaps this child had sadistic pleasures in mind, or perhaps her thought was only that, for example, if I have an extra piece of pizza, which I find delicious, you may be left hungry. In any case, her idea was that the pleasures we enjoy that cause pain or suffering do not yield perfect happiness, even for us. Callicles, in Plato's dialogue, would have rejected this idea. He is what we might call an 'egoistic hedonist' about happiness. That Chinese fifth-grader made it clear that, in her view, a purely egoistic account of happiness cannot be correct.

On another occasion I discussed perfect happiness with a class in an elementary school near my home in Massachusetts.

Very early on in that discussion Juliane made clear how limited Tony's conception of happiness really is. According to him, as she put it, 'Total happiness is just enjoying what you are doing right now and not thinking of all the other things that you want.' This is a very trenchant remark. It invites us to reflect on an important assumption that gives Tony's conception of happiness whatever plausibility it has. If we want to give that assumption a name, we can call it 'solipsism of the present moment'.

Unqualified solipsism is the view that only I and my impressions and thoughts exist. The world, other people – everything else besides me – is only a thought or impression I have, or perhaps a collection of my thoughts and impressions.

Solipsism, so understood, is not, of course, a position any important philosopher defends. There would be no point in defending solipsism. If solipsism were true, there would be no one else to convince of its truth. What could be the point of my trying to convince you that you are only a figment of my imagination? In fact, the only challenge that unqualified solipsism poses is the challenge of proving that it is wrong.

Solipsism of the present moment is more interesting. It is the claim that there is nothing of value or importance except what one can appreciate at the moment. On this assumption, it is quite plausible to conclude that, if I am now enjoying something in such a way that, at the moment, I don't want anything else, I am totally happy. Juliane's comment should remind us that there may be many things we want that we are not even thinking about just now. But if those other things we want are put out of our mind by some simple pleasure we are now enjoying, we should not conclude, according to her, that this simple contentment amounts to perfect happiness.

Andrew underlined Juliane's point with an example. 'You could be playing with something at your desk,' he said as he himself played at his desk with his pencil, 'and not paying attention to anything else'. He then added in disbelief, 'And that would be perfect happiness?' The implication of his tone of voice was that such a supposition was quite implausible. The broader implication was that solipsism of the present moment must be rejected.

Matt tried another tack. He, too, wanted to focus on much more than a pleasure of the present moment. But what he required for total happiness was some major accomplishment in one's life. His idea was that the satisfaction of having accomplished some major goal in life would give one happiness for a lifetime. His own choice for a major accomplishment was to become a football star, in fact, to become, as he put it, 'the very best wide receiver ever.'

Nathan seemed to agree with Matt. 'Even after you retire,' he said, 'you could have the satisfaction of knowing that you were the very best'. But Marissa was not convinced that one major achievement in life would guarantee total happiness. 'You can get bored doing what you do best,' she insisted.

Kristle was also sceptical about Matt's proposal. But the grounds for her scepticism were different from Marissa's. 'You can't be happy forever,' she said; 'sad things will happen.' Here again, these children touched on a theme philosophers have pursued since ancient times. Plato thought that an ideally good person would be invulnerable to misfortune. Goodness, and with it, happiness, he thought, are a condition of one's *psyche*, or inner self. According to Plato, if one has achieved an ideally good state of one's *psyche*, not even torture will be a threat to one's happiness.

Of course, the achievement Plato was talking about was different from the achievement Matt had in mind. Matt thought that excellence at football, what we might call 'football virtue', would be an achievement that would guarantee happiness for a lifetime. Plato thought that the needed achievement was virtue or excellence of soul, or inner self. Yet, structurally, Matt's and Plato's suggestions were similar.

Aristotle, in contrast to Plato, thought that even the most virtuous of us is vulnerable to the vicissitudes of fortune. Mary, another pupil in that class echoed Aristotle's caution. 'Something bad can always happen,' she warned, 'something not in your control'.

The verdict of most of the kids in that class was not just that Tony had the wrong conception of what perfect happiness is. Rather, in their view it is a mistake to aim for perfect happiness. They considered that an unattainable goal. 'You can be overall happy,' they agreed, 'but not perfectly happy'.

So those are two different discussions of happiness – one in China and one in the US. My aim has not been simply to report the responses of children in these groups to my story about perfect happiness. Instead, what I have tried to do is something more ambitious. I have tried to locate the comments of these children within the tradition of philosophical thought about happiness that begins with Plato and continues up to the present day. I do not, of course, mean to suggest that the children whose comments I have reported here have well-worked-out positions on the nature of happiness. That, of course, is not the case. What is true, however, is that their thoughtful comments can easily be understood to belong to a rich conversation about happiness that is now almost two-and-a-half millennia old.

In a way, the ease with which I have been able to link up these children's words with the grand philosophical tradition should come as a surprise. After all, none of these children had studied philosophy. And none of them would have been able to write a treatise on happiness.

Yet there is also a way in which the naturalness with which we can link their remarks to the views of traditional philosophers should not come as a surprise after all. As Aristotle pointed out, we all want to be happy – we old folks and those children alike. Moreover, even young children can recognize that wanting to be happy is so basic that it is absurd or nonsensical to ask, 'Why do you want to be happy?' If children can thus identify happiness in at least what I have called a formal way, and if the desire for happiness motivates their lives, as it does ours, they should have some thoughts on what the nature of happiness is, and perhaps even on what it would be to be perfectly happy.

My message here, however, is not just that it is *possible* to have an interesting and valuable discussion with young children about what happiness is, or about whether time exists. Rather, my message is that it is both good for them and good for us adults to have such discussions with them. It is good for them, since being unreflective or even confused about what they consider happiness to be can be a major hindrance to their leading a good life. Having such discussions with them is also good for us, since it both gives us a new respect for our children and also forges a relationship with them that both allows for, and also encourages, much more reciprocity and mutual respect than we are accustomed to think possible. That's a win-win result.

More broadly, the possibility of having good philosophical discussions with young children suggests that we should replace the deficit conception of childhood with what I have sometimes called a 'mirror-image' conception of childhood. Instead of viewing children as beings whose essential nature it is to lack knowledge and skills that adults normally have, we should think of them as having valuable abilities that adults lack, as well as lacking valuable abilities that adults normally have. I mentioned at the beginning that children are, in general, better at learning languages than adults are. They are also, on average, better at producing aesthetically interesting drawings and paintings than they will be, on average, as adults. Furthermore, they are much more likely to be interested in philosophical questions than the average adult. Being more likely to get interested in philosophical questions than they will be as adults, they make surprisingly good conversation partners in thinking about the great questions of philosophy.

What difference would it make to parents and teachers if they could be convinced that children make good philosophical conversation partners? It might make a great deal of difference to the way we think about our children and to the ways we treat them. Being in a real philosophical discussion with children offers both child and adult an opportunity for mutual exchange and mutual respect that is otherwise rare in our society.

Yet no parents or teachers will invite the possibility of doing real philosophy with children unless they can get beyond the deficit conception of childhood. I hope that my experiences with children will encourage some parents and teachers to do just that.

Chapter Four

Religion and Philosophy in Schools

Stephen Law

Is philosophy in schools a good idea? The extent to which early exposure to a little philosophical thinking is of educational benefit is, of course, largely an empirical question. As a philosopher, that sort of empirical study is not my area of expertise.

But of course there is also a philosophical dimension to this question. As a philosopher, conceptual clarification and the analysis of the logic of the arguments on either side certainly is my field. That is where I hope to make a small contribution here.

This chapter is in two parts. In the first, I look at two popular religious objections to the suggestion that all children ought to be encouraged to think independently and critically about moral and religious issues. In the second part, I explain a well-known philosophical distinction – that between reasons and causes – and give a couple of examples of how this conceptual distinction might help illuminate this debate.

Two popular religious objections

Philosophy in the classroom involves children thinking critically and independently about the big questions. These questions include questions about morality and the origin and purpose of human existence. Examples are: 'Why is there anything at all?', 'What makes things right or wrong?' and 'What happens to us when we die?' These questions are also addressed by religion. The subject matter of philosophy and religion significantly overlap. And where there is overlap, there is the possibility of *disputed territory*. Proponents of philosophy in the classroom may find themselves coming into conflict with at least some of the faithful. While many religious people are enthusiastic about philosophy in the classroom, there are also many who are either totally opposed to it, or else want severely to restrict its scope. Some Christians, Muslims and Jews consider the introduction of philosophy an unwelcome intrusion into those parts of the curriculum that have traditionally been deemed theirs. They have developed a whole range of objections.

I want to look at two very popular objections to the suggestion that all children should be encouraged to think critically and independently about moral and religious questions. The first is: *to encourage a thinking, questioning attitude on these topics is to promote relativism.* The second is: *parents have a right to send their child to a school where their religious beliefs will not be subjected to critical scrutiny.*

Here is an illustration of both worries being expressed simultaneously. In 2004, the UK's Institute for Public Policy Research (IPPR) proposed that all children should be exposed to a range of religious faiths and atheism, and also that they be taught to think critically about religious belief. The IPPR recommended that the focus be on

> learning how to make informed, rational judgements on the truth or falsity of religious propositions. . . . Pupils would be actively encouraged to question the religious beliefs they bring with them into the classroom, not so that they are better able to defend or rationalise them, but so that they are genuinely free to adopt whatever position on religious matters they judge to be best supported by the evidence. (Hand, 2004)

What the IPPR proposed is, in effect, a form of philosophy in the classroom: the philosophical examination of religious belief.

Many religious people were entirely comfortable with this proposal. But not all. The *Daily Telegraph* ran a leader condemning the IPPR's recommendations. Here is *Daily Mail* columnist Melanie Phillips quoting from it approvingly:

> As [this] *Telegraph* leader comments, this is nothing other than yet another attempt at ideological indoctrination: 'It reflects the belief that parents who pass on the Christian faith are guilty of indoctrinating their children, and that it is the role of the state to stop them. The IPPR and its allies in the Government are not so much interested in promoting diversity as in replacing one set of orthodoxies by another: the joyless ideology of cultural relativism.' (Phillips, 2004)

Here we find both of the concerns mentioned above expressed simultaneously. Surely parents have a right to send their children to a school where their religious beliefs will be promoted without being subjected to this sort of independent critical scrutiny. The state has no right to interfere. And in any case, isn't encouraging such critical thought *itself a form of indoctrination* – in this case, indoctrination with the poisonous dogma of relativism?

The charge of relativism

I'll consider that charge of promoting relativism first. Relativism, as Melanie Philips and the *Daily Telegraph* use the term, is the view that the truth in some particular sphere is relative.

Some truths are indeed relative. Consider wichitti grubs – those huge larvae eaten live by some aboriginal Australians. Most Westerners find them revolting (certainly, the model Jordan did when she was recently required to eat one on *I'm a Celebrity, Get Me Out of Here*). But at least some native Australians consider them delicious.

So what is the truth about wichitti grubs? Are they delicious, or aren't they? The truth, it seems, is that, unlike the truth about whether wichitti grubs are carbon-based life forms or whether they are found in Australia, there is no objective, mind-independent truth here. The truth about the deliciousness of wichitti grubs is relative. For Jordan, that wichitti grubs are delicious is false. For others, it's true. When it comes to deliciousness, what's true and false ultimately boils down to subjective opinion or taste.

The relativist about morality insists that the truth of moral claims is similarly relative. There's no objective truth about whether female circumcision, stealing from supermarkets, or even killing an innocent human being, is morally wrong. Rightness and wrongness ultimately also boil down to subjective preference or taste. What's true for one person or culture may be false for another.

The relativist about religious truth similarly insists that the truth about whether or not Jesus is God is relative. That Jesus is God is true-for-Christians but false for Muslims. The 'truth' about religion is simply whatever the faithful take it to be.

Often associated with relativism is a form of *non-judgementalism* – if, say, all moral and religious points of view are equally valid, then we are wrong to judge those who hold different moral and religious views.

This brand of non-judgementalist relativism about truth is widely considered to be eating away at the fabric of Western civilization like a cancer. It is supposed to be deeply destructive – resulting in a culture of selfish, shallow individualism in which personal preference trumps everything and, ultimately, anything goes.

Relativism is certainly commonly supposed to have infected the young. Schools are often blamed. Marianne Talbot of Brasenose College Oxford, says about her students that they

> have been taught to think their opinion is no better than anyone else's, that there is no truth, only truth-for-me. I come across this relativist view constantly – in exams, in discussion and in tutorials – and I find it frightening: to question it amounts, in the eyes of the young, to the belief that it is permissible to impose your views on others. (quoted in Phillips, 1996, p. 221)

The US academic Allan Bloom writes:

> [t]here is one thing a professor can be absolutely certain of: almost every student entering university believes, or says he believes, that truth is relative. (Bloom, 1987, p. 25)

The new Pontiff is also deeply concerned. He says,

> We are moving towards a dictatorship of relativism which does not recognize anything as for certain and which has as its highest goal one's own ego and one's own desires. (Ratzinger, 2005)

Relativism even gets the blame for the rise of dangerously rigid political and religious dogmas. It was recently reported that the UK Ministry of Defence believes that:

> the trend towards moral relativism and increasingly pragmatic values [is causing] more rigid belief systems, including religious orthodoxy and doctrinaire political ideologies, such as popularism and Marxism. (quoted in Baggini, 2007)

Interestingly, when Nick Tate, head of the SCAA (the UK body responsible for devising and assessing the National Curriculum) introduced compulsory classes in citizenship for all pupils attending state-funded schools, he was explicit that one of his chief concerns was to 'slay the dragon of relativism' (Tate, 1996).

So, relativism is supposed to be rampant. But where did it come from?

The roots of relativism

In the minds of many, the blame lies with the Enlightenment. Take the UK's Chief Rabbi, Jonathan Sacks, for example. He finds particular fault with the Enlightenment philosopher Immanuel Kant. Kant provides the classic definition of Enlightenment. He says individuals should think independently and make their own judgement, rather than defer more or less uncritically to some external authority:

> [Enlightenment is the] emergence of man from his self-imposed infancy. Infancy is the inability to use one's reason without the guidance of another. It is self-imposed, when it depends on a deficiency, not of reason, but of the resolve and courage to use it without external guidance. Thus the watchword of enlightenment is: *Sapere aude!* Have the courage to use your own reason! (Kant, quoted in Honderich, 1995)

It is no coincidence that 'Sapere' and 'Aude' have been adopted as the names of two Philosophy for Children (P4C) organizations.

The Chief Rabbi considers Kant's thinking dangerous. He says that:

> according to Kant . . . to do something because others do, or because of habit or custom or even Divine Command, is to accept an external authority over

the one sovereign territory that is truly our own: our own choices. The moral being for Kant is by definition an autonomous being, a person who accepts no other authority than the self. By the 1960s this was beginning to gain hold as an educational orthodoxy. The task of education is not to hand on a tradition but to enhance the consciousness of choice. (Sacks, 1997, p. 176)

It's this Kantian rejection of any external moral authority that might decide right and wrong for us – Kant's insistence on the moral autonomy of the individual – that is the root cause of our problems. It's here that we find the origin of today's relativism. For to teach in accordance with Kant's thinking, says Sacks, requires, 'non-judgementalism and relativism on the part of the teacher' (ibid.).

Melanie Phillips concurs. 'It seems reasonable,' she says 'to regard the Enlightenment as the defining moment for the collapse of external authority' (Phillips, 1996, p. 189). The problem with Enlightenment thinking, she argues, is that 'instead of authority being located "out there" in a body of knowledge handed down through the centuries, we have repositioned it "in here" within each child' (ibid., p. 28). Because each individual 'has become their own individual arbiter of conduct', so relativism and the view that 'no-one else [is] permitted to pass judgement' have become the norm.

For Sacks, Phillips, and many other religious conservatives, Kant's '*Sapere Aude!*' – the battle cry of the Enlightenment – lies at the very heart of the West's 'moral malaise'. It is not surprising, then, that Phillips would oppose the IPPR's recommendations that children be encouraged to think critically about their own religious beliefs and traditions.

According to Sacks, Phillips and very many others, encouraging children to think independently, particularly about moral and religious matters, is precisely what got us into the awful mess in which we now find ourselves. They believe the time has come to move back in the direction of traditional, authority-based moral and religious education.

Philosophy in the classroom promotes relativism?

I have sketched out just one of the many reasons social and religious conservatives will give when explaining their hostility to the suggestion that all children ought to be encouraged and trained to think critically even about moral and religious beliefs. Such encouragement, they claim, promotes relativism. But need it?

No. In my book *The War for Children's Minds* (Law, 2006), I deal with this sort of objection – as well as many others – in much greater detail. Here I will merely sketch out three very obvious reasons why to encourage and teach children to think critically even about morality and religion need not entail the promotion of relativism and non-judgementalism.

1. Relativism entails no point to thinking critically.

   If relativism were true, there would be *no point* in engaging in the kind
   of critical thinking that proponents of philosophy in schools recommend.
   For if relativism is true, the belief that you arrive at after much very careful
   critical thought will be no more true than the one you started with. Those
   who recommend we think critically about the big questions – including moral
   and religious questions – even from a young age are, in effect, *opposed* to relativism insofar as they think that this sort of activity is able to get us closer to
   the truth.

2. Philosophy can combat relativism.

   Secondly, a children's philosophy programme is free to include critical discussion of relativism. A little close critical scrutiny is able pretty quickly to
   reveal precisely why the usual politically motivated arguments for relativism
   (such as that only relativists can promote tolerance) are, frankly, awful. I
   believe children should have the failings of moral relativism explained to
   them. That should form part of their education.

3. Relativism and respect for religious authority.

   Thirdly, there's at least anecdotal evidence that, rather than relativism being
   a product of a thinking, questioning culture, embracing relativism may be a
   strategy teachers embrace in order to *avoid* thinking critically about – and, in
   particular, questioning the authority of – any given religious tradition. If a
   teacher is required to teach a range of faiths, children are likely to spot that
   they contradict each other, and will inevitably ask, 'Which is actually *true?* Is
   Jesus God, as Christians claim, or merely a prophet, as Muslims claim?' Suggest that one religion must be mistaken and phone calls may ensue ('My
   daughter has been told the Pope might be mistaken'). Embracing relativism
   provides teachers with an easy escape from this dilemma. They can say 'That
   Jesus is God is true-for-Christians, but false-for-Muslims'. Religious relativism
   conveniently makes all religious beliefs come out as true. As Marilyn Mason
   (former chief education officer for the British Humanist Association) here
   explains, rather than promoting relativism, clear philosophical thinking is
   actually well placed to *combat* this sort of shoddy, relativistic thinking:

   I used to wonder where my students' shoulder shrugging relativism and sub-
   jectivism about knowledge came from, though I think I now know: talk of
   'different truths' or 'subjective truth' seems to have become the accepted RE
   way of demonstrating tolerance and mutual respect when confronted with

differing and sometimes conflicting beliefs and views on morality or the supernatural . . . Here is an area where the clear thinking characteristic of philosophy at its best would surely help. (Mason, 2005, p. 37)

Regarding the last two points, I should add, incidentally, that I do not mean that children should simply be told that they must more-or-less uncritically accept that relativism is twaddle. The idea is not to encourage independent critical thought about everything except relativism. But I see no reason why children cannot be given the very good arguments against relativism (which, presented correctly, are both engaging and fairly easy to grasp) to reflect on at an appropriate stage in their development.

I should perhaps also add that the kind of philosophy programme I would recommend is not, then, an exclusively hands-off affair in which topics are always chosen by children, in which children are never taught basic skills, positions and styles of argument, and in which supposedly philosophical discussion is allowed to take the form of a free association of ideas, with little or no logical structure. So while I am enthusiastic about class discussions on the P4C model (which are often excellent), they do need to be paired at some stage with some teaching of the basic skills, arguments and positions – including relativism. (This is not to say that I favour a dry academic approach – I think we need to develop new, engaging ways of teaching skills, arguments and positions.)

I don't deny, of course, that this sort of teaching would need to be carried out by people who are at least reasonably competent in the area, by teachers who, for example, are well-versed in the arguments for and against relativism. Nor do I deny that an intellectually flabby P4C programme might inadvertently end up promoting relativism. But there is certainly no necessity that philosophy in the classroom should promote relativism. As I say, done correctly, philosophy in the classroom is actually well-placed to *combat* the kind of relativism that is allegedly carrying Western civilization to hell in a hand basket.

A parental right to a philosophy-free religious and moral education?

Now let's turn to the second objection I mentioned at the beginning of this section – that parents have a right to send their child to a school where their religious beliefs will not be subjected to critical scrutiny.

Of course, many who favour philosophy in schools will agree with this. They may say, 'I believe philosophy in schools is a very good idea, but I don't think it should be *forced* on religious parents if they don't want it.'

My view is that the IPPR recommendations are sound: all children should, without exception, be encouraged to think critically – and thus philosophically – even about the moral and religious beliefs they bring with them into the classroom. Religious parents should not be able to opt out. But I am not here going to attempt to make much of a positive case for that perhaps rather illiberal-sounding assertion. I will simply offer a challenge to those who, like Phillips and the *Daily Telegraph*, believe schools that promote a religious faith in a wholly uncritical way are acceptable.

Suppose political schools started springing up – a neoconservative school in Billericay followed by a communist school in Middlesbrough. Suppose these schools select pupils on the basis of parents' political beliefs. Suppose they start each morning with the collective singing of political anthems. Suppose portraits of their political leaders beam down from every classroom wall. Suppose they insist that pupils accept, more or less uncritically, the beliefs embodied in their revered political texts. If such schools did spring up, there would be outrage. These establishments would be accused of educationally stunting children, forcing their minds into politically pre-approved moulds. They're the kind of Orwellian schools you find under totalitarian regimes in places like Stalinist Russia.

My question is, if such political schools are utterly unacceptable, if they are guilty of educationally stunting children, why on earth are so many of us still prepared to tolerate their religious equivalents? Why, if we cross out 'political' and write 'religious', do these schools suddenly strike many of us as entirely acceptable? Assuming that Phillips and the *Daily Telegraph* would consider such political schools unacceptable (irrespective of the desire of parents to send their children to them), the onus is surely on them to explain why we should consider their religious equivalents rather more acceptable – indeed, even *desirable*.

One move they might make would be to say that our political beliefs are clearly far too practically important – they are far too likely to have a concrete impact in terms of the kind of society we live in – to be left in the hands of the indoctrinators. Religious beliefs, on the other hand, are more other-worldly, and so less of a concern. But this would be to overlook the fact that religious beliefs are often intensely political. Clearly, religious points of view on homosexuality, charity, a woman's place in the home, abortion, the State of Israel, jihad, and even poverty and injustice, are all political. There are few aspects of religious belief that don't have an important political dimension. In which case, my challenge becomes sharper still: if such authoritarian political schools are unacceptable, then why are their religious equivalents acceptable, particularly as these religious schools are, in effect, highly political?

I see no reason, incidentally, why an enlightened, liberal approach to moral and religious education of the sort recommended by the IPPR cannot be conducted in religiously affiliated schools. It is not incompatible with a religious upbringing. Teachers at a Christian school, for example, might say: 'This is what we believe, and these are the reasons why we believe it. Obviously we would like you to believe it to, but not just because we tell you to. We want you to think and question and make up your own minds.' A school can have a strong Christian ethos even while encouraging independent critical thought – indeed, even while promoting philosophy in the classroom.

So I don't see that the appeal to relativism and parental rights justifies either the view that philosophy in the religious classroom is largely undesirable or the view that it be made, at most, an optional extra.

Reasons and causes

In this second part of this chapter, I want to make a well-known philosophical distinction – that between reasons and causes – and then draw out a couple of conclusions concerning philosophy in the classroom.

People's beliefs can be shaped in two very different ways, as illustrated by the two different ways we might answer the question 'Why does Jane believe what she does?'

First, we might offer Jane's reasons and justifications – the grounds of her belief. Why does Jane believe our CO_2 gas emissions are causing global warming? Well, she has seen the figures on how much CO_2 we are putting into the atmosphere, and she has seen the graphs based on Antarctic ice cores showing how global temperatures have closely tracked CO_2 levels over the past 600,000 years. So, concludes Jane on the basis of this evidence, the rising temperatures are very probably a result of our CO_2 emissions.

Another example: why does Jane believe there is a pencil on the table in front of her? Because there appears to be a pencil there. She remembers just putting a pencil there. And she has no reason to suppose that there's anything funny going on (that she's hallucinating, the victim of an optical illusion, or whatever).

Of course, explaining why someone believes something by giving their grounds or reasons is not yet to say that they are good reasons. Mary may believe she will meet a tall, dark, handsome stranger because that's what a psychic hotline told her.

So we can explain beliefs by giving people's reasons. But this is not the only way in which beliefs can be explained. Suppose John believes he is a teapot. Why? Because John attended a hypnotist's stage-show last night. John was pulled out of the audience and hypnotized into believing he is a teapot. The hypnotist forgot to un-hypnotize him, and so John is still stuck with that belief.

John need not be aware of the true explanation of why he believes he is a teapot. He may not remember being hypnotized. If we ask him to justify his belief, he may find himself oddly unable. He may simply find himself stuck with it. He may well say, with utter conviction, that he *just knows* he is a teapot. In fact, because such non-inferentially held beliefs are usually perceptual beliefs, it may seem to John that he can *see* he's a teapot. 'Look!' he may say, sticking out his arms, 'Here's my handle and here's my spout!'

So we can explain beliefs by giving a person's *reasons, grounds and justifications*, and we can explain beliefs by giving purely *causal* explanations (I say *purely* causal, as reasons can be causes too (see, for example, Davidson, 1963)). Purely causal explanations range from, say, being hypnotized or brainwashed to caving in to peer pressure or wishful thinking. These mechanisms may even include, say, being *genetically* predisposed to having certain sorts of belief (it has been suggested by Daniel Dennett (2006) and others that we are, for example, genetically predisposed to religious belief).

Of course, both kinds of explanation may be relevant when it comes to explaining why Sophie believes that P. Sophie may believe that P in part because there is *some* evidence for P, though not enough to warrant belief in P, and in part because she is, say, biologically predisposed to believe P. It may be that neither factor, by itself, is sufficient to explain Sophie's belief.

We may well flatter ourselves about just how rational we are. Sometimes, when we believe something, we think we're simply responding rationally to the evidence, but the truth is that we have been manipulated in a purely causal way. I might think I have decided that sexism is wrong because I've recognized the inherent rationality of the case against it, when the truth is that I have simply caved in to peer pressure and my unconscious desire to conform.[1]

Brainwashing

So there are two ways in which we might explain belief. There are, correspondingly, at least two ways in which we might seek to induce belief in someone. We might attempt to make a rational case, try to persuade them by means of evidence and cogent argument. Or we might take the purely causal route and try to hypnotize, apply peer pressure, and so on instead.

One of the most obvious ways of engaging in purely causal manipulation of what people believe is, of course, brainwashing. Kathleen Taylor, a research scientist in physiology at the University of Oxford who has published a study of brainwashing, writes that five core techniques consistently show up:

> One striking fact about brainwashing is its consistency. Whether the context is a prisoner of war camp, a cult's headquarters or a radical mosque, five core techniques keep cropping up: isolation, control, uncertainty, repetition and emotional manipulation. (Taylor, 2005)

The *isolation* may involve physical isolation or separation. *Control* covers restricting the information and range of views people have access to, and includes censorship. Cults tend endlessly to *repeat* their beliefs to potential converts. This repetition may include, for example, very regular communal chanting or singing. Under *uncertainty*, Taylor discusses the discomfort we feel when presented with uncertainty: by providing a simple set of geometric certainties that cover and explain everything, and also constantly reminding people of the vagaries and chaos of what lies outside this belief system, cultists can make their system seem increasingly attractive. *Emotional manipulation* can take many forms – most obviously the associating of positive feelings and images (for example, uplifting or serenely smiling icons) with the belief system, and fear and uncertainty with the alternatives.

Of course, the extent to which these techniques are applied varies from cult to cult. Clearly, they are also applied by non-religious cults and regimes. A school in Mao's China or under the present regime in North Korea would almost certainly check all five boxes. But it is an indisputable matter of fact that religious schools of the sort that tended to predominate in the UK up until the 1960s also very clearly checked all five boxes.

That these and other purely causal mechanisms are effective at influencing belief even outside a cult's headquarters or a prisoner of war camp is surely undeniable. We are all very heavily influenced by them. The success of the advertising industry is testimony to their effectiveness. Indeed, many advertising campaigns check many, if not all, of Taylor's five boxes for brainwashing.

When challenged on this, the industry typically insists that it is *primarily* concerned with 'informing' the public – providing good reasons and evidence on which consumers can base a rational and informed choice. Nevertheless, the main tools of the advertising trade are for the most part purely causal. An advertisement for soap powder, lipstick, a car or a loan typically contains very little factual information or argument. The power of these adverts to shape our thinking and behaviour is mostly purely causal – they play on our uncertainties and rely very heavily on repetition and emotional manipulation.

The question of balance

That such purely causal mechanisms are going to shape what people believe is something that is, to some extent, unavoidable. Even in a very liberal educational setting in which philosophy is involved, there will inevitably be many purely causal factors also influencing belief. Certainly, we should admit that a classroom is not wholly given over to the space of reasons. All sorts of causal and psychological pressures are applied, knowingly and unknowingly, within a school. This may even, to a very significant extent, be desirable. The question is how these purely causal influences should be *balanced* against giving reasons and justifications, encouraging rational reflection, and so on.

Now I would suggest that the extent to which religious people tend to favour or oppose the introduction of philosophy in the classroom (and the extent to which they would recommend a return to more traditional religious educational methods) tends to a very large extent to correspond with the degree to which they prefer reliance on techniques that are, in effect, purely causal. Philosophy in the classroom is about thinking critically and independently about many of the same issues in which religion has a stake. Free and open discussion, in which all views are open to close critical scrutiny (religious views included), means operating within what Wilfred Sellars called 'the logical space of reasons' (Sellars, 1956, p. 169) On the other hand, while traditional religious education might also involve a degree of free discussion (typically within certain parameters: children may be subtly or not so subtly steered away from asking certain sorts of question or making certain sorts of point), it is generally orientated far more towards purely causal techniques of influencing belief. Daily repetitive acts of worship, repetitive prayer, isolation from other belief systems (including physical isolation from those who hold them), control over the range of materials children have access to (such as writings critical of that faith), the punishment of those who dare to question (a colleague of mine educated in a Catholic School in the 1960s was punished simply for asking *why* the Catholic Church opposed contraception) and emotional manipulation (associating 'all things bright and beautiful' with the faith, images of moral chaos and hell with the alternatives) – these techniques are the mainstay of traditional religious education.

So while every style of moral and religious education inevitably involves a blend of both engaging children's rational, critical faculties *and* (whether or not intentionally) applying purely causal mechanisms, one of the fundamental issues dividing proponents of philosophy in the classroom from religious traditionalists is how these two ingredients should be balanced.

Truth-sensitivity

I want now to look at some of the ways in which reason-involving educational methods differ from purely causal mechanisms for shaping belief. Let's begin with *truth-sensitivity*. One interesting fact about these two ways of getting someone to believe something is that, generally speaking,[2] only one is truth-sensitive. The purely causal mechanisms of isolation, control, repetition, uncertainty and emotional manipulation, for example, can be used to induce the belief that Paris is the capital of France. But they can just as easily be applied to induce the beliefs that Paris is the capital of Germany and that Big Brother loves you. The attractive thing about appealing to someone's power of reason, by contrast, is that it strongly favours beliefs that are *true*. Cogent argument doesn't easily lend itself to inducing false beliefs. You are going to have a hard time trying to construct a strong, well-reasoned case capable of withstanding critical scrutiny for believing that Swindon is inhabited by giant wasp-men or that the Earth's core is made of cheese.

Sound reasoning and critical thought tend to act as a filter on false beliefs. Of course, the filter is not foolproof – false beliefs will inevitably get through. But it does tend to allow into a person's mind only those beliefs that have at least a *fairly* good chance of being correct.

And, unlike the purely causal techniques of inducing belief discussed above, the use of reason is a double-edged sword. It cuts both ways. It doesn't automatically favour the teacher's beliefs over the pupil's. It favours the truth, and so places the teacher and the pupil on a level playing field. If, as a teacher, you try to use reason to persuade, you may discover your pupil can show that it is *you*, and not them, that is mistaken. That's a risk some 'educators' are not prepared to take.

Causal vs normative determination

Some post-modern thinkers insist, of course, that 'reason' is a term used to dignify what is, in reality, merely another purely causal mechanism for influencing belief, alongside brainwashing and indoctrination. Reason is no more sensitive to the 'truth' than these other mechanisms (for of course there is really no truth for it to be sensitive to). Reason is, in reality, just another form of power – of thought-control. It is essentially as manipulative as any other mechanism.

But this is to overlook the fact that while a rational argument can in a sense 'force' a conclusion on you, the 'force' involved is *normative, not causal.* Causal determination determines what will happen. For example, given the causal power of these rails to direct this train, the train will go Oxford. Indeed, it is causally forced or compelled to. Normative determination, on the other hand, determines not what will happen, but what ought to. It is an entirely distinct kind of determination involving an entirely different sort of compulsion or force.

A rational argument shows you what you *ought* to believe if you want to avoid contradiction and give your beliefs the best chance of being true. Take this valid deductive argument:

All men smell
John is a man
Therefore, John smells.

To recognize that this argument is valid is just to recognize that, if you believe that all men smell and that John is a man, then you *ought to* believe that John smells. But of course this argument doesn't *causally* compel you to accept that conclusion even if you do accept the premises. You're free to be irrational.

This isn't to deny that rational arguments have causal power. Of course they do. A good argument can have the power to change history (consider the wonderful arguments of Galileo, or the campaigner against slavery William Wilberforce). But when rational arguments have the causal power to shape people's thinking, they typically have it as a result of their having normative power. People change their opinions precisely because they recognize the *normative* force of the argument.

Notice, by the way, that we can easily demonstrate that a rational argument doesn't have normative power simply in virtue of its having the causal power to shape people's thinking (though critics who fail to understand the difference between normative and causal determination typically miss this point).

The obvious counter-example is *fallacious argument*. A fallacious argument lacks any normative power, but, if the fallacy is seductive, it will still have considerable *causal* power to shape belief.

So far, I have stressed how rational argument differs from purely causal mechanisms for influencing belief. In particular, rational argument is truth-sensitive, while purely causal mechanisms are typically not. Also, rational arguments, while possessing causal power to shape belief, typically have this power in virtue of their normative power. The kind of 'determination' a rational argument 'imposes' on us is, in the first instance, normative, not causal. Rational argument is certainly not a form of coercion or manipulation in the way that purely causal mechanisms are.

Let's now develop that last point a little further. As I explain below, it seems to me that rational arguments allow for a form of *freedom* in a way that purely causal mechanisms do not.

Reason and freedom

Enlightenment liberals like myself tend to feel uncomfortable about heavy reliance on purely causal mechanisms. Here's one reason why.

When you use reason to persuade, you respect the other's freedom to make (or fail to make) a rational decision.[3] When you apply purely causal mechanisms, you take that freedom from them. Your subject may think they've made an entirely free and rational decision, of course, but the truth is that they're your puppet – you're pulling their strings. In effect, by ditching reason and relying on purely causal mechanisms – peer pressure, emotional manipulation, repetition and so on – you are now treating them as just one more bit of the causally manipulable natural order – as mere *things*.

On one of the formulations of his categorical imperative, Kant says that we ought always to treat both others and ourselves always as ends in themselves, and never purely as means to an end. We should not treat others or ourselves in an entirely instrumental way, as we might treat a screwdriver or car, to get the result we want. We should have 'respect for persons' – for their inherent freedom and rationality, which, according to Kant, is what distinguishes them from mere things.

Here's an illustration (not Kant's) of the kind of respect Kant has in mind. Suppose I need food to feed my starving children. I might get food from the local shop by lying – by saying that I will pay for it next week knowing full well that I won't. Or I might try to get food by honestly explaining my situation to the shopkeeper and hoping she will be charitable. In both cases, I 'use' the shopkeeper to get what I want. But, unlike the first option, the second does not involve using the shopkeeper *purely* as a means to an end. I respect her rationality and freedom to make her own decision about whether to provide food without payment. Kant says that only the second option shows the shopkeeper the proper respect she is due as a person. The first treats her purely instrumentally, as if she were merely a thing.

Avoiding the purely causal route so far as influencing the beliefs of others is concerned is, presumably, one of the things that Kant would insist on. Indeed, if Kant is right, it seems that reliance on purely causal mechanisms to shape belief also involves a fundamental lack of respect for persons.

How to influence belief

It is undeniable that, as educators, we do want to influence children's beliefs. Influencing beliefs is not all there is to education, not by a very long way. But that this is *one* of the things we are interested in doing in the classroom is beyond dispute. We don't want to send children out into the world believing that a woman's place is behind the sink, that it's morally acceptable to torture animals, that Jewish people are untrustworthy, or that the entire universe is just six thousand years old. Well I don't, anyway. So the question is not *whether* we should influence what children believe, but *how*.

I have tried to show how the philosophical distinction between reasons and causes can help illuminate this question. We have seen that rational argument differs from taking the purely causal route in at least three important ways:

1. It is *truth-sensitive* (whereas purely causal mechanisms typically are not).
2. While rational arguments can be causally powerful, their causal power typically derives from their *normative* power – which is a categorically distinct *non-causal* form of 'power'.
3. Rational argument allows for an important form of *freedom* – a freedom that the purely causal mechanisms actually strips from us.

We have also seen that religious traditionalists lean rather more towards purely causal mechanisms for influencing belief than do proponents of philosophy in the classroom. Indeed, this is one of the fundamental issues, perhaps *the* fundamental issue, dividing them.

To finish, I want to provide a couple of examples of how thinking about the debate between proponents of philosophy in the classroom and religious traditionalists in these terms might shed some light on some of the arguments offered on either side.

First, the distinction makes a little clearer, perhaps, why taking the purely causal route can be *tempting*. When you open up debate and critical discussion, you run the risk that people won't believe what you want them to believe. If we suppose that certain beliefs are very important indeed, perhaps even vital for the survival of Western civilization, well then the temptation to take the purely causal route can become very strong indeed.

For example, some argue that, whether or not religious belief is true, it is socially necessary. Remove it, and society will eventually fall apart. So we must rely on traditional religious education to instill it. Bring reason into religious education, and, given its truth-detecting power, the dubiousness of religious belief might be exposed. The results may be disastrous. So philosophy in the classroom – and certainly in the classroom where religion is discussed – is a bad, if not downright dangerous, idea. Many American neoconservatives take this view.

Second, a failure properly to understand the distinction between reasons and causes may lead defenders of traditional religious educational techniques to think that their methods are, in essence, really not so very different to what proponents of philosophy in the classroom have in mind. At bottom, aren't both really just forms of causing-people-to-believe-what-you-want-them-to-believe? As we saw above, Melanie Phillips considers what the IPPR proposes (critical scrutiny of religious beliefs in the classroom) to be, just 'another attempt at ideological indoctrination'. In Phillips' mind, philosophy in the classroom is not an alternative to indoctrination. It's just a *different kind* of indoctrination.

It is certainly in the interests of religious opponents of philosophy in the classroom to obscure the distinction between educating within the logical space of reasons, and educating via the purely causal route. In particular, it is in their interests to obscure the fact that the distinction raises some very fundamental questions about freedom, and also about what Kant calls 'respect for persons'.

That many proponents of traditional religious educational methods (who would oppose philosophy in the classroom) fail fully to realize the extent to which they are applying purely causal mechanisms to induce belief is indicated by the fact that when the beliefs in question are political, not religious, and when the techniques are applied in political schools rather than religious schools, they consider these same techniques brainwashing. That many of the faithful simply don't recognize that their preferred educational methods come at least very close to brainwashing is, I suspect, largely due to the fact that, within the religious setting of convent schools, madrassahs, and so on and within their own upbringing ('After all, it never did me any harm'), these techniques have acquired the rosy glow of comfortable familiarity.

Notes

[1] That what we believe, or at least what we will say we believe, is shaped far more by peer pressure than we might imagine was suggested by the experiments of Solomon Asch (1951) in the early 1950s. Asch found that, in order to avoid being out of step with what their peers believe, the majority of his subjects denied what was clearly before their eyes.

2 *Some* purely causal mechanisms are truth sensitive. For example, a thermometer is a fairly reliable mechanism for indicating temperature. Similarly, our perceptual mechanisms are fairly reliable mechanisms for producing true beliefs. They 'track the truth', as it were. Notice, however, that the purely causal techniques typically applied by cults, and indeed, in religious schools, are not truth-sensitive. They can just as easily be applied to induce false beliefs as true ones.

3 Someone might raise the worry: If we are physically determined, then we don't have free will, and if we don't have free will, then we cannot make free, rational judgements and decisions after all. Well, yes, perhaps there is, for the above reason, a sense in which none of our judgements is 'free'. But there remains a sense, I think, in which rational persuasion allows for a *kind* of freedom that the purely causal mechanisms strip from us. And this kind of freedom might be compatible with for example physical determinism.

Part Two

Making the Case for Philosophy in Schools

Chapter Five

The Role of Philosophical Thinking in Teaching Controversial Issues

Harry Brighouse

Moral philosophy is an activity that every reflective person begins engaging in at a very young age. As soon as a child asks why she should share her toys, or why she should refrain from responding in kind to a cruel playmate, or why she should refrain from being cruel to a kind playmate, she is asking a philosophical question. Even the crudest answers to these questions – 'because you will get on better in the world if you do so' – are philosophical in kind.

Most teachers deal to some degree with moral philosophical issues within their subject matter. But within the school curriculum they arise in their most sophisticated forms in humanities subjects such as English and History. The evolution of subjects such as PSHE and Citizenship in the UK and the increased emphasis on civic education in the US pose moral philosophical issues very sharply. Some examples: In Citizenship: What kind of deliberation should voters engage in before voting? Should they vote in their own interests, or for the sake of the common good? In PSHE: Is abortion a moral choice? Is extra- or pre-marital sex a moral choice, and if so, when is sex not a moral choice? In the US: all those questions plus Was the US right to invade Iraq? Even if it was wrong, would withdrawal now be right? Is it right to love your country when your country is doing wrong?

There are reasons for the recent increase in teaching about controversial issues in the contexts I've mentioned. One is that it is more widely recognized than it once was that citizens have a responsibility not merely to press their own interests, but to deliberate in a more impartial, and well-informed, manner about issues at stake in public life. In a democracy everyone shares responsibility for the way things go, and so everyone has an interest in being able to think responsibly about how things should go. Second, there is a recognition that new issues face us as individuals and voters, especially those raised by developments in medical technology, which the moral apparatus developed by our religious and moral traditions do not fully equip us to deal with. Finally, it is no longer the case in any developed country that a single well-defined religious tradition dominates the terms of public debate or private morality, so that even if a child is raised within a wide-reaching religious tradition she will certainly have to encounter and think through moral perspectives quite unlike her own. Teaching about these issues in schools is supposed to help children to carry out their obligations as citizens and to cope with diversity in civil society in a way that better enables them to flourish as individuals.

Philosophical education concerning controversial issues is urgently important in a democracy. Democratic polities disperse moral responsibility for political decisions by giving all citizens a formal mechanism for contributing to political decision-making, the vote. Citizens who vote for a winning party, or a successful policy option in a referendum, are responsible for that decision. Of course, they must therefore make their best effort to assess the probable effects of the decision; but they must also make their best effort to evaluate the moral reasons that count for and against it. Identifying and evaluating moral reasons is the stuff of moral philosophy; when we do it, we are doing moral philosophy whether we recognize that or not.

In principle, schools needn't be the locus of this aspect of education. More imaginative readers can probably think of a society which contains numerous and publicly unavoidable models of careful moral reasoning – on television, in newspapers, in parliament and on the street corner – and in which children come, as they develop into adults, to be morally responsible reasoners about public matters and discerning thinkers about morality in their own lives. But even those readers will doubt that they inhabit such a society, and, like many other tasks that could, in principle, be done through other institutions, it makes sense in our society to burden schools with this one.

Yet most teachers have received no education in moral philosophy either in secondary school or during college, let alone education in how to lead discussions within diverse classrooms on moral philosophical questions. Recent UK-based research into the teaching of social and ethical issues arising from developments in biomedical research found that teachers deal with such issues in very different ways (Levinson et al., 2000). To summarize: Science teachers felt that it was their role to teach *the facts* and that they were insufficiently equipped to deal with the ethics involved. Humanities teachers on the other hand viewed the teaching of controversial issues as relatively unproblematic but often felt that the scientific facts in accessible form were not always readily available to them. From looking at this research, and from numerous discussions with teachers on both sides of the Atlantic, I suspect that few are well-equipped to teach about values. Too many teachers on both sides of the science/humanities divide seem to think that there is a simple 'fact/value' distinction, and that the standards for thinking about each side of the distinction are completely different. Too many slide from a commitment to toleration to a presumption of relativism. And too few have been exposed to more rigorous ways of thinking about value-related matters than one would glean from attending to better newspapers.

In the US (though not in the UK) there is a large pool of expertise in teaching philosophically about moral issues to young people who have no previous exposure to philosophy. Most universities in the US have 'contemporary moral issues' courses, usually housed in Philosophy departments, which fulfil requirements within a wide range of majors. I have taught such a course for many years, and although my students are university students, very few have studied, or will study, any other philosophy; they are usually in nursing, business studies, pre-law, pre-medicine or other professional trajectories. I have also run sessions at a local high school, with students who were not bound for elite universities. So what follows is largely an account of my approach, with the hope that it, or at least some of it, can be useful to others.

The chapter has the following structure. First I argue that moral relativism is false, and that teachers should enter moral philosophical discussions by explicitly disavowing (and arguing against) relativism. I then explain how philosophical methods can be used in teaching about moral issues. A basic understanding of philosophical methods helps teachers to organize their own thinking and guide the discussions of their students to facilitate serious reflection. Finally I give two specific examples of how philosophical methods can be used in organizing discussion of abortion and 'designer babies'.

Moral relativism

Moral relativism is the thesis that there are no moral truths. Why is it so important to demonstrate that moral relativism is false? If moral relativism is true, then there is no foundation for reason-giving debate about moral matters. We can, as it were, make it all up. To take a simple matter, when we engage in a debate about whether the earth is flat, there is a fact of the matter about which we are disagreeing, and evidence bearing on that fact constitutes one source of reason-giving. When we engage in a debate about the causes of WWI we marshal evidence, organizing the facts about the prior trajectories and strategies of the major actors, and entertain counterfactuals for the sake of illuminating the evidence. We can do this in a reasonable way because we agree that there is a truth of the matter independent of our own beliefs, and which has authority over our beliefs if only we can find it. But if there is no truth – as the moral relativist believes there is not in the moral case – then there is nothing with authority over our beliefs, and all we have is a clash of attitudes, entirely unchecked by the world, and largely unchecked by reason.

One helpful way of making the contrast is by appeal to models of thinking. The teacher can present two models, the taste model and the scientific model, and test the students' intuitions about them.

The taste model

Julian likes coffee but hates tea
Sandy likes tea but hates coffee

In the taste model there is no room for reason-giving debate. Julian and Sandy understand that what each other has is a taste. They might feel sorry for each other, believing that the other is missing out on some great experience that everyone should have, but neither believes his own taste to have authority over the other, and neither believes that there is any external evidence to appeal to in trying to argue for the superiority of his own taste. Indeed, neither believes his own taste to be superior, or that there is any true disagreement here.

The science model

> Ermintrude believes that all swans are white.
> Florence believes that there are black swans.

In the science model, there is a genuine disagreement. They disagree about a matter of fact, for which it makes sense to seek further evidence, and each understands what evidence might dissuade her from her current belief. They understand that it is not possible that both of them are right, because they both understand that the facts about the world have authority over their beliefs. If they want to resolve the dispute then Ermintrude gives her reasons for thinking all swans are white, Florence hers for thinking there are black swans, and they investigate further.

If the taste model were appropriate to moral issues, there would be no standards of reasoning to apply. It would make no more sense to run a course in a university called 'Contemporary Moral Issues' in which students are educated to reason carefully about abortion, racism, euthanasia and justice in taxation than it would to run a course called 'Contemporary Gustatory Issues' in which students are educated to reason carefully about the relative tastiness of smoked salmon, stilton cheese, tea and coffee.

But if it is more like the science model, there are standards to apply. A central purpose of teaching about controversial issues is to teach these standards – to induct students into the practices of reasoning and thinking about these issues.

How does one persuade students that they already, despite the claims some of them make to the contrary, believe that moral relativism is false? The best way is to ask them whether they believe that certain propositions are true or false, or just matters of taste. For example:

A. It is wrong to torture babies simply for enjoyment.
B. Slavery was morally right and there was no reason to abolish it.
C. The Holocaust was a great moral good.

These statements express propositions which are not like the proposition that coffee tastes really good, in that they have a truth value which in no way depends on the standpoint, traits, perception or personality of the person making them.

A is true, and B and C are false. They have those properties because there is a corresponding reality against which we can evaluate them.

Even the most determinedly relativistic students tend not to dispute this. But when they do, it makes sense to ask them how they would respond to people who disagreed with them about these statements. Would they walk away saying 'oh well, he's got strange tastes' or would they argue, and try to give reasons for why? Most of them think these issues, at least, are ones over which disagreement needs to be confronted by reason-giving. Fortunately, most people, even if they say they are relativists about morality, find, on reflection, that they are not.

There is a large difference between statements A–C and the moral issues that usually arise in discussion among teenagers and in the school curriculum. The statements work as ways of pointing out that there are moral facts precisely because there is no longer any dispute about them. But it can be helpful to point out that slavery, at least, was once thought to be morally acceptable by many people, and that they defended their view with reasons – reasons which were wrongheaded, but were invoked nevertheless. Just because an issue is controversial that does not mean there is no fact of the matter at stake; it just means that, whatever the moral facts are, they are not clear to everyone in those circumstances.

Moral reasoning for everyone

The key question, though, is how do we get at the moral facts that the anti-relativist argument claims must be there to be got at? 500 years of hard work have built up a tradition of scientific reasoning which amounts to a method to get us closer to the truth in scientific matters. Those who want to get toward the truth in science get trained in those methods and participate in a community of scholars who use the methods, monitoring themselves and each other, sometimes explicitly and sometimes implicitly. But even those who agree that there are moral truths do not all agree on a method for arriving at them. Some consult holy books or gurus, others reflect on their own experiences, still others seem to intuit the truth without much reflection at all. So how, in a classroom consisting of children reared with very different approaches, is the teacher to prompt genuinely philosophical collaborative discussion and reflection?

In fact contemporary philosophy has developed a set of techniques for addressing moral matters in a responsible way, and although naming it for one's students probably doesn't make much sense, understanding what it is probably does help one to teach them more effectively. We call it the method of reflective equilibrium. The method of reflective equilibrium invites us to explore our moral beliefs in the following way. We list our considered judgements about particular cases, and look at whether they fit together consistently. Where we find inconsistencies we reject those judgements in which we have least reason to be confident (for example, those in which we have reason to suspect there is an element of self-interest pressing us to the conclusion we have reached). We also list the principles we judge suitable to cover cases, and look through those principles for inconsistency, again rejecting those we have least reason to be confident in our judgements about. Then we look at the particular judgements and the principles in the light of one another: are there inconsistencies?; do some of the principles look less plausible in the light of the weight of considered judgements, or vice versa?

Of course, all that this method gives us is, at best, a consistent set of judgements. But if we engage in the process collectively, in conversation with others who are bound by similar canons of rationality, we can have increasing confidence in the truth of the outcomes. Other people can bring out considerations we had not noticed; they can alert us to weaknesses in our own judgements; they can force us to think harder and better. If we converge on conclusions about particular cases with people with whom we otherwise disagree a great deal, we should have more confidence in our judgement. We cannot ever be certain that we have arrived at the ultimate truth. But this method at least gives us a way of making some progress.

What do I mean by 'judgements about particular cases' and 'principles'? An autobiographical comment which, I'm afraid, does not reflect particularly well on me, will help. In the late 1970s I held a pre-theoretical view concerning freedom of expression that, I think, was quite common among British teenagers with my political outlook. I believed that there was no reason to grant free speech to racists, or anyone with anti-social views, and that it was entirely fine for the government to censor offensive films. So, the principle I held was something like this: 'Governments should have the power to censor expression when it meets some objective criteria for being anti-social'. One morning I turned on the radio and heard Jimmy Young (a BBC Radio 2 disc jockey) announce that he was soon going to be talking to a Church of England vicar who was trying to have a new film, 'Rimbaud', banned from his local cinema. My reaction was outrage – 'how dare this busy-bodying minister try to shut down a film about the great homosexual French poet Rimbaud?' (The judgement was about an individual case: 'It is wrong to censor *this* film'). When the discussion began, however, it turned out that the vicar objected not to its portrayal of homosexuality, but to its excessive violence – the film starred Sylvester Stallone (who would have been an eccentric choice for Rimbaud), and in fact the film was called Rambo, not the homophonic Rimbaud. The film was (I believe, though I should confess that I never saw it) entirely devoid of reference to homosexuality or poetry, and I knew that had I heard the vicar without having been confused about his topic, I would have agreed with every word he said (the judgement about the individual case I *would* have had: 'It is fine to censor *this* film'). There was not, in fact, a conflict between my principle and my judgement about the individual cases, but being forced by the situation to think through the principle and both judgements together, I realized that I had no good grounds for my adherence to the principle, and have ever since had a much more liberal (and, dare I say, rational) attitude towards freedom of expression.

As a teacher, one way of making it hard for students to engage in this method is by giving them the impression that you know the truth about the matter at stake with complete confidence. Of course, it would be odd if you were leading a discussion about the morality of abortion in a classroom without having thought about the topic a good deal more than your students, and without having arrived at some tentative conclusions, and it is sensible not to pretend to be an ingénue. But three things help to draw out discussion.

First, it is important to make the distinction to the students between making arguments and asserting conclusions. I say that for all of the moral issues we discuss I think there are interesting arguments on more than one side. So although I sometimes have a strong view about an issue, I recognize there are strong (though obviously not conclusive), or at least interesting, arguments against my view.

Second, it is important to make it clear that you have no interest at all in what conclusions they draw about the issues; only in the quality of the arguments they make for the conclusions. They will not be judged for their conclusions, but for the quality of their thinking, the care they take in trying to avoid mistakes in reasoning, and their willingness to offer reasoned responses to the questions at stake. Of course, some students will find it confusing at first to be told that these are matters about which there are truths, but in addressing which the quality of their reasoning, rather than the conclusions about the truth they draw, is what is at stake. But any other message increases the ever-present risk that the teacher will be seen as (or will actually be) a de facto moral authority, rather than an imperfect authority in the practice of moral reasoning.

The third preliminary is to point out at the outset what counts as giving reasons, and to help students see what kinds of reasons are likely to be in play. But what is it to give reasons? I tell my students that reasons are explanations of why someone should do something. Some reasons appeal to the interests of the agent: for example, 'You should go to Restaurant X because you like the kind of food they serve, and they do it really well'. Others appeal to moral claims: 'You shouldn't do that because, even though it will help your career, it is dishonest'. But reasons depend on reasons – the reason you shouldn't be dishonest is because it is wrong (or at least wrong in many situations). Ultimately, to demonstrate the most fundamental moral claims, we need to do some deep moral philosophy. But in discussing a particular issue it is helpful to think about how widely a reason is held. The fact that everyone agrees on a reason is not a guarantor of its truth, but it is a good practice to appeal to widely held reasons, especially when you are trying to prove controversial claims. If your audience disagrees with you about a claim, but you can show them that it is implied by some value they hold very strongly, you've made an interesting argument.

So 'The Bible says so' is not a reason, unless you can give reasons for seeing the Bible as authoritative: it is not going to persuade non-believers. But if you are trying to persuade a Christian of some claim, it probably helps. 'It leads to human suffering' is a reason only if you think human suffering is bad (which, fortunately, most of us do). The key is to offer reasons for your conclusion that are as widely acceptable as possible, without making it impossible for you to say anything interesting. But even if you think human suffering is bad, that X leads to human suffering is only a reason not to do it, not a conclusive reason not to do it – maybe the alternatives lead to more human suffering, or lead to other worse things.

I think of reasons as lying on a spectrum, which roughly tracks their persuasiveness

Idiosyncratic Reasons . . . . Completely Impartial Reasons
(E.g. it makes me laugh)   (E.g. it causes widespread suffering)

Of course, not everyone accepts completely impartial reasons. But the more widely the reason an argument appeals to is accepted, the more impartial the argument will seem.

Five kinds of moral reason will frequently occur in carefully orchestrated moral debates, and it is worth alerting students to them at the outset, so that they can be reflective about them.

Consequences

Students will often appeal to the consequences of a policy or action. So, for example, one reason a student might oppose the war in Afghanistan is that it will have bad consequences for the Afghans, or, possibly, for the Middle East as a whole. Think of two possible consequences: the destruction of the Taliban would be seen as bad by a supporter of the Taliban; the rise of militant Islam in the Muslim world would be seen as bad by secularists. Both were possible consequences of the war. You have to identify that a consequence is being appealed to, help the student to see the moral aspect of their evaluation (they think the Taliban are good/bad), and talk about how difficult it sometimes is to identify consequences in advance of actions. Furthermore, consequences themselves are objects of moral evaluation; most actions produce some good and some bad consequences, but one has to look at which are good and which bad, and how good and bad they are, in order fully to evaluate them.

Motives

Sometimes students will appeal to the motives of the actors performing the actions. If motives are tainted they will often condemn actions with good consequences, if pure they will often excuse actions with bad consequences. So someone might argue that Bush and Blair are motivated in pursuit of the war in Afghanistan not by the good of the Afghans, but by domestic considerations – shoring up support for their own governments. Sometimes motives are decisive: for example, in homicides we ask whether the killer intended the death – if so it's murder, if not it isn't. But sometimes – especially in the case of government policy, large-scale action – it is hard to believe that it can be so decisive. Partly because motives are mixed (different policy-makers and different voters have radically different motives for supporting a single action), but also partly because of the scale of action, and the fact that so many people involved are distant from those who act. If it were really the case that an action saved millions of lives, we would not want to reject it even if we knew that the policy-maker who advocated it was motivated purely by career considerations, or greed.

Action-types

Sometimes a student will say: 'well that's murder, and murder is always wrong' or 'that's lying, and lying is always wrong'. There are two questions to ask here. Is the action really as they have described it (whether abortion is murder is what is at issue in the abortion debate – calling it murder doesn't get us very far). The other is whether the action-type is always wrong. Murder probably is; similarly rape. But lying? killing? war? Think of examples of these actions which are either obviously right, or where it is at least not clear.

Character

Sometimes students will condemn something because of the character of the person performing the action. In between the collapse of the twin towers in Manhattan on 11 September 2001 a special advisor at the much-troubled Department of Transport sent an email to colleagues suggesting that day would be a good one to disclose bad news, because it would be ignored by the press. A furore erupted when the email came to light a month later, and the advisor's job was saved only because her boss, the Transport Minister, fought for her at the highest level. Defending herself against blanket press criticism she said, variously, that it was an 'error of judgement', 'a terrible act' and 'something I will have to live with for the rest of my life'. But the email had no bad consequences – it harmed no-one. Sending an email is not a forbidden action-type.

Her motives were to help the government, or to do her job well or some other not entirely dishonourable motive. And her judgement was, contrary to her claim, not in error – her job was to know how to present news, and she was right that it was a good day to bury bad news. What was 'wrong' was her character. The action revealed, for the world, a poisonous personality, a character sufficiently indifferent to human tragedy that she was able to use clear and sharp judgement about her own job, which had nothing to do with relieving suffering. (Note, that insensitivity to human suffering can be part of a great virtue: the fire-fighters and police officers who entered the building to save lives on the same day had similarly sharp and clear judgement, but we admire that, because they have trained their characters to respond insensitively to human suffering in order more effectively to relieve it.)

Desert

Desert considerations are close to character considerations. For example, it is reasonable to think that Osama Bin Laden deserves severe punishment. Not only for his actions but also for being the person he is. This is why character considerations sometimes figure in sentencing decisions – because someone who is normally upstanding and does wrong in a moment of great stress seems to deserve less severe treatment than someone who has no reservation about wrong-doing and no regrets. Passionate defenders of moral positions often try to bring desert and consequence considerations together. For example, defenders of capital punishment usually say that murderers deserve death *and* that the death penalty deters murderers. But the considerations are clearly distinct. My own view on capital punishment is that some murderers *do* deserve death, but there's no evidence that the death penalty deters, and the systems needed in order to protect those who do not deserve death from capital punishment are so expensive that it's not worth society's while to execute those who deserve it. So one view about the issue is that the death penalty is a case where the best policy, all things considered, is one that does not give people what they deserve.

Two examples: abortion and designer babies

I want to finish by offering two brief discussions of contemporary moral controversies which illustrate some arguments that are worth presenting to, and can be engaged with by, students.

Abortion

I'm going to focus on just two arguments about abortion, both because they are interesting and because I know from experience that they can be used with 15- to 17-year-old students. Much of the debate about abortion focuses on whether the fetus is a human being. But, of course, it is a human being on any reasonable understanding. We need to avoid getting hung up on semantics. The issue is fundamentally moral – is the fetus the kind of being that it is wrong, and that we do not have a right, to kill. I'm going to describe two arguments, one of which says that it is wrong, and the other of which says that the woman in whom a fetus resides has a right to remove it.

Here's the argument that abortion is wrong:

First we need to ask what makes killing an innocent adult human being wrong. The answer is that killing him deprives him of a valuable future, one in which he will have valuable self-conscious experiences. Unlike the view, often invoked by opponents of abortion, that all human life is sacred, this argument allows that some killings, such as voluntary euthanasia, are not wrong (because the person who chooses euthanasia is not being involuntarily deprived of anything), and nor does it invoke a religious commitment which non-religious people do not share. It also allows us to think that killing some animals – dolphins, whales, the higher primates – who may have self-consciousness, is wrong. But if that is what is wrong with killing, then abortion seems to be wrong, because abortion deprives someone – the fetus – of a valuable self-conscious future. (Marquis, 1989)

What's nice about this argument is that it doesn't need to claim that the fetus is a human being, or fuss about when life starts – it only depends on the obviously true claim that it is capable of having a valuable human future, and will have that if it is not aborted. It does not even have to claim that abortion is an act of killing, because whether or not it is an act of killing, it *is* an act of depriving a being of a valuable self-conscious future. And if this is what makes killing wrong, it makes other actions which involve it – like abortion – wrong as well.

How can we respond to this argument? One possibility is to say that depriving someone of a valuable self-conscious future is not what is wrong about killing them. But this response is only going to be compelling if we can say something convincing about what *is* wrong with killing.

A second response is to deny that fetuses (at least in the early stages) really are the kinds of beings that have valuable self-conscious futures ahead of them. They are not self-conscious in the early stages, and have not, for example, developed brains, which seem to be at the core of our personal identities. This response has to say something about when the fetus becomes a being that has a valuable self-conscious future. Any account will have to appeal to the science and to philosophical argument, and is bound to be contentious, but so is the view that they are, even in early stages, such beings. But one thing to say is that any reasonable account is likely to give the date as some time quite a bit earlier than 22 weeks, which is a common age after which abortion becomes illegal.

The argument that women have a right to abortion that I'm going to present was made in 1971 by the American philosopher, Judith Thomson. Thomson explains that most opposition to abortion has relied on the idea that fetuses have a 'right to life'. And if they have a right to life, it must be wrong to abort them, since this deprives them of life. She defers to the assumption that fetuses do have a right to life, and argues that it is permissible to abort them anyway (Thomson, 1971).

She constructs an analogy as follows (which I've adapted slightly to make it less complex):

Imagine that there is a world famous violinist, who is suffering from a rare and fatal blood disease. You are the only person who can save him, because your blood is the only match for his. The only way you can save him is by having your kidney attached to his by a tube for nine months. Suppose you wake up one morning, having had sex with someone the previous night, and find that you are hooked up to the violinist, and this was somehow caused by you having sex. The tube is very long, flexible, and unintrusive, so for the first few months you can go about your normal life, with only moderate inconvenience, but as the months pass it will shorten and become less flexible, making the inconvenience ever greater until the last few weeks when you will just be longing for it to be removed. The violinist will be unconscious throughout the period, so he will not intrude on your privacy. It will merely be increasingly inconvenient and increasingly painful. Detaching the tube now will be relatively painless for you, but it will get more painful as time goes on, and after nine months it will be very painful, but will only involve a tiny risk of serious illness or death (in fact, exactly the same risk as childbirth under modern medical conditions).

Do you have a right to detach yourself from the violinist? Thomson thinks it is obvious that you do. She says it would be *very nice* of you *not* to detach yourself, and we should give you credit for that. But you are not obliged to remain hooked up – you have a right to detach. But, she says, the situation is exactly analogous with that of abortion: the act of sexual intercourse causes another being to be dependent on your body for its life for nine months. If you have the right to detach yourself from the violinist, then you have the right to detach yourself from the fetus – to prevent, in both cases, the other being from using your body to ensure his survival.

How can we respond to the argument? First, you can attack the claim that the cases are analogous. The violinist is, after all, an adult and not vulnerable in the way a fetus is. He could have bought insurance against such a disastrous disease and has had some of his life already. But why should this make a difference? He is going to *die* unless you offer up your body for his use, just as the fetus will.

Second you can say that there is a special bond between mother (and father) and child, a genetic bond, say, or a bond of love. Obviously, if a woman wants an abortion, she doesn't love her fetus, and although people do undoubtedly become deeply attached to fetuses it is very odd to love them – you don't know them. And why should the fact that a being carries your genetic material be decisive? We can understand that people do, in fact, often care about their genetic relations more than other people, but it is hard to see why such an urgent matter as saving someone's life should be obligatory when that person is related to you, but not when they are not.

Finally, both of these responses concede something very important: that whatever it is that makes abortion wrong it is not the right to life of the fetus. The violinist has a right to life, but he does not have the right to use your body to sustain his life. In general the right to life does not involve the right to whatever is needed to sustain life. Both these responses to the analogy imply that it is something else – being vulnerable, or being genetically related – and not the right to life – that justifies the right not to be aborted.

Another response to this argument concedes that the cases are analogous, but says, against Thomson, that you do *not* have a right to detach yourself from the violinist. In my experience people are initially rarely willing to say this, but this may be culturally specific, because I have always taught about this in the US. How would we support an obligation to remain attached to the violinist? The most obvious way is to say that we have very extensive obligations to help other people in need. So if we can save someone's life, especially if it only involves us in the kinds of risks and inconveniences involved in an ordinary pregnancy, we are obliged to do that. Thomson never discusses this possibility, and I have a suspicion that this is because in the US, which shapes her thinking, opponents of abortion tend to be conservatives, and (American) conservatives tend to believe that we do not have extensive obligations to help other people. According to them it is ok to let others suffer, and die, as long as we do not directly cause their misfortune. So admitting such vast obligations as seem needed to support the idea that we are obliged to remain attached to the violinist is not acceptable to them. So although someone could make this response, Thomson knows that almost no-one will. (Some Roman Catholics, of course, do make this response, and that is entirely consistent.) My experience, however, is that once students who oppose abortion see this route they are often willing to embrace it; preferring to accept that there are much more extensive moral demands to help other people than they had previously thought than to accept that there is a right to abortion.

Designer babies

Technology now exists that allows parents to choose – or at least dramatically increase the probability of their children having – certain genetic traits. There are three central mechanisms:

1. Selective abortion (which enables parents to abort fetuses found to have certain disabilities, such as Down's Syndrome and Cystic Fibrosis; or, in the most common case, to abort female fetuses when a boy is wanted).
2. Selection of the other biological parent. This is routine, of course, when people choose their partners, who are typically of the same race, social class and national identity as they are. But in the US, for example, it is legal to pay for the services of sperm donors and egg donors, and it is therefore possible to select the traits of those donors without having actually to marry, or in any way attract, them. A famous advertisement in the daily newspaper of an Ivy League university sought an egg donor who was at least 5ft 10 in, had a family history free of congenital disease, and a high IQ; the promised fee was $50,000. In 2000, Sharon Duchesneau and Candy Mcullough, a lesbian couple, sought a sperm donor with five generations of deafness in his family to increase the probability that their child would, like them, be deaf.
3. Gene therapy. This is the fastest-growing form of designing babies – gene therapy can be used to avoid certain traits, and to select others, such as eye colour. In our lifetimes it is likely that scientists will have sufficient understanding of the human genome to support the development of technology that will allow parents to prevent some disabilities and to choose many desirable traits (eye colour, IQ, height, etc.) without rejecting a given fetus.

Unlike abortion, this is a moral issue concerning which there is not yet a large and sophisticated philosophical literature to draw on, so rather than focus in depth on particular arguments, it is more fruitful to try to elicit considerations pointing one way or another. In that spirit here are some arguments for and against allowing parents freedom, with some discussion.

Arguments for allowing people to design their babies:

- Parents should be allowed to do their best for their children. We allow them to buy them private schooling, which helps them to earn more money and have more rewarding jobs. We allow them to buy cosmetic orthodontistry, to make them more confident and more attractive to potential mates. We even allow adults to buy all sorts of cosmetic surgery to make them more attractive. Selecting traits is not fundamentally different: it is just allowing parents to do their best for their children. If we have the technology people should be allowed to use it. (Note that there is economic research showing that men who are taller, and people who are more conventionally attractive, earn more money than others over the course of their lives, controlling for social class background, schooling and IQ.)
- Parents should be allowed to choose traits of their children, so that the children will be more like, or perhaps less like, them. We allow them to choose what sort of schooling their children get; what sort of church if any they will

go to; what sort of communities they will grow up in (for example, they can raise them in a Kibbutz, or a hippy commune, or a strict religious order). If they are allowed to do it by choosing their environments, why shouldn't they be allowed to do it by choosing the child's traits?

- Regardless of what we actually allow right now, human freedom is a great good, and respecting it requires that we allow parents to use available technology without the government intruding by asking about their motives and effects, as long as in doing so they do not cause serious harm to their children or others.

Arguments against allowing it:

- Human beings should not interfere with nature. This is the most common response, but it is not really an argument. First of all, human beings are part of nature, and whatever they do is 'natural'. So saying that they should not interfere with nature does not rule anything out. Of course, people usually mean something else by 'nature' in this context, but it is not clear what. If it means whatever is outside human beings, the principle would disallow all of modern technological society, and would especially disallow medical interventions to cure disease and lessen suffering. 'Not natural' is often a not very good way of articulating a sense of deep unease for which one cannot actually provide an argument.

- Human diversity is very important. If parents were allowed to select traits, diversity would diminish, because there would be a 'race to the top' as it were, in which everyone had a few, highly valued, traits. This argument is stronger against selection of some traits than others. For example, sex selective abortion is used widely in Asia to select against girl children, who are less economically valuable to their parents than boy children. It is easy to see the potential for social disaster if the ratio of women to men fell dramatically.

  But what about other traits? Why would it matter if, for example, there were less diversity of eye colour, or of height, or even of IQ. And even for those traits that we do want diversely dispersed, this doesn't rule out the use of trait-selection. The government could auction rights to select traits for example, and limit the supply of rights so that the distribution of traits remains diverse. This would allow the rich to get what they wanted for their children, so might be thought to be unfair. But it could use the income from the auction to provide a basic income for all those children who do not get the most highly valued traits. Or the government could organize a lottery to distribute rights to select traits, in which every parent has an equal stake.

- We don't know what the consequences would be for natural selection, and for society, of allowing widespread trait-selection. So we should not do it. This argument needs spelling out a bit more. Ask students what sort of bad consequences they might expect. The science is certainly young and the technology is bound to be a bit uncertain, and it is reasonable to apply a certain principle of conservatism to these sorts of matters. But as the science and technology improve won't the strength of this objection fade?

- American philosopher Michael Sandel has recently advanced an argument against allowing people to design their offspring grounded in the motives involved (Sandel, 2007). He argues, broadly speaking, that what is wrong with designing children is the hubris of the activity, the attempt to master what is and ought to be a mysterious process. To the response that parents exhibit similar hubris by, for example, intensively subjecting their children to high pressure schooling, and trying to control their friendship networks etc. Sandel says, certainly, they do these things, and in doing so they exhibit the same vice; intensive parenting is bad for the same reason that designing children is.

An argument for allowing some design interventions but not others:

- The claim here is that society should allow parents to eliminate disabilities by whatever route is possible, but not to select advantageous traits and abilities, and not to force disabilities on their children. Why? Because people have a right to live a normal life, if it is possible, and this means they have a right to be rid of disabilities (if technology allows) and not to have disabilities forced on them. But they do not have a right to have advantages over others, like being taller and more attractive. The natural objection is that some people are, in fact, taller and more attractive than others, because they are lucky enough to have tall, or attractive, parents (or short or unattractive parents who accidentally passed on a combination of traits that underwrite height or attractiveness). Why should *these* advantages be restricted to people lucky enough to have the necessary genetic heritage?

  What about Sharon Duchesneau and Candy McCullough? Most students, hearing of their choice, will think that they were doing something profoundly wrong, and will agree with Baroness Nicholson's comment that 'If they succeed, that child should have the right to sue its parent for imposing on it a disability'. (Nicholson is deaf herself; and they did succeed, and have a son). But in fact deafness is rather a special disability. Many deaf adults believe that they participate in a community with other deaf adults, and say, apparently sincerely, that they do not regard their deafness as a disability, or defect, at all. There is no other (apparent) disability which is so widely embraced by those who suffer it. The deaf have, furthermore, one of the standard markers of culture, a distinctive language. There is a real case against the claim that deafness is a disability at all. Furthermore, it is very hard to see what complaint *the deaf child* has in this case. If his mothers had not selected that donor he (the deaf child) would never have been born. He would never have existed. Surely it is better for him that he is alive than that he had never been alive. We could only deny this if we thought that the life of someone who was profoundly deaf was not worth living, which is obviously false.

Conclusion

In neither of my examples have I tried to bring out the full range of moral considerations in play; that would take a book for each example, rather than a few pages. In each case I've tried to offer a model for discussion; a way of starting a class off by presenting them with an argument, and inviting them to reason about it, providing some dialectic along the lines that I have encountered when doing this myself, all in the context that I have laid out in the preceding sections.

Chapter Six

Why Teach Epistemology in Schools?

Harvey Siegel

It is not infrequently suggested that philosophy ought to be included in the school curriculum. The highly successful Philosophy for Children (P4C) programme is one common locus of this view, and important books by Gareth Matthews another (Matthews, 1980, 1994; Lipman, 1988, 1991). In western Europe it is not uncommon to teach philosophy during the secondary school years, and the worldwide International Baccalaureate Program makes one course in what they call Theory of Knowledge a requirement for its coveted IB Diploma. So neither the existence of philosophy in the school curriculum, nor advocacy for its inclusion, is unknown.

Nevertheless, they are less common than they ought to be, and I am happy to be part of this book's effort to advance the cause. I have great sympathy for the view that including philosophy in the school curriculum is a good thing, for all the usual reasons: exposure to some of the world's greatest thinkers and thoughts; introduction to rigorous argumentative and analytical methods; encouragement of habits of self-reflection and self-criticism; enhancement of traits such as open-mindedness and intellectual humility and so on. Other important reasons are advanced in the chapters included in this volume. But in what follows I restrict myself to epistemology, one of the core sub-disciplines of philosophy. Ought we to teach epistemology in schools? In a word: Yes. In this paper I offer five reasons for doing so, reasons specific to epistemology, that I hope supplement the more general reasons just mentioned for including philosophy in the school curriculum.

1. Epistemology capitalizes on natural student interest

Helping students to understand some basic epistemological matters, for example, those concerning knowledge, truth, justification, evidence, rationality and relativism – including what is more or less settled and what is philosophically controversial in this domain – is highly desirable. These matters are of basic interest to many young people, and treating them in the school curriculum can help to encourage students to think about something in which they're already interested in a more systematic and deep way than they would or could if left to their own devices.

The claim that many students are in fact interested in such matters is an empirical one, of course, and is open to challenge on empirical grounds. I have no serious empirical evidence to offer on the matter; what evidence I have is mainly anecdotal. (But see Lipman, Sharp and Oscanyan, 1980, for some related data. The website of the Institute for the Advancement of Philosophy for Children (IAPC) contains a long list of related research, some of which is supportive of the claim, as well as a wealth of additional information concerning the value of including philosophy in the curriculum.) It nevertheless seems to me uncontroversial and widely accepted that students do wonder, not just about what is true, but about what truth is and whether or not anything can be said to be true; about whether such truth (if there can be said to be any) is 'absolute' or 'relative'; about whether we know anything at all, in the face of Evil Demon, Mad Brain Scientist and Matrix-like possibilities, and if so how we know that we do; about whether or not, and if so how, their own beliefs as well as the beliefs and claims of others can be justified; about what (if anything) might make candidate beliefs justified and so worthy of belief; and so on.

Students are also often aware of features of their own cognitive lives that give rise to such epistemological worries. For example, students often tenaciously hold beliefs concerning controversial moral issues (e.g., the permissibility or otherwise of abortion, or of pre-marital sex or drug use), scientific/technological issues (e.g., the strengths/weaknesses of evolutionary vs. 'intelligent design' explanations of biological phenomena, or the wisdom or otherwise of investing in nuclear vs. renewable energy sources), political issues (e.g., the legitimacy of the current US invasion/occupation of Iraq, or the wisdom or otherwise of restricting immigration in order to combat terrorism), personal issues (e.g., whether or not their parents and/or teachers have any legitimate authority over them to enforce behavioural codes ('Be home by midnight!'; 'Don't talk in the corridor!')). But they also often realize that such tenacity of belief is apparently incompatible with other, broadly epistemological views that they are also inclined to endorse, for example, that everyone is free to believe whatever they like, and that beliefs are 'personal', 'subjective' and so not open to criticism by others. Such apparent incompatibility obviously gives rise to a range of fundamental epistemological questions: What is it for such beliefs to be justified? Can such justification be 'objective,' or is the justification of beliefs irredeemably 'subjective' or 'relative'? In what might such objectivity consist? Can beliefs be legitimately thought to have truth values, that is, to be true or false? If so, what makes them true or false, and in what does such truth/falsity consist? If not, can they nevertheless enjoy some measure of justification? And so on. Such issues as these arise as soon as students reflect on their own beliefs and the relations obtaining both among their own beliefs and between their own beliefs

and those of others. So ordinary features of cognitive life seem straightforwardly enough to give rise to epistemological issues and set the stage for
epistemological reflection.

If this much is right, many students at least are as a matter of course confronted
by epistemological questions and curious about the best ways to resolve such
questions. At the same time, though, it comes to most students as something
of a revelation that there is an academic subject – epistemology – that
addresses these questions in a systematic way. A considerable number of students will have the opportunity to encounter the subject in their post-secondary
educational careers, at least in the US. But of course many students will
either be unaware of the opportunity or will decline it, often for reasons
unrelated to its potential ability to scratch their particular epistemological itch
(no room in their schedule; too many requirements for their major; lack of
understanding of the content of such a course etc.). University students in
the UK, who are forced to specialize earlier, may well find themselves unable
to avail themselves of such courses. Of course, a very large number of students simply don't go to university. All this makes exposure to systematic
reflection concerning epistemological matters far too hit-or-miss – a bad
thing, given both the intrinsic worth of the subject matter and the obvious
educational advantage of addressing topics in which students are antecedently interested. To make the prospects of such reflection less a matter of
accident, including the systematic study of epistemology in the school curriculum seems the obvious remedy. Given antecedent student interest in the
topics such a curriculum subject would address, the potential educational
benefit of so including it seems limited only by the possible limited quality of
such a course. A good course in epistemology, pitched at the right level for
students and taught by a well-trained, engaged teacher, promises enormous
educational benefit.

2. Epistemology is essential for a proper understanding of critical thinking

A widely held educational aim is that of *critical thinking*. It is widely believed
by educators that we ought to educate so as to enhance our students' critical
thinking abilities. Indeed, it is hard to think of a more widely held educational
aim on the current educational scene. But what exactly does 'critical thinking'
mean? What does this widely held aim come to?

According to the view most widely held by relevant theorists, critical thinking
centrally involves two things: *abilities* and *dispositions*. On this view of the matter,
a critical thinker is one who is (1) able to reason well – to construct and evaluate
reasons and arguments for and against candidate beliefs, judgements and
actions; and (2) disposed to believe, judge and act in accordance with such
reasoned evaluations. There is of course much more to say about the nature

and desirability of critical thinking (Siegel, 1988, 1997, 2003; Bailin and Siegel, 2003). But saying this much is enough to indicate the centrality of epistemology to the proper articulation and defense of this basic educational aim. For critical thinking is a normative notion; critical thinking is (to over-simplify a bit) *good* thinking – and good thinking is thinking that is properly guided by epistemological criteria governing reason assessment; it is good to the degree that it satisfies or meets epistemic criteria concerning the goodness of reasons. (See Bailin and Siegel, 2003 for further discussion of the normative character of the notion of critical thinking.)

If this is right, we do not understand our own favoured educational aim unless we understand its essentially epistemological character. In the same way, students – whose critical thinking we are endeavouring to foster – will not properly understand what it is we are endeavouring to foster in/for them, unless they similarly understand its essentially epistemological character. Grasping that character is essential to their understanding of the nature of critical thinking. In short: If we regard critical thinking as an important educational aim, it is incumbent upon us to understand and keep in view the centrality of epistemology to its proper understanding – that is, the way in which critical thinking is responsive to and guided by epistemological criteria concerning the goodness of candidate reasons for beliefs, actions and judgements. It is also incumbent upon us to convey that understanding to students, given that we want them not only to become critical thinkers, but to understand and reflectively endorse that very aim. Our regarding critical thinking as an important educational aim thus gives us a good reason to include epistemology in the school curriculum.

3. Epistemology is essential for a proper understanding of the desirability of education for critical thinking

We want students, we say, to be critical thinkers. Why? Why do we think this is a *desirable* educational outcome? After all, there are many other putative educational aims on the market. Why single out critical thinking?

This is an important question, which the advocate of critical thinking must take seriously. Happily, there is a straightforward answer: any answer to the question must inevitably prove itself in the give-and-take of reasons. The desirability of the educational aim of critical thinking can be seen in the fact that appeal to it is inevitable in that only by way of it can any candidate educational aim be established as desirable. Suppose that someone advocated an alternative aim, for example, the fostering of creativity, or imagination, or caring, or social justice or what-have-you. How could one or another of these aims be established as desirable, or as more desirable than that of critical thinking? Only, it seems, by advancing reasons for regarding the favoured aim as desirable. But to so advance reasons would be straightforwardly to engage in critical thinking. The desirability of the aim, in other words, is presupposed by the very taking seriously of the question. In the most extreme case: attempting to demonstrate that critical thinking is *not* desirable could only be carried out by engaging in it, thus presupposing that it *is* (at least for the purpose of showing that it is not.)

This may strike the reader as a kind of a logical trick: the aim of critical thinking, I am arguing, can be challenged only by presupposing it. In fact, the argument has a fairly common, though controversial, form: that of a *transcendental* argument – roughly, that something (in our example, the desirability of critical thinking as an educational aim) is *necessary* for something else (in our example, the questioning of its desirability, or the advocacy of an alternative educational aim) to be *possible*. Such arguments have a long and complex philosophical legacy and an uncertain philosophical stature. I will not attempt to address that legacy or stature here, except to say that despite some well-known objections to such arguments, this particular one seems to me quite strong. (See Siegel, 1988, 1997, 2003 for further articulation and defense.)

I should also make clear that I am not rejecting any of the alternative aims mentioned. On the contrary, I have argued for a plurality of plausible educational aims, arguing only that critical thinking be regarded as 'first among equals' in virtue of its status as a prerequisite for the defense of any other (Siegel, 1988, p. 137).

If I am right that critical thinking is a desirable educational aim, that that desirability is established (at least in part) by the transcendental argument just rehearsed, that we want students to be able critically and reflectively to endorse the ideal and appreciate its desirability, and that the character of critical thinking is itself fundamentally epistemological, we have yet another reason for including epistemology in the curriculum.

4. Critical thinking presupposes contentious epistemological positions

Suppose that the case has been made for the desirability of critical thinking's status as a fundamental educational aim, and the desirability of students' understanding and reflective consideration (and, ultimately, endorsement on the basis of reasons) of that aim. A key dimension of the ideal's epistemic character is its presupposition of some contentious answers to some fundamental epistemological questions.

I have argued elsewhere that a commitment to critical thinking requires:

a) *A distinction between justification and truth*: a candidate belief may be justified, even though false, and by the same token may be true although unjustified.

b) *A rejection of relativism*: the epistemic strength of a candidate belief is a function of the epistemic features of the reasons relevant to its proper evaluation, which is not relative to individual reasoners or groups of reasoners; reasons have *probative force*, which force is independent of the reasoner considering the reasons in question, and education for critical thinking should centrally involve the effort to enable students to accurately assess the probative or evidential strength of candidate reasons for/against belief.

c) *The relation between justification and truth*: while justification and truth are *independent* of one another, the former is nevertheless a *fallible indicator* of the latter.

(Siegel, 1997, ch.1)

All these are contentious epistemologically. I think that they are correct. But the present claim is the weaker one that their presupposition is required for the advocate of critical thinking as a fundamental education aim. I won't defend this claim here. Rather I wish to point out just this: if this weaker claim is correct, and if we want students to understand (and ultimately reflectively endorse on the basis of the reasons that can be offered in its defence) the character of critical thinking, then teaching epistemology – and in particular relevant arguments for/against the three presuppositions just mentioned – is essential. Here is yet another reason for including epistemology in the curriculum.

5. A proper understanding of the desirability of education for critical thinking is itself required if school education is to meet its obligation to treat students with *respect as persons*

Finally, and perhaps most importantly: Educators, like everyone else, are morally bound to treat students with *respect as persons*: as independent centres of consciousness, entitled in virtue of their personhood to be treated in ways that acknowledge and honour their moral worth, the equal legitimacy of their needs and interests, and their right to decide for themselves (to the extent possible) what to believe, how to act, what to value and how to live. In the educational context, this moral requirement requires teachers and others involved in educational efforts to deal with students honestly, in ways that recognize students' independent judgement and honour their demands for reasons, justifications and explanations. To fail to treat students in this way is to fail to treat them with respect, as persons; it is in so far to treat them in a morally unacceptable way (Siegel, 1988, pp. 56–7).

Here, as above, much more needs to be said in defence of this rather grand assertion; but, again as above, this is not the place to say it. Instead I concentrate on the point of immediate relevance: if this assertion is correct, it is morally required that students be taught so as to foster and enhance their abilities and disposition to think critically. If educators fail to try to so educate their students, they fail to honor the moral imperative to treat them with full respect as persons, entitled to believe, judge and act in accordance with their own reasoned evaluation of the matter at hand. If students are so entitled, educators have an obligation to help to enable them to do so *well*. And since doing so well involves believing, judging and acting in accordance with the probative force of reasons, a key part of their education will involve learning how to assess reasons with competence and skill. And this requires mastery of criteria of reason assessment, which in the end is an epistemological matter. And so: for educators to meet their moral obligation to treat students with respect, they must strive, among many other things, to teach them some epistemology.

I should acknowledge that the last four reasons offered for including epistemology in the curriculum share a presupposition that is so far undefended: that educating for critical thinking requires that students be educated not simply to *be* critical thinkers, but to understand and reflectively endorse that educational aim as well, on the basis of reasons that warrant its status as an educational ideal. Is this presupposition itself justified? I think it is. Here's why: Critical thinkers seek reasons and justifications for their beliefs, judgements and actions, and are disposed to believe, judge and act on the basis of the justification afforded by those reasons. When confronted with efforts by their teachers to encourage them to be critical thinkers, they should – if their education for critical thinking has succeeded to this point – seek reasons for that as well. That is, they should ask: Why should I engage in critical thinking? Why think that critical thinking is a worthy educational ideal? Addressing these questions requires attention to the epistemological character of critical thinking and the epistemological presuppositions underlying it. If we're serious about educating for critical thinking, we have to encourage students' questioning of that very aim. (And we should regard it as evidence of our educational success that students press these questions, thereby demonstrating the abilities and disposition we hope to foster.) Enabling them to pursue these questions requires attention to that epistemological character and those epistemological presuppositions. So, again, epistemology should be included in the school curriculum. (See Siegel, 1997, pp. 23–5 for further discussion.)

I have offered five reasons – the last four of which centre in various ways on the educational aim of critical thinking – for including epistemology in the school curriculum. If these reasons are good ones, epistemology should be part of that curriculum. While I support the teaching of philosophy generally – not *just* epistemology – in the school curriculum, the reasons I have offered render epistemology especially suitable for inclusion.[1]

Note

[1] Thanks to Michael Hand for excellent advice on improving the penultimate draft of this chapter.

Chapter Seven

Philosophy and the Development of Critical Thinking

Carrie Winstanley

This chapter defends the inclusion of philosophy in the school curriculum on the grounds of its capacity to develop children's thinking. The argument is that philosophy is a powerful subject and that philosophizing, or philosophic enquiry, is the optimum pedagogy for fostering the essential skills and dispositions of critical thinking. Critical thinking is developed more effectively through philosophy than through other school subjects, or indeed through programmes specifically designed to enhance thinking.

In the UK in recent years, there has been increasing concern about the quality of children's thinking in schools. In order to become discerning users of information, children need to hone their abilities to evaluate the ideas and views with which they are presented. How best to assist them in this is hotly contested, with researchers, teachers and policymakers investing considerable energy and finances in schemes and projects designed to find the most cost-effective and useful way to support children's development as critical thinkers.

What is critical thinking?

Arguments for and against the teaching of thinking in schools have tended to focus on whether thinking skills exist and, if they do, whether they can be generalized across different areas of enquiry and study. The use of the word 'skills' is perhaps part of the problem and in some of the more persuasive literature the word is rarely used. Here, for example, Scheffler is emphasizing the role of critical thinking as a vital educational aim:

> The fundamental trait to be encouraged is that of reasonableness. . . . In training our students to reason we train them to be critical. (Scheffler, 1989, pp. 142–3)

Siegel reinforces the difference between this broader conception and the narrower model suggested by the term 'skills':

Advocates of efforts to foster critical thinking in schools sometimes conceive this aim narrowly, in terms of imparting skills which will enable students to function adequately in their jobs, and in so doing be economically productive. More often however, the proponents of the educational aim of critical thinking have in mind the broader view of critical thinking as more or less equivalent to the ideal of rationality. (Siegel, 2003, p. 307)

It is common, however, to find critical thinking discussed only (or predominantly) as a set of skills, as in the influential 1999 DfEE report *From Thinking Skills to Thinking Classrooms* (McGuinness, 1999). The report makes two main claims about the nature of thinking:

1. Thinking-as-a-skill is uncontested and is to do with 'knowing how' rather than 'knowing that'.
2. Developing thinking is like other forms of skill learning, because:
   a) it is made up of components;
   b) learning is through observation and modelling, with practice and feedback;
   c) there is transfer of learning.

(McGuinness, 1999, pp. 4–5)

In the literature on teaching critical thinking it is not, in fact, uncontested that 'thinking-as-a-skill is to do with knowing how rather than knowing that', in the sense of theoretical and practical reasoning being easily separable. This kind of statement exposes the idea of teaching critical thinking to unnecessary criticism. Johnson, for example, describes this first contention in the report as 'educationally unhelpful':

It may, for instance, divorce beliefs from actions, and drive a wedge between mental processes, which are taken to be active, and knowledge, which is taken to be inert. (Johnson, 2001, p. 6)

Other defenders of critical thinking are more careful. Higgins and Baumfield (1998), for example, pointedly emphazise the importance of knowledge and understanding, noting that expertise is defined through subject knowledge and experience. They maintain that novices need both knowledge and general skills in order to develop mastery. White explains how the two areas interact: 'practical reasoning depends on theoretical reasoning, because thinking out what is to be done relies upon thought about what is the case' (White, 2002, p. 110).

So, while McPeck is clearly right to point out that 'thinking is always thinking about something' (McPeck, 1981, p. 3), this carries less force than he thinks it does as a criticism of critical thinking. It is true that no thinking is content-free, but it does not follow from this that we cannot apply the same methods or procedures of thought to very different contents. While it is certainly the case that analysis in music theory differs in various respects from analysis in African history, ice-dancing or molecular biology, people *can* nevertheless be reasonably described as thinking analytically in all of these cases. Siegel remarks:

> It makes perfect sense for example, to claim that one teaches critical thinking simpliciter, when one means that one helps students to develop reasoning skills which are general in that they can be applied to many diverse situations and subject matters. Contra McPeck, there is nothing vacuous or unintelligible about such a claim. This is supported, moreover, by the fact that there are readily identifiable reasoning skills which do not refer to any subject matter, which do apply to diverse situations, and which are in fact the sort of skill which courses in critical thinking try to develop. (Siegel, 1988, p. 20)

It makes sense, then, to describe analytical thinking as a critical thinking skill, but only under certain conditions. Bailin and Siegel, for example, find the description of thinking-as-a-skill acceptable, 'as long as it is taken as referring to thinking that is skilled in the sense that it meets relevant criteria' (Bailin and Siegel, 2003, p. 182). These criteria include the application of theoretical reasoning to practical situations, avoiding the separation of 'knowing how' and 'knowing that'.

Higgins and Baumfield (1998) argue that domains of knowledge are closely related and that the onus is on their detractors (e.g. McPeck, 1981; Barrow, 1993; Gardner, 1999; Johnson, 2001) to prove that there are no connections between fields. Even though fields of learning are distinct, there are shared aspects that can be highlighted by teachers. Different subject areas are closely related, with knowledge from one field informing several others and with notable similarities in the methods used to approach tasks and problems. Bailin and Siegel recognize that subject areas differ in important ways, but emphasize that:

> . . . it simply does not follow that nothing general can be said about the activity of thinking, conceived as the general activity of which all particular episodes of thinking are instances. That particular episodes of thinking always have particular content is perfectly compatible with there being general thinking skills or abilities that are applicable to a wide range of domains, subjects, or contexts. (Bailin and Siegel, 2003, p. 184)

They identify arguments that are 'applicable across a range of reasoning contexts' (p. 184), suggesting, for example, similarities in different types of fallacies. That they recognize the value of subject content contradicts Johnson's suggestion that supporters of the notion of being able to teach critical thinking dismiss 'the importance of school subjects' (Johnson, 2001, p. 36).

Critical thinking is applicable to all other aspects of school learning because it involves methods of thought – for example, those of reason assessment – that are integral to all subjects. Contrary to what is claimed by advocates of some thinking skills programmes, there is no coherent distinction to be drawn between teaching critical thinking and teaching its 'transferability' to other domains: critical thinking is 'transferable' by its very nature. If, for example, Feuerstein's Instrumental Enrichment programme was successful in developing critical thinking, there would be no need for his elaborate 'bridging' activities, designed to connect learning across subjects.

The McGuinness report's second claim, that developing thinking resembles other forms of skill learning in the sense of being amenable to improvement through observation, modelling, practice and feedback, is less problematic. These methods are indeed useful for fostering all aspects of critical thinking.

Apt to cause confusion is the prevalence in the literature on thinking skills of 'taxonomies of thinking that categorize critical thinking alongside terms such as *problem solving, decision making* and *inquiry*. Thus critical thinking is seen as one form of thinking among many' (Bailin and Siegel, 2003, p. 187). Bailin and Siegel view these other terms as descriptions of *contexts* for thinking, rather than *kinds* of thinking, and point out that thinking in each of these contexts can be critical or uncritical.

It is largely in psychological and professional literature that one encounters these taxonomies, catalogues and hierarchies of thinking skills. Some are skewed towards curriculum subjects, others focus on different thinking habits, and still others are orientated towards employability and key skills. In the UK, as part of the focus on improving children's thinking, several such lists have appeared in recent years. Here is one example (for which neither origin nor rationale is given):

> The following thinking skills complement the key skills and are embedded in the National Curriculum: Information-processing skills/Reasoning skills/Enquiry skills/Creative thinking skills/Evaluation skills. (DfES, 2005)

The skills contained in each of these sub-categories are then listed. The class of 'Enquiry skills', for example, includes the following:

> Asking questions/defining problems/questions for enquiry/choosing equipment/tools/planning research/predicting outcomes/consequences/carrying out research/drawing conclusions/testing conclusions/evaluating process/improving ideas. (ibid.)

Although it is admirable that children's thinking has come under the spotlight and is a required focus for teachers, there are some deep confusions behind lists of this kind. On one hand they are presented as lists of 'essential' or 'key' skills; on the other, practitioners are advised when setting out to teach these skills, that 'what is included and excluded can be arbitrary' (McGuinness, 1999, p. 5). Bailin and Siegel argue that within these taxonomies most of the terms refer not to thinking processes 'but rather to particular outcomes that result from the application of certain critical standards' (Bailin and Siegel, 2003, p. 188), and point out that the activity and the nature of associated tasks will differ in relation to the context.

Many thinking skills programmes are problematic in this regard, offering their own apparently arbitrary and sometimes self-referential lists of skills (see, for example, de Bono, 1969, 1970, 1976, 1992, 1995). The enterprise of developing children's critical thinking is seriously compromised by the proliferation of such lists, with their varied emphases on widely differing aspects of thinking.

Rather more illuminating than these taxonomies and hierarchies is recent philosophical work on critical thinking. Theorists such as Ennis, Siegel, Bailin and McPeck have argued over different conceptions and these debates have allowed more nuanced accounts to emerge, helping educators to understand children as critical thinkers in a more holistic way. Conceiving of critical thinking merely as a set of skills is inadequate because it obscures the pivotal role of the *propensity* or *disposition* to think critically. Whereas, in 1962, Ennis defined critical thinking simply as 'the correct assessing of statements' (Ennis, 1962, p. 83), in his more recent writings he has emphasized the dispositional aspects of being a critical thinker that were missing in his earlier work. He writes:

> Critical thinking is [here] assumed to be reasonable reflective thinking focused on deciding what to believe or do. . . . Under this interpretation, critical thinking is relevant not only to the formation and checking of beliefs, but also to deciding upon and evaluating actions. It involves creative activities such as formulating hypotheses, plans, and counterexamples; planning experiments; and seeing alternatives. Furthermore critical thinking is reflective – and reasonable. (Ennis, 2004)

These ideas are not exclusive to Ennis. In 1984, Paul insisted that critical thinking is 'ultimately intrinsic to the character of the person' (Paul, cited in Siegel, 1988, p. 18). The idea of the 'critical attitude' or 'critical spirit' is introduced and developed by Siegel (1988, 1992), who suggests that the 'skills of reason assessment and the attitudes, dispositions and character traits constitutive of the 'critical spirit' are the real, underlying traits' (Siegel, 1992, p. 72). Siegel's definition of a critical thinker is as follows:

> A critical thinker, then, is one who is appropriately moved by reasons: she has the propensity or disposition to believe and act in accordance with reasons; and she has the ability properly to assess the force of reasons in the many contexts in which reasons play a role. (Siegel, 1988, p. 23)

Bailin and Siegel emphasize that merely 'fostering in students the ability to assess the probative strength of reasons' is not enough to make them critical thinkers, which requires both 'the ability to reason well and the disposition to do so' (Bailin and Siegel, 2003, p. 182). They note that 'a given thinker may have the ability but not (or not systematically or routinely) use it' (ibid., p. 183). They argue that helping children to develop the right dispositions is fundamental to the enterprise of teaching critical thinking, and identify the requisite dispositions as follows:

> . . . valuing good reasoning and being disposed to seek reasons, to assess them, and to govern beliefs and actions on the basis of such assessment . . . open-mindedness, fair-mindedness, independent-mindedness, an enquiring attitude, and respect for others in group inquiry and deliberation. (ibid., p. 183)

The development of dispositions is also emphasized by White:

> Thinking is an activity. It is something that goes on in the mind. It is an occurrent phenomenon. But it is something at which children can improve. The activity can get better with practice. This is why thinking is sometimes characterized as a skill. It has a continuant as well as an occurrent side to it. Part of the educator's task is to build up children's thinking skills through engaging them in thinking activities . . . We want them to use their skills on a more regular basis, to get into the *habit* of thinking clearly about what they are to do and believe. We want to develop thinking *dispositions* in them. (White, 2002, p. 104)

This dispositional aspect of critical thinking is largely missed by most thinking skills programmes, which tend to focus on improving cognitive processes, building strategies for generating ideas or speeding up decision making, rather than forming the habit of acting and believing in accordance with reasons.

A useful summary of what constitutes critical thinking, and of the qualities possessed by critical thinkers, is presented by Ennis:

> Assuming that critical thinking is reasonable reflective thinking focused on deciding what to believe or do, a critical thinker:

1. Is open-minded and mindful of alternatives
2. Tries to be well-informed
3. Judges well the credibility of sources
4. Identifies conclusions, reasons, and assumptions
5. Judges well the quality of an argument, including its reasons, assumptions, and evidence
6. Can well develop and defend a reasonable position

7. Asks appropriate clarifying questions
8. Formulates plausible hypotheses; plans experiments well
9. Defines terms in a way appropriate for the context
10. Draws conclusions when warranted - with caution
11. Integrates all items in this list.

(Ennis, 2004)

Why is philosophy the best way to develop critical thinking?

I turn now to the question of why philosophy might plausibly be thought to develop children's critical thinking more effectively than either the traditional subjects of the school curriculum or artificially constructed thinking skills programmes. I advance two reasons in support of this contention: (i) that critical thinking is the essence of philosophy, and (ii) that philosophy is not dependent on a substantial empirical knowledge-base.

Critical thinking is the essence of philosophy

While other subjects require the application of critical thinking, none actually explores the idea of what it is to think critically as one of its central foci. Some curriculum subjects and thinking skills programmes now append to their core tasks structured activities designed to develop metacognition, but in philosophy this is already at the heart of the discipline, since the validity of inferences, the quality of arguments and the meanings of words are constantly under scrutiny. Consider this example of a discussion with some six-year-old children trying to be clear about specific words and their meanings, paying careful attention to the subtle differences. They are discussing the merits of Magritte's surreal 1958 painting *Les Idees Claires* (Clear Ideas), in which a rock hovers between the sea and a cloud:

Child 1:   It's mysterious how it hangs.
Child 2:   No, it's not mysterious, not to me.
Child 1:   How can it hang? It would fall.
Child 2:   That doesn't make it mysterious, it just makes it impossible in life. You can do anything in a picture.
Child 1:   Yes, I know; so it's a mysterious picture, then.
Child 2:   No, because a real mystery would make you think 'Um, how did that happen?' but this is a picture so it never happened so I don't think 'Um, how did that happen?' at all, I just think, 'Why did he paint it hanging in the sky? What's the idea?'
Child 1:   Why isn't that mysterious then?

Child 2:   Well maybe the idea is mysterious, but the picture isn't mysteri-
             ous, it's just like a kind of dream picture.
Child 1:   Yes, I have mysterious dreams.

The careful definitions of critical thinking (e.g. those of Ennis and Siegel) considered in this chapter highlight the fact that philosophy (in particular
epistemology) is the embodiment of the abilities of exploring ideas with logic
and rationality, with the added important aspect of imbuing pupils with the disposition of being a critical thinker. This makes philosophy uniquely well-suited
to the development of critical thinking. Critical thinking concerns, for example,
the identification of 'conclusions, reasons, and assumptions, and judgements of
the quality of an argument, including its reasons, assumptions, and evidence'
(Ennis, 2004). Philosophy addresses itself precisely to these issues: it is about the
nature of reasoning and it invokes the critical spirit or attitude. Siegel suggests:

> In so far as rationality consists of believing and acting on the basis of good
> reasons, and in so far as we accept [McPeck's] epistemological approach – or
> any approach which makes reason assessment central – we must perforce
> regard critical thinking not as a dimension of rationality, but as its equivalent
> or educational cognate. Otherwise we are forced to regard instances of believ-
> ing and acting on the basis of good reasons as non-instances of critical
> thinking. (Siegel, 1988, p. 30)

Philosophy is not dependent on a substantial empirical knowledge-base

Philosophy liberates children from needing a substantial knowledge base in
order to discuss complex issues and their consequences. Having limited subject
knowledge can inhibit discussion in a way that is not characteristic of philosophical enquiry with children, in which ideas rather than facts are under
discussion. The basis of the agreements or disagreements concerns concepts,
ideas and the logic of arriving at the views held. The teacher gently probes the
children to give reasons for their views and explain the route of their thinking.
The emphasis is on explaining reasons, coherence of argument and the rationality of the notions under examination. In knowledge-based subjects, the
discussion is skewed in favour of the participants with the most facts at their
fingertips. The first discussant postulates an idea that is dismissed by another
group member for being predicated on false or limited data about a situation.
The conversation founders and becomes about the verifiability of facts rather
than about ideas.

In philosophical enquiry, the child who is challenged on their view can
explain how they arrived at that particular notion. It is the ins and outs of their
argument that is under scrutiny. If a detractor disagrees, the child must strive to

clarify their position. This is feasible because avenues for discussion are still open, unlike conversations in which a proven fact suddenly puts a stop to further hypothesizing.

A popular animated film character has the catchphrase 'to infinity and beyond', which for a while became a feature of many playground games. Here are some five-year olds discussing its meaning:

Child 1:	Infinity is the biggest number there ever can be and no number can ever be bigger.
Child 2:	Oh yeah, but whatever number you say I can do a bigger one.
Child 3:	Three million million.
Child 2:	Three million million, and one.
Child 3:	Um, ten thousand and fifty.
Child 2:	Ten thousand and fifty, and one.
Child 1:	Infinity.
Child 2:	Infinity, and one.
Child 1:	That is just a trick because there is no thing that is bigger than infinity.
Child 2:	But you can have 'infinity and beyond' so that *is* bigger than it.
Child 1:	Oh, but infinity is space. It is infinity in space and nothing is bigger.
Child 3:	You can't be bigger than space. It is everything. And it just goes on.
Child 2:	Where is the end of space? Is it in infinity?
Child 1:	Yeah, when does space run out?

These children are not inhibited by their lack of knowledge when discussing the confines of space and the nature of numbers. The same group talking about the Elizabethan era were having a similarly wide-ranging speculative conversation about what life was like in the past, following a visit to a royal palace. It was abruptly ended by a well-meaning teacher interjecting that their ideas about the queen powering along the Thames to the Tower were anachronistic, since boat travel was only ever as fast as men could row. The focus of the conversation shifted to power and electricity. What had started as a moral discussion about the right of the monarch to take the life of a criminal ended as a conversation about what time Elizabethan people went to bed: a question that could be easily answered with recourse to a book. So, what followed an initially complex exchange of views was a more stilted conversation with numerous dead ends caused by facts needing verification before ideas could be pursued. In history, knowledge is vital for understanding, but in terms of encouraging imaginative conjecture and exploring ideas, limits are imposed through a lack of information.

Some children are hesitant to join in classroom discussions that require a wide knowledge base for fear of making an embarrassing factual error in a classroom context. Some of these children have less access than the norm to acquisition of general knowledge, for reasons of their background or dominant language for example, and are aware that this disadvantages them in class. For these and other reasons, some students have an acute awareness of the gaps in their knowledge base and so become tentative, displaying a lack of confidence in discussion. It can be freeing for them to engage in discussion without the concern that they will be corrected in public for lack of factual accuracy.

The opportunity to explore ideas more freely is welcomed by children, and this is where philosophy can really help. Released from the concern of feeling ridiculed, they are on an equal footing with other children and are able to participate with confidence.

Conclusion

Teachers and policymakers are currently (and properly) concerned with improving the quality of children's thinking in schools. According to the UK Department for Children, Schools and Families (DCSF):

> Since the explicit inclusion of thinking skills in the National Curriculum, interest in the teaching of thinking skills has burgeoned in the UK. Thinking skills approaches are emerging as a powerful means of engaging teachers and pupils in improving the quality of learning in classrooms. (www.standards. dfes.gov.uk/thinkingskills)

The time is right, therefore, for the introduction of philosophy into the school curriculum. At present, the DCSF recommends philosophy as one approach alongside others to developing thinking skills, and makes no attempt to rank the various approaches in terms of quality or efficacy. While the Government's interest in philosophy is to be welcomed, and has been helpful in reigniting the debate about philosophy in schools and bringing the idea of children learning philosophy to a wider audience, lining up 'philosophical approaches' with 'cognitive intervention approaches' and 'brain-based learning approaches' to the development of thinking skills is problematic. It leaves philosophy outside the structure of the school curriculum and aligns it with a set of programmes of questionable educational worth.

There are at least two concerns here. First, there is a danger that the demand for sketchy, quick-fix training will result in philosophy being relegated to an after-school, extra-curricular optional add-on, or squeezed into spare moments. Philosophy in this guise is highly unlikely to be taught in an ideal or appropriate fashion, despite teachers' best intentions. The subject's low value will be betrayed by its lack of appearance as a clear, compulsory curriculum subject.

The second concern is raised by the 'infusion approach' sometimes suggested for philosophy and for thinking skills programmes. This method is to incorporate philosophy across all existing subjects, using each area to draw out the philosophical aspects of the different fields. Each teacher is required to emphasize the philosophical aspects of their subject, whether or not they feel this to be fitting. The infusion approach serves to dilute philosophy and presents an impoverished model of the discipline.

Both approaches, add-on and infusion, rely on teacher enthusiasm and have no real checks on the quality of delivery or the consistency of the pupil experience. If empirical methods are used to collect data on the effectiveness of these approaches, the results are likely to be disappointing as philosophy will not have been presented as a useful and relevant subject. What is needed is the adoption of philosophy as a full curriculum subject, taught systematically by appropriately trained staff. Only then will be it be possible to make a fair empirical assessment of the benefits it brings to children.

Philosophy is the best possible subject for helping children become effective critical thinkers. It is the subject that can teach them better than any other how to assess reasons, defend positions, define terms, evaluate sources of information, and judge the value of arguments and evidence.

A final thought. The P4C movement has been extraordinarily successful in getting philosophy into schools, and having a distinctive label was no doubt important when the movement's ideas were a radical innovation in the 1960s and 1970s. The 'community of enquiry' pedagogy and other aspects of the P4C approach are as useful as ever for helping teachers present philosophy to children, particularly in the younger age ranges. It may be, however, that the P4C label, which serves to distance schoolroom philosophy from philosophy proper, is now outdated. We do not speak of G4C (Geography for Children) or MwC (Music with Children). So perhaps we could now dispense with '4C' and revert simply to 'philosophy', and give the subject its rightful place in the school curriculum.

Chapter Eight

Philosophical Intelligence:
Why Philosophical Dialogue is Important in Educating the Mind

Robert Fisher

During a discussion of intelligence one child suggested that: 'It's like voices in your head telling you things - the more intelligent you are the more voices you have'.[1] The metaphor of the mind as having many voices reflects a frequently expressed intuition that the mind has many expressive facets. Nearly a century ago Edmond Holmes argued that these facets reflected intellectual dispositions he called 'instincts', which he identified as the communicative, dramatic, artistic, musical, inquisitive and constructive, all of which he argued can be expanded by education (Holmes, 1911). In the late twentieth century, Howard Gardner developed the more elaborated theory of Multiple Intelligences (MI), which has now become hugely influential (Gardner, 1983). This chapter develops Gardner's ideas about Existential Intelligence (EI) to make the case for a capacity of mind called Philosophical Intelligence (PI). It contends that if education is about the whole person and all their capacities of mind, then the existence of PI provides a justification for including philosophical enquiry on the curriculum in all schools.

Existential Intelligence

Gardner makes the general claim that there are many ways for human beings to be intelligent, and this claim seems undeniable (Gardner, 1983). He further argues that humans have eight or more modules or 'frames' of mind, each of which embody different aspects of intelligence. EI is the last intelligence on his list and is for him the most problematic. Gardner finds it problematic for a number of reasons. First, unlike other intelligences, he can find no discrete locational evidence for EI in the brain. However critics challenge Gardner's claim that intelligences are situated in discrete modules in the brain. They cite neurological research suggesting that all of Gardner's intelligences rely on connections that are distributed across the brain (Klein, 2003). There are some functions localized in regions of the brain but these are limited. The whole brain system is required for each of Gardner's intelligences to function fully, including EI. The case for EI therefore does not rely on any specific locational evidence of neurological activity in the brain. The appeal to neuro-biological evidence in the early formulations of MI theory has been shown to be weak.

Second, Gardner has some conceptual worries about EI because he finds it hard to define and because he thinks it does not correspond to a school subject (Gardner, 1999). Because he cannot fully describe EI or locate it in an academic tradition, he is reluctant fully to endorse it. The solution to these problems, however, may lie in changing the designation from Existential Intelligence to Philosophical Intelligence. The label PI ties Gardner's eighth intelligence to a long and well-defined academic tradition, to a rich literature and established procedures of enquiry.

Gardner offers a preliminary definition of EI as the human 'proclivity to pose and ponder questions about life, death, and ultimate realities' (Gardner, 1999). He argues that children show EI when they raise, and sometimes answer, life's larger questions, such as:

- Why are we here?
- Are there other dimensions, and if so what are they like?
- Are there really ghosts?
- Where do we go when we die?
- Why are some people evil?
- Does God exist?

Traditionally these kinds of questions have been called philosophical. Gardner suggests that EI is a universal human sensitivity to and capacity for tackling deep questions about human existence: again, questions generally understood as falling within the field of enquiry of philosophy. The case for EI, then, can be made more robust and conceptually intelligible if the capacity is renamed PI.

It is worth saying something here about Gardner's use of the term 'intelligence'. Critics have challenged this use, arguing that the modular functions Gardner describes are primary abilities that educators and cognitive psychologists have always acknowledged (Schaler, 2006). These functions are common capacities of human minds to respond to stimuli in different and in more or less effective ways. But little turns on whether we label these functions 'primary abilities', 'intellectual capacities', 'mental abilities' or 'intelligences'. Gardner's critics may argue that MI theory simply serves up old wine in new bottles, but the crucial question is whether this vocabulary offers us a clearly defined model of the capacities of the human mind and a basis for planning educational programmes to develop those capacities.

Philosophical Intelligence

Philosophical thinking is fundamentally about the creation of organizing ideas or concepts. It arises from the capacity of the mind to free itself from its dependence on sensory experience and to create new knowledge using concepts as tools for thinking. PI is called into play when thinking goes beyond mere information processing, beyond the given. Philosophizing is not based on empirical observation and has no need of instruments or specialized knowledge. It is informed but not constrained by outside authority. It is about conceptual understanding, about how the world is conceived and given meaning in words. Philosophy also involves an attitudinal stance, characterized by a curious, questioning, speculative disposition and a desire to understand. Philosophers advance knowledge by building on concepts or configuring the contours of new concepts – as in this example from a classroom dialogue:

Child:	I am iffing.
RF:	What do you mean by 'iffing'?
Child:	It's when you say 'Suppose if trees could talk, or birds ruled the world'. So if someone says 'That's crazy!', you can say 'I am only iffing'.

The central motivation of philosophy derives from the consciousness of the incompleteness of human knowledge and from the mind's ability to reflect on its own thinking. All human knowledge remains partial because of the ambiguity of experience, the unreliability of our perceptions and the fallibility of the reports of others. In representing the world in words we are faced with ambiguity, uncertainty and vagueness of meaning. The following is an example from classroom discussion illustrating one struggle to explain the relationship between the world and mental experience:

RF:	What is a horizon?
Child:	A horizon is as far as you can see with your eyes.
RF:	So you can't see beyond the horizon?
Child:	You can sort of see beyond the horizon, but you have to use your imagination.
RF:	So is your imagination like an eye?
Child:	Yes, you have a kind of eye in your mind.
RF:	Like a camera?
Child:	Yes . . . no, not like a camera, because a camera can't see what's not there, but your mind can.

Philosophy begins with the recognition of a problem or a cluster of problems arising from our experience as beings-in-the-world and the various claims or beliefs that people make or hold about being in the world. Among such problems are the following:

- the problem of the nature and structure of reality
- the problem of the relation between the mind and the world
- the problem of the nature and scope of human knowledge
- the problem of the nature of the human person
- the problem of free will
- the problem of the basis of moral action
- the problem of how best to organize human society

A. J. Ayer says of philosophical problems:

> It is not further scientific information that is needed to decide such philosophical questions as whether the material world is real, whether objects continue to exist at times when they are not perceived, whether other human beings are conscious in the same sense as oneself. These are not questions that can be settled by experiment, since the way they are answered itself determines how the result of any experiment is to be interpreted. What is in dispute in such cases is not whether, in any given set of circumstances, this or that event will happen, but rather how anything at all that happens is to be described. (Ayer, 1956, p. 7)

Philosophical enquiry would not occur if there were no problems about describing things or if the meanings of words and the logical relations between the concepts we use were consistent and transparent. One kind of philosophical investigation is prompted by the fact that there are some underlying inconsistencies in the meaning and use of certain concepts. Philosophy is needed because words and concepts can confuse the speaker or the listener or can be manipulated for undeclared purposes. As Wittgenstein put it: 'Philosophy is a battle against the bewitchment of our intelligence by means of language' (Wittgenstein, 1953, p. 109).

In philosophy it is the concepts or categories with which we think about the world that are the topics of enquiry. The mark of a concept being philosophical, in any field of enquiry, is that it is common, central and contestable (Splitter and Sharp, 1995). St. Augustine was exercising his PI when he asked: 'What then is time? I know well enough what it is, provided that nobody asks me; but if I am asked what it is and try to explain, I am baffled' (*Confessions*, Book XI, Section xiv).

Formal and informal philosophy

I should like to distinguish between two kinds of philosophy, which I shall label formal and informal. By formal philosophy I mean philosophy as an academic discipline, as the field of study enshrined in the great books of philosophy that constitute the heart of our received tradition of philosophical wisdom. This tradition depends primarily upon the printed word, so that when G. E. Moore was asked 'What is philosophy?', he pointed to the books in his philosophy library and said 'It is all of these'.

To ensure that enquiry is systematic, the field of formal philosophy is traditionally divided into four main areas of study: epistemology, metaphysics, ethics and logic.

- *Epistemology* is the study of knowledge, what we can know about the world and how we can know it. Typical epistemological questions are: What is knowledge? How do we know what we know? Can we ever be certain?
- *Metaphysics* is the study of the nature of reality, what exists in the world, what it is like, and how it is ordered. Metaphysical questions include: What is a person? What is a mind? Is there a God?
- *Ethics* concerns what we ought to do and what it would be best to do. Ethical questions include: What is good? What is right? How should I treat others?
- *Logic* is the study of the nature and structure of arguments and reasons. Questions relating to logic include: What is the meaning of what is stated? What is truth? How can we verify or prove the conclusions?

Philosophical questions also fall into other categories such as aesthetics (e.g. What is art? What is beauty?), political philosophy (e.g. How should society be organized? How should decisions be taken?), philosophy of science and so on.

By informal philosophy I mean discursive or dialogic engagement with conceptual problems and questions of existential concern without recourse to the specialist resources of academic philosophy. The inquiries of formal philosophy depend on and derive from prior and more informal inquiries into the basic problems of human experience and knowledge. Such informal inquiries precede acquaintance with traditions, texts or authorities. Where formal philosophy is a continuing conversation with the famous dead that can illuminate and inform perennial human concerns, informal philosophy is the encounter with and exploration of those same concerns prior to engagement with the philosophical canon.

PI may be construed as our basic capacity for and inclination to informal philosophy. It describes the set of cognitive abilities that enable us to ponder existential questions and to express ideas in abstract concepts. It is our capacity to reflect upon the philosophical ideas and questions that arise from our own experience, as distinct from those presented to us by the philosophical tradition.

One model of informal philosophy is provided by the Ancient Greeks, for whom philosophy was an exercise in arguing with an educative purpose. Socrates showed how philosophizing is a way to pursue the truth through analytic discussion.

Informal philosophy is natural to human beings in general, and to children in particular. It can be activated in children by using a series of questions and prompts that move children's thinking from the concrete and literal stages of enquiry through to abstract and conceptual speculation. These processes are characteristic of Philosophy for Children (P4C) programmes, which successfully engage children in philosophical discussion of questions of their own devising.

All children have a propensity for philosophical thinking, for asking probing questions and experimenting with ideas and possible solutions. Some children, like some adults, find philosophizing easier than others, but since PI is a capacity all of us possess, those who find it harder can still be helped to think philosophically, to broach problems in more systematic and logical ways.

Philosophy begins in wonder and in the propensity of the human mind to ask questions, like Tom, aged 5, who asked: 'Where does time go when it is over?'. But it is more than asking questions: philosophy also involves reflecting on experience in order to seek solutions to the recurrent problems of human experience. Some of these human problems stem from the activity of the mind contemplating its own existence, others from seeking knowledge about the world and responding to the challenges of life. Scientific method can help us investigate the tangible world of nature, but philosophical reflection is needed to organize our ideas and concepts into mental maps and models of the world.

Kant said, 'Philosophical knowledge is the knowledge gained by reason from concepts' (Kant, 1781). Philosophy involves questioning and speculating (creative thinking), generating and building on ideas, posing hypotheses, applying imagination, making links to new ideas and reflecting on alternative possibilities ('possibility thinking'). It involves discovering or inventing relationships between ideas, reasoning to test the validity of these, and 'thinking-outside-the-box' about what might exist beyond the given. A philosophical enquiry ends in a judgement, even if a provisional one, which seeks to build on our understanding of a particular concept or problem.

'Philosophy informs us,' said Hume, 'that every thing, which appears to the mind, is nothing but a perception, and is interrupted, and dependent on the mind' (Hume, 1739). We need to apply judgement in assessing perceptions, arguments and evidence. What seems obvious to our senses cannot always be trusted. Nor can the views of academic philosophers, who as a group have held very divergent views. In place of the authority of others, those who exercise PI must exercise this capacity *for themselves*, and be able to justify their views with reasoning and argument.

In summary, philosophy begins in wonder, in curiosity and in questioning ideas about the world, but it also requires the exercise of certain habits of intelligent behaviour in building concepts and seeking justification for belief, including:

- defining clearly the meanings of words and concepts we use
- creating, extending and developing ideas, concepts and theories
- using reasoning and argument with logic and consistency
- making judgements on the strength of reasons and evidence

What are the implications of PI for schools?

How should we seek to develop this intelligence in our students? Gardner argues that 'students should probe with sufficient depth a manageable set of examples so that they come to see how one thinks and acts in the manner of a scientist, a geometer, an artist, an historian' (Gardner, 1999). For PI, this means showing students what it is to think and act like a philosopher. Research suggests that an ideal pedagogy for developing PI is philosophical dialogue undertaken in 'communities of enquiry' (Fisher, 2003a,b; Lipman, 2003; Trickey and Topping, 2004).

Philosophical dialogue has no fixed curriculum – it can be applied to conceptual content in any subject area (Fisher, 2003a). In schools this may mean setting aside special lessons for philosophical enquiry, as advocated by Lipman and his followers, or making space for philosophical enquiries within existing curriculum subjects (Fisher, 2003b). Philosophical dialogue is most suited to subjects naturally requiring conceptual exploration, such as English literature, religious education and citizenship, but can arise in response to any concept which stirs curiosity and invites reflection. Philosophy is the struggle for conceptual understanding and can be prompted by personal or communal concerns, by ideas in fiction or poetry, song lyrics, paintings or films, or by problems encountered in social relationships and activities.

While methods of teaching philosophy in schools are well-established, methods of assessing and testing the development of PI are less well-developed and remain an important focus for continuing research. Research evidence from a wide range of small-scale studies across the world indicate that P4C programmes, when implemented over time, can, like other thinking skills programmes, enhance various aspects of a child's academic performance (McGuinness, 1999; Fisher, 2005a). Collaborative philosophical enquiry with children has been shown to produce gains along a range of educational measures, including verbal reasoning (Trickey and Topping, 2004). And findings from my *Philosophy*

in Primary Schools research project echo worldwide research into P4C programmes, showing that the *Stories for Thinking* programme has a positive effect
on students in the following ways:

- achievement in academic tests
- self-esteem and self-concept as thinkers and learners
- ability to engage effectively in discussion with others
- fluency and quality of questioning
- quality of creative thinking and verbal reasoning
- ability to think in abstract and conceptual terms

All these factors are important in education, and the last three are central to
the development of PI. Project evaluations confirm that students enjoy a *Stories
for Thinking* approach to philosophic discussion and find discussion in communities of enquiry motivating (Fisher, 1996). Teachers claim that philosophical
discussion adds a new dimension to their teaching and the way their pupils
think. The evidence suggests that pupils become more ready to ask questions
and develop the skills of intelligent discussion. As Kim, aged 9, put it, 'The
important thing is not to agree or disagree but to say why'.

There appears to be a widely held view that philosophy ought not to be
included on the school curriculum because it is too difficult for children. But if
all children have some capacity for exercising their PI, then though philosophy
may be difficult and challenging it cannot be said to make impossible cognitive
demands on children. Indeed there is a long-established and well-researched
tradition of including philosophical discussion in primary school curricula
through various P4C programmes. Against the view that philosophy is unduly
difficult for children, it may be countered that the young actually have an
advantage in learning to philosophize, since their thinking patterns are relatively untouched by learned reactions, knowledge and prejudices. They are
genuinely surprised by everyday events; they question, have unusual thoughts
and like to be involved in open-ended enquiry.

There is no better preparation for being an active, responsible and creative citizen than for a child to participate with others in a community of
enquiry founded on reasoning, freedom of expression and mutual respect
(Fisher, 2003a). The effects of philosophical discussion extend across the
curriculum, as children become better at giving reasons, asking questions,
forming concepts, planning, reasoning, imagining, solving problems and
making decisions and judgements. Thinking together in serious, sustained
and systematic ways helps children to internalize the habits of intelligent
behaviour, enquiry and discussion (Fisher, 2005b; Alexander, 2006). As
Jemma, aged 10, said, 'Philosophy can help in all your lessons, no matter
what you're learning'. When asked why this was so, she said, 'Because it gets
you questioning and wondering why'.

PI is an identifiable form of human intelligence, and the development of children's PI an area of education with a sound theoretical and pedagogical basis. Developing PI should therefore be a goal for all schools and curriculum time should be given to the practice of philosophical dialogue. A well-researched pedagogy shows how communities of philosophical enquiry can be created in classrooms with children from the age of five. Later, at college level and beyond, students can further develop their PI by studying formal philosophy, while retaining their informal philosophical capacity to question, speculate and reflect. As Whitehead said: 'Philosophy begins in wonder. And at the end, when philosophic thought has done its best, the wonder remains' (Whitehead, 1938).

Note

[1] Quotations from teachers and children in this paper are taken from the author's *Philosophy in Primary Schools* research project.

Chapter Nine

Autonomous and Authentic Thinking through Philosophy with Picturebooks

Karin Murris

This chapter puts forward some intricately related political, social, moral and philosophical reasons for introducing philosophy as a foundational, compulsory subject (the fourth R: reasoning). It deliberately resists the temptation to offer instrumental reasons. The arguments are broader, bolder and more controversial. A deeper understanding of the critical pedagogy of Philosophy for Children (P4C) – the 'community of enquiry' methodology – opens up a space to think afresh about the aims of education, the role of schools as institutions and the kind of conversations we should have with younger people. It also demands classroom resources of a particular form and content.

Philosophy for Children

Philosophy for Children was pioneered by Matthew Lipman some 50 years ago in the USA. His conception of philosophy as an oral practice has its philosophical roots in the figure of Socrates, the main character in Plato's famous dialogues. Although Socrates also existed in flesh and blood as Plato's tutor, we have little information about him as a historical figure apart from what Plato tells us. Significantly, he never wrote his philosophical ideas down on paper (the removal of an educational stumbling block much appreciated by many students). Matthew Lipman compares academic philosophy to memorizing the inscriptions in a graveyard: memorizing a collection of names and dates. He urges us not only to rethink what constitutes philosophy, but also to address the need to use a pedagogy that does justice to philosophizing as an activity – philosophy as 'a way of life' (Lipman, 1991; Murris, 2000). Another philosophical root is Immanuel Kant, whose maxim '*sapere aude*' – have the courage to think for yourself – is central to philosophical practice (Martens, 1999; Geschwindt, 2007).

The P4C pedagogy – building a community of philosophical enquiry (Lipman, 1991; Cam, 1995; Murris and Haynes, 2000) – is whole-class dialogue with participants sitting together in a way that enables each of them to hear and see all the others properly, usually a circle. Ground rules, developed if and when the community needs them, focus on responsive listening, inclusiveness of everyone's needs, and avoidance of bias (e.g. preference for friends over others). The individual's right to remain silent is respected, though everyone is gently encouraged to participate. The work is genuinely collaborative: everyone in class is encouraged to listen responsively, to build on each other's ideas, and to investigate the issue at hand rigorously, developing in the process the social skills and attitudes for working in and as teams. Despite surface similarities with 'circle time' or discussion (e.g. circular seating, emphasis on speaking and listening), P4C is unique in its collaborative and creative pursuit of rigour and justified true beliefs. Participants are openly encouraged to disagree with each other and to critically reflect on the dialogue through meta-dialogical activities (dialogues about the dialogue), thereby taking an active role in shaping the content of the lesson and evaluating the investigative strategies used.

Conceptual enquiry

Another characteristic of P4C is its critical reflection on everyday language. When analysing the meaning of words, philosophers 'spiral together' into a deeper understanding of the language they use when they talk, think, or think about thinking (Murris and Haynes, 2000). Philosophical concepts, such as 'beauty', 'fair', 'good', 'poor', 'stranger', 'knowledge', 'clever' and 'rubbish', are explored, deconstructed and reconstructed in enquiries, aided by knowledge of the history of philosophical ideas. These concepts are common to all English language users, central to the way we think about ourselves and others, but also contestable. Their meanings are 'fuzzy at the edges' because of their generality. Crisp definitions of them fail because of the necessity in philosophical analysis to connect with the person who is doing the thinking. Each individual in class needs to situate the investigation in their own concrete historical, emotional, social and cultural context, bringing a unique perspective to the enquiry. Differences between people are not a hindrance, but an asset. They force participants to find strong reasons for their beliefs and to justify them openly and courageously. Although experiences may be private, meanings are not. In our conversations with others, we construct who we are and what we know. We also find out what others think and value and modify our own opinions accordingly, progressing from mere opinions to reasoned points of view. The use of analogies, examples and counter-examples, thought experiments and metaphors, also plays an important role in this philosophical process.

Teaching philosophy requires the right kind of environment, a critical pedagogy, and resource material that is in line with the pedagogy's epistemology. Factors that contribute towards becoming a reasonable thinker are: an atmosphere in which making mistakes and feeling frustrated is normalized; acceptance of forms of expressing thoughts other than language; listening responsively to what others are saying; and participants saying only what is worth listening to. Such thinking is 'contaminated' by passion, compassion and care for truth. It is not reasoning alone that leads to reasonableness, but the experience of reasoning together, as a community, that leads to reasonableness in each participant (Field, 1995).

In the early stages of a community of enquiry it is usually the teacher who brings into the circle a starting point for philosophical questioning, soon including pupils in this decision-making process. When pupils' questions have been recorded, the community of enquiry chooses one of them to start the enquiry. This is usually done by majority vote. The teacher facilitates this process, but does not cast a vote. The teacher's role is to support and guide discussion, not to manipulate or steer it. This has implications for planning and preparation as well as for the styles of teaching. Teachers have to be willing to treat pupils' questions without prejudice, to be genuinely committed to the enquiry, but resist the desire to drive the discussion in a pre-planned direction or to give answers. The teacher's presence, attention and responsiveness during the enquiry are of utmost importance to support the young people's experience of thinking (Murris and Haynes, 2000). Such enquiry differs from mere discussion in the rigour with which concepts are explored, shaped and reshaped and in being informed by the history of philosophical ideas and arguments (Murris, 1997, 2000).

Philosophy with picturebooks

P4C's democratic and egalitarian community of enquiry pedagogy allows pupils to ask the questions that the community will try to answer. Pupils are also included in decisions about the best strategies for broaching the questions. In line with such an ethos, suitable starting-point material for philosophical enquiry should contain plenty of ambiguity and complexity. Resource material should not spoon-feed ready-made philosophical questions: it should offer thought-provoking ideas with no prescriptive content, in the manner of literary texts and works of art – and of picturebooks, which combine the two.

Traditionally, philosophical texts are surprisingly devoid of wonder, complexity and mystery, and are inattentive to the concrete and the everyday. Also, the removal of emotion from thought is typical in philosophy. Martha Nussbaum offers an alternative form of philosophical texts. She explains:

> Style itself makes its claims, expresses its own sense of what matters. Literary form is not separable from philosophical content, but is, itself, a part of content – an integral part, then, of the search for and the statement of truth. (Nussbaum, 1990, p. 3)

However, the use of literature for P4C has been strongly rejected by Matthew Lipman and others (Lipman et al., 1980). Although in many ways work with picturebooks builds on the P4C tradition, its theory and practice has opened up discussions about the nature of philosophy, the criteria of a good philosophy teaching resource and the relationship between educational resources and the pedagogy of P4C (Murris, 1992, 1997; Murris and Haynes, 2000; Haynes, 2002; Haynes and Murris, 2006). In British primary schools picturebooks are now popular texts with which to generate philosophical enquiries.

In the field of children's literature, a 'quiet revolution' has taken place in the production of good quality, contemporary picturebooks (Arizpe and Styles, 2003). Typically, serious study and appreciation of this new cultural form has lagged behind its initial appearance (Lewis, 2001), so it is not surprising that picturebooks have escaped the general notice of philosophers. For many educators, picturebooks are still pigeon-holed as resources for teaching literacy to young readers, rather than being recognized as aesthetic objects that can provoke deep philosophical responses. Philosophical work on and with picturebooks is new in a field that is dominated by aesthetic, literary and psychological approaches (e.g. Wallen, 1990; Doonan, 1993; Baddeley and Eddershaw, 1994; Styles et al., 1996; Hunt, 1999; Nodelman, 1999; Arizpe and Styles, 2003).

Constructing meaning with carefully selected picturebooks is not just a process of finding out what the pictures denote or literally represent. The reader is pulled in two different directions of meaning-making by the use of the different sign systems, creating 'a kind of miniature ecosystem' (Lewis, 2001, pp. 48, 54). The linear direction of the text wants us to continue reading while the pictures compel us to ponder. We need to care about the subject of our thought in our efforts to be critical. Importantly, the 'gaps' between text and image may be experienced differently as we grow older and as we bring our established habits of thought to the reading of the narrative, forging a new relationship between teacher and pupil. With their multiple narratives, ambiguity and contradictions, picturebooks are emotionally and cognitively demanding texts for all ages, forcing us to rethink what children's literature is and who it is for. Similarly, P4C is not something adults do for children, but *with* children, themselves and others.

Suitable picturebooks are interrogative texts that do not moralize or patronize, but communicate to young readers that they are taken seriously as thinkers. They have no didactic purposes and are what John Stephens calls 'carnivalesque texts', inspired by Bakhtin's use of 'carnival'. He explains:

> Carnival in children's literature is grounded in playfulness which situates itself in positions of non-conformity. It expresses opposition to authoritarianism and seriousness, and is often manifested as parody of prevailing literary forms and genres . . . [It has] linguistic and narrative resources through which to mock and challenge authoritative figures and structures of the adult

world – parents, teachers, political and religious institutions – and some of the (often traditionally male) values of society such as independence, individuality, and the activities of striving, aggression and conquest. (Stephens, 1992, p. 122)

The choice of characters in interrogative texts problematizes social assumptions by blurring the borders between the serious and comic, reality and fiction, creating in effect 'anti-heroes'. Such picturebooks playfully challenge the reader to question their most basic and precious habits of thought.

Carnivalesque picturebooks provoke communities of enquiry to pay attention to particulars, to have respect for emotions and to have what Nussbaum describes as 'a non-dogmatic attitude to the bewildering multiplicities of life' (Nussbaum, 1990, p. 27). Their interpretation requires a kind of reasoning that is personal and experiential, flexible and not formulable; the kind of reasoning that Aristotle calls 'practical reason' or '*phronesis*'. A philosophical investigation into the meaning of, for example, the concept 'love' would involve an analysis of the use of the term in particular, concrete cases as expressed in everyday language. This is not a search for definitions: such searching is based on the erroneous, but for centuries very popular, idea that there must be an essence (pure love) possessed by all instances of a concept (love of nature, of chocolate, of God, of one's unborn child). Wittgenstein urges us to ask instead how the word 'love' is actually used in everyday language: 'don't think, look!' (Wittgenstein, 1953).

Awareness of how grammar misleads us into thinking that we need to access the abstract through the abstract (few philosophy texts contain concrete examples or illustrations) opens up fresh ways of thinking about the possibility that fictional, concrete settings and characters may be capable of disclosing abstract truths. P4C demands resource materials of a particular kind. An abstract philosophical treatise on the concept 'love' would lead us into darkness.

On the other hand, the powerful portrayal of Frog's plight in the picturebook *Frog in Love* – written and illustrated by Max Velthuijs – is a concrete expression of 'that strange unmanageable phenomenon or form of life, source at once of illumination and confusion, agony and beauty' (Nussbaum, 1990, p. 4). Frog's contradictory emotions and mad behaviour in the text, images and 'gaps' in between set up a dialectical relationship with the reader, inviting reflection on the meaning of 'love'.

In the story, Frog notices that he does not know whether he is happy or sad (see Figure 9.1). He feels funny. He has been walking about in a dream all week. He feels like laughing and crying at the same time, turns sometimes cold, sometimes hot, and observes that there is 'something going thump-thump inside me'. Hare diagnoses him as being in love, but Frog doesn't know whom he is in love with. When he finally discovers that he is in love with Duck, Piglet comments: 'A frog can't be in love with a duck. You're green and she is white'. But Frog doesn't care about that and declares his love to Duck.

FIGURE 9.1   '*Frog in Love*', by Timothy Geschwindt, aged 6.

Using *Frog in Love* in classrooms, I have found that it can start challenging discussions about racial hatred based on different skin colour (Haynes and Murris, 2006). For example, the majority of children in an inner-city primary school class in Leicester thought it a bad idea to have a white husband or wife because 'blacks are better' and 'only whites are racist'. Philosophy lessons give space and opportunity to pupils to express what they really think, rather than what they think their teacher wants to hear.

In a school in inner-city Salford, the picturebook inspired an eight-year-old girl to ask the question 'How do we know what we feel?'. Her profound doubt led to a long enquiry about how language may mislead us into thinking that the identification of emotions is straightforward. Distinguishing between emotions can be problematic, even between such apparently opposite emotions as happiness and sadness. Some people cry their hearts out when immersed in a narrative, yet at the same time they evaluate the experience as a happy one, one to deliberately seek out and look forward to. Human emotional life is full of complex contradictions.

On another occasion, a five-year-old child remarked: 'I am in love with Rebecca, but my heart doesn't go thump-thump'. In the subsequent enquiry, everyone in class was forced to examine whether physiological expressions of love are universal. Even the teacher became increasingly puzzled about how, as a matter of fact, we indeed do know that we are in love.

How accurate a portrayal of love is *Frog in Love*? The artwork entices the reader to address the question of what 'love' means by drawing on their own concrete experiences of loving relationships. This imaginative connection with the personal engages the self and makes the reasoning passionate – there is a care about the focus of the investigation. Text and image are interdependent. This provokes further questioning and opens up opportunities to sympathize and to empathize. Frog's experiences are like our own, or maybe not, or maybe just in some respects. We need to find out. Literature can spur us into philosophical action.

An example of a philosophical dialogue

Picturebooks, then, are powerful stimuli for philosophical enquiries; but their use should not prevent P4C facilitators from being responsive to whatever opportunities may arise in the classroom for philosophical dialogue and reflection. With a mixed-age primary class I had planned the reading of a picturebook as a starting point for a philosophical enquiry. Instead we spent some forty minutes engaged in spontaneous philosophical conversation followed by making drawings. I started the lesson by asking them what they thought philosophy was. I reconstructed some of the dialogue afterwards as follows:

Boy 1:	It's about meaning.
Boy 2:	About thinking.
Me:	What do you think philosophers might be thinking about?
Boy 3:	Space?

Me:	Yeah, philosophers do think about space, e.g. whether space goes on forever and ever. What do you think?
Girl 1:	Yeah, it goes on forever.
Boy 4:	[Struggling to pronounce the word] Infinity.
Boy 3:	No, coz there are black holes and stuff.
Boy 5:	Yeah, but you can go round them and then it goes on forever.
Girl 2:	Are there corners in space?
Boy 5:	No, otherwise it wouldn't go on forever.
Boy 6:	[Showing with his hands] Yeah, coz if you put your hand like this and the other hand like that it makes a corner and then space stops.
Girl 1:	Space goes on after the corner. Everything goes on. Numbers go on.
Me:	Everything goes on?
Boy 7:	Yeah, coz when you are dead, your birthday goes on. My uncle died and on his birthday we gave him a present.
Me :	So you get older even when you are dead?
Boy 8:	Yeah, your skin gets older, rots and stuff, but you don't grow or anything when you are in your grave.
Me:	So who do you give presents to when someone is in their grave?
Girl 3:	To the bones, coz that's what's left when you are in a grave. Like the dinosaurs. We still have their bones.
Me:	So that's all there is left of you?
Girl 3:	You also have a soul and that goes to heaven.
Boy 9:	Only when you have been good. When you kill someone you go to hell.
Me:	What is a soul?

Various possible answers were offered to this last question: one's personality, genes, feelings, moods. 'It is invisible.' 'You can't see it, but you can feel it.' I asked the children to get up, move around the circle and find an empty seat if they believed that there is indeed a heaven. With the exception of three children, all got up and swapped places. I invited the 'non-believers' to start us off again. A boy explained that your spirit leaves your body and moves into a newborn baby's body (see Figure 9.2). After all, people are born after people have died. He explained that he was born five days after his uncle had died, so perhaps he was his uncle. Some got excited about this idea. 'Perhaps I am my grandfather!', a boy exclaimed. They were all keen to make drawings. In a subsequent lesson I explored 'cause confusion' with them, also known as the *post hoc ergo propter hoc* fallacy (Warburton, 2000). This common fallacy among young and old is the mistaken belief that just because one event follows another that one is the cause of the other.

FIGURE 9.2 'When you die your spirit leaves your body and moves into a newborn baby's body', by Ben Evans, aged 8.

The young people in the transcript interwove different perspectives and points of view into a new fabric, linking their personal, private knowledge with public knowledge. They listened carefully and responded to previous points made. The facilitation was effortless. They respectfully took turns, openly agreed and playfully disagreed with others. They expected to be listened to by peers and adults, and felt free to ask questions they were genuinely puzzled about. Their answers invited further philosophical questions, probing deeper into what was assumed to have straightforward meaning: what space is, or infinity, or soul. The idea of still having a birthday when you are dead surprised and fascinated me. They seemed to thoroughly enjoy following the enquiry where it led them, and the carefully chosen questions in the moment increased their interest and engagement. In the review, observing teachers who knew the children well reported amazement at the level of participation, particularly from some usually very reluctant speakers.

The freedom to roam in philosophical space

Giving up the attempt to steer pupils to the (written) production of 'right' answers has a liberating effect on them. Their self-esteem grows dramatically, but only if the topics they are enquiring into arise out of their own puzzlement and their own search for meaning. The experience of not knowing something becomes less frightening and is seen as an invitation to construct meaning with others. But this clear link between pupil engagement and the open-ended nature of philosophical questioning is not obvious to everyone. The teacher of the class in the example above, despite recognizing the pupils' enjoyment and participation, expressed her unhappiness with what she called my 'avoidance of their questions'. She saw the role of the teacher as being to answer pupils' questions, not to respond with further (probing) questions. Is this an expression of the belief that education is about pouring correct answers into empty minds?

My experience of working in secondary schools is somewhat different. When I teach a secondary class for the first time, the pupils are often suspicious of my intentions and the genuineness of my open-ended, searching attitude, not really believing that I myself, as the teacher, do not know the answers to any of the philosophical questions I (initially) generate. As victims of an educational system that does not value independent thought, they feel insecure about their own abilities. This is despite my reassurances that they can connect a narrative with their own thoughts and feelings. Uncertainty is not celebrated in schools, and is often confused with insecurity (Haynes, 2005). Philosophical questioning and the unexpected directions enquiries often take can cause anxiety and uncertainty, especially with older pupils and teachers. Pupils' original curiosity, sense of wonder, and enthusiasm for intellectual enquiry dramatically diminishes as they progress through school (see, for example, Lipman et al., 1980; Reed, 1983).

Sitting in a circle is an alien experience for most secondary pupils and they are reluctant to speak their mind in front of peers. Starting with philosophy at nursery is ideal, but even at a much later age their confidence can reawaken once they experience a community of enquiry's power to generate and explore problems, and once they begin to appreciate the significant role they themselves can play within that community.

The significant effects of P4C on raising school standards, IQ and self-esteem are now well documented (Trickey and Topping, 2004). Some teachers enjoy a pedagogy that does not assume they are the epistemological experts, always knowing better or more or best. Teachers too seem to be victims of an educational system that has, as one teacher put it, 'straight-jacketed' them and made them 'teach-for-testing'.

Philosophy teaches better thinking through enquiry and dialogue. Young people internalize the procedures of dialogue over time, which is the key to internalizing the dialogue itself. 'Outer' dialogue becomes 'inner' dialogue (Lipman et al., 1980; Morehouse, 1993; Cam, 1995; Murris, 1997; Haynes, 2002, 2007). Reasoning well with others takes time and requires good examples. When teaching reasoning the social structure is crucial. The current educational emphases on individual work and one-to-one teacher–pupil interactions reflect reductionist metaphors of mind and modernist conceptions of the relationship between talking and thinking. The metaphysical assumption that the existence of thoughts in individual minds precedes their expression in communal talk inhibits recognition of the fact that reasoning develops in conversation with others, in the space *between* people (Murris, 1997).

The damaging effects of schooling

Pupils' boredom and apathy in schools is often attributed to their home environment. If this were true, many young children would not enter nursery schools bursting with questions, being curious and playful with ideas. Slowly, and from an early age, children's confidence as independent thinkers disappears under the waves of closed questions asked by teachers and assumed by curriculum materials, whatever the subject.

Growing up does not guarantee better, more reasonable thinking. On the contrary, it needs to be explicitly taught, as the art of philosophical questioning is difficult and fragile. The relevance for other subjects is clear: being educated in the disciplines means 'knowing how and when to ask questions' (Splitter and Sharp, 1995, p. 59), not merely being able to solve problems created by others. Schooling has a damaging effect on pupils' ability and courage to question what nobody else is questioning.

Philosophical questions are profound and complex. Philosophy as a subject does not prescribe set methods for answering the questions it raises. A philosophical problem, Wittgenstein observed, has the form 'I don't know my way about' (Wittgenstein, 1953). The 'my', significantly, includes both pupils and teachers. Despite good exam results and positive inspection reports, pupils' speaking and listening skills – especially in secondary schools – are generally poor: they show little respect for each other, and their verbal reasoning is weak. At the same time their teachers identify these skills as basic for any learning.

Many teachers and pupils have become dependent upon the certainty of right and wrong answers and feel lost and confused when questions elude simple resolution. They have become victims of a mostly answers-based curriculum that offers an ill-founded sense of security (Haynes and Murris, 2006). A. V. Kelly argues that adults' psychological need to be in control has contributed to a curriculum that is focused on subject and knowledge content, and to the questionable but popular conception of knowledge as infallible, as an ever-expanding body of facts that can be readily transmitted (Kelly, 1995).

Knowledge acquisition is a public process with people agreeing and disagreeing about what counts as knowledge. Knowledge claims can be questioned, challenged, evaluated and modified by everyone, including young children. It follows that knowledge should be presented to children as contestable and always open to revision. Any opposition to this, Kelly says, is opposition to the very notion of democracy itself.

Autonomy and authenticity

The person who asks the questions determines to a great extent who holds the power and is in control in a classroom. In such a disempowering situation for pupils, the emphasis is placed on the answers that are seen to be important to teachers. In that sense, Sharp and Splitter claim, the education children get is close to indoctrination, 'since many of the answers insisted upon are, in reality, open to question but are, in practice, rarely questioned' (Splitter and Sharp, 1995, p. 51). Answering closed questions requires playing the game of 'guess-the-answer-in-the-teacher's-head'. Such games jeopardize trust, corrupt authentic relationships between teachers and pupils and prevent young people from taking personal responsibility for their own learning. As Michael Bonnett and Stefaan Cuypers identify, space needs to be created for students to be authentic, that is, true to themselves; and this requires the fostering not only of autonomy or self-determination but also of social interdependence and care and commitment to others:

> . . . interpersonal relationships require a developed sense of ownership and responsibility for one's own life and its consequences upon others, as a pre-requisite both for showing consideration to others and for understanding them – knowing from the inside what it is to be responsible and thus to participate in the human condition. (Bonnett and Cuypers, 2003, pp. 336–7)

The emphasis on closed questioning in schools gives a false picture of what knowledge is. Whatever the discipline, 'facts' should always be tentative. Members of any community, whether scientific or philosophical, need to think with others, be responsive to different points of view and be open-minded when evaluating new information. Meanings cannot be given or handed out: they need to be *acquired.*

Emotional disturbance cannot be avoided. On the contrary, it can be a sign that 'demanding thinking' is taking place (Bonnett, 1995). For Socrates, the educated mind can cope with living 'in a state of creative ignorance, inner perplexity and the emotional unease such perplexity creates' (Abbs, 1993, p. 17). The result of this 'existential perplexity' is critical self-reflection and autonomous thinking – necessary conditions of what Peter Abbs calls 'authentic education' (ibid., p. 18).

In the dialogue *Meno*, Socrates uses the stingray as a metaphor for the teacher: anyone who comes close and touches it feels numb and unable to speak. Importantly, this includes the stingray itself: the teacher is numbed too (Matthews, 2003). This can be uncomfortable and produce resistance in teachers.

It is telling that the notion of academic freedom is not used in the context of children's education. If we allow children the freedom, in the existentialist meaning of the word (Bonnett and Cuypers, 2003, p. 328), to choose and to be responsible for their responses to the situations they find themselves in, we enable them to be authentic in class. Observing teachers' interactions with children raises profound questions about the ownership of knowledge, teaching and learning (Standish, 2005).

Facilitating authentic learning then, according to Bonnett and Cuypers:

> ... requires the teacher to empathise with the learners – to develop a feel for the quality of their current engagement by 'listening' for what is incipient in it: the issues and possibilities that their current thinking inherently holds within itself, and to challenge them to acknowledge and pursue them. To do this the teacher must also attend to what things they themselves (including the traditions of thought in which they are embedded) have to contribute, so that she or he can provide invitations for the refinement and deepening of the learner's thinking. Thus the teacher is concerned to focus neither on the learner in isolation, nor on some prespecified piece of knowledge, but on the engagement of the learners with whatever seriously occupies them. The teacher's task is to help the learners to identify and to develop their own sense of what calls to be thought in this situation and to give the space for this to occur. (Bonnett and Cuypers, 2003, p. 339)

Philosophy is in a uniquely strong position to open up such a space. The sciences (including the social sciences) are motivated by the desire to control, predict, generalize and explain; they rarely acknowledge the ways in which the world we encounter, and we ourselves, ultimately remain mysterious. Philosophical questioning presupposes flexibility of thought, openness to new ideas and the cultivation of 'non-attachment' to beliefs. Such questioning cannot be taught mechanically. It has a genuine 'itch', what Derrida calls 'aporeia', as its source (Buckreis, 2005, p. 3). The teacher cannot possibly be in control of the content: in philosophy classes everyone is 'itching'.

Political correctness in Britain can be a barrier to authentic enquiries in class. There is an assumption that children should not question their faith (Haynes, 2005), talk about taboo subjects, or be exposed to literature that gives the 'wrong message'. Although teachers have a duty to protect the young in their care, too much care and protection can suffocate expression of original ideas (Haynes and Murris, 2006). It is crucial that the integrity of philosophical enquiries is not compromised by subtle manipulation (steering enquiries into 'safer' territory), by plain cheating (pretending a question did not get the majority in blind voting), by avoidance (of what may upset children or parents), or by projection (of a need for answers and certainty). Teachers' urge to protect must not be allowed to stifle independence of thought and autonomy.

Although there is a legal document (the United Nations *Convention on the Rights of the Child*) offering a moral code for how young people should be treated, our educational institutions, as a result of some engrained assumptions about childhood, are not living up to it. Children are seen as 'egocentric' or 'inexperienced', unable to distinguish between right and wrong and inclined to do the right things only out of fear of punishment. When 11-year-olds agree that it would be uncomfortable to live in a peaceful world because 'you would have to drink cups of coffee all the time' (see *Your Granny or Your Goldfish* at http://www.jnpartnership.co.uk/main.php/237/371), adults smile, but continue to develop educational resources that presuppose peace as a desirable global objective. Children's ideas make no real difference. They are harmless and cute. Romantic notions about children and their innocence are still prevalent, as is the opposing belief that they are 'uncultivated' and 'wild' and need to be tamed. Both perspectives fail to regard children as responsible, reasonable partners in discussions about important decisions. Yet children are citizens, not just citizens-to-be, and they are able to exercise their freedom to help shape the rules they themselves will be subjected to.

Conclusion

Philosophical enquiries, stimulated by carefully selected literature, can be deep, meaningful dialogues, forging epistemologically and morally different teacher–pupil relationships. New ways of using children's literature and conversing with young people become possible when teachers stop being concerned about predetermined teaching objectives, exam results and league tables and prioritize listening to and respecting young people's own ideas and perspectives. Schools tend to be undemocratic institutions and as such don't do justice to the plurality of beliefs young people hold and their capacity to generate new thinking. But young people have a moral right to a curriculum that relates to their needs. By creating a space for authentic intellectual and moral exploration, schools and teachers are challenged to be more inclusive and less hierarchical in the execution of power. Philosophy, reconstructed in the form of P4C with picture-books, includes raising standards, but also goes far beyond. It gives people the courage and opportunity to think for themselves and strengthens the skills and attitudes essential for authentic and independent thinking. It is education for living and for life.

Acknowledgements

I would like to thank the young people and teachers referred to in this chapter for their support and valuable insights. In particular, I would like to thank Tim Geschwindt and Ben Evans for their permission to publish their wonderful drawings.

Chapter Ten

Philosophy in Children's Literature

Lynn Glueck and Harry Brighouse

I could spend a happy morning
Seeing Roo,
I could spend a happy morning
Being Pooh.

(A. A. Milne, *The House at Pooh Corner*)

Although it is taught as a separate and well-defined discipline within univ rsities, and predates pretty much all other disciplines, most children do not encounter philosophy separately in schools. Of course, though, they do encounter philosophy through other disciplines, though often not under that description. Ideas that are fundamentally philosophical – susceptible of rational evaluation, but not empirical confirmation – are encountered in the sciences and in mathematics, but they are probably most vividly encountered in courses based around literature, in which questions of right and wrong, being, and the meaning of life, are often central to the subject matter. When studying Hardy, the Brontes, Thoreau, Donne and Eliot, the centrality of philosophical ideas is obvious. In this chapter we want to explore some less obviously philosophical texts. We think, in fact, that philosophy plays a major role in children's literature, as much in Milne (see epigraph) and Sendak as in Eliot and Hardy.

First we explain what philosophy is and argue that when teachers teach litera-ture they should be sensitive to, and alert their students to, the philosophical dimensions. We do not place a lower-bound age limit on this claim, but we advocate it for the children who would usually be regarded as of an appropriate age to read the texts we discuss. Then we shall look at some of the books in the canon of children's literature, illustrating how they are philosophical and offering interpretations that we hope will be provoking and useful for classroom teach-ers. We end by confronting a number of possible objections to using philosophy with young children. The central objection is that children of the age to enjoy children's literature are incapable of appreciating philosophy. If so, then although philosophy could still play a role, in literature, its role could not be appreciated by children, and so it would be a mere adult indulgence to discuss it. But even if children can appreciate philosophy, as with other potentially valuable educational subjects, the opportunity costs may be such that it is not worth teaching it. Finally, some children might be harmed by teaching them philosophy, even through children's literature.

Why teach the philosophical aspects of children's literature?

Philosophical questions are questions susceptible of evaluation through reason, but the truth of which cannot in principle be settled by empirical evidence or mathematical reasoning. So whether God exists is a classic philosophical question; as are the nature of causation, whether there are moral truths and if so what they are, and whether it is possible to know the contents of other minds. Some questions seem philosophical until a science develops that renders them, sometimes surprisingly, susceptible to empirical investigation. For a contemporary example think about debates concerning the nature of the human mind; a century ago such debates were firmly philosophical, but many claims that we once thought were philosophical are now beginning at least to be explored using brain science.

We do not propose that young children be invited to evaluate and reason about the classic philosophical arguments concerning God's existence, or that they be asked to explore the mind-brain identity problem. Children's literature can be used, instead, gently to introduce children to a certain category of intellectual question, just as early mathematics and early social and natural science teaching do not demand of children that they learn the subject with full rigour, but rather introduce questions and make children familiar with the kinds of questions they will investigate at an age-appropriate time. There are three rather obvious reasons why this should be done. The first is that, for reasons elaborated elsewhere in this volume, philosophical skills are a vital part of the armoury of the responsible democratic citizen, just as literacy and numeracy skills are. The idea is that when discussing reading we draw out children by inviting them to explore the realm of reasons around the question, for example, of whether it is morally right to kill animals for the purpose of feeding human beings. This question (which, as we shall see, arises in *Charlotte's Web*) is one that most children can see as needing an answer. But it leads into deeper philosophical questions such as what constitutes full moral standing, and when it is legitimate to impose costs on others; children should not be expected to settle such questions, but exposing them to these questions and inviting reflection can be seen as analogous to reading and basic mathematics. Second, given that it is valuable for children to learn philosophy, the setting of children's literature is a particularly nice place to begin. Children like stories to be repeated, so the setting of a book like *The House at Pooh Corner* or *Bootsie Barker Bites* is already familiar; the introduction to the subject is gentle, rather than harsh, and helps children to see that philosophical questions arise in relatively familiar settings. Finally, we conjecture that where children's literature contains philosophical reflection some children will find it enjoyable, just as some enjoy art, others music, and still others mathematics. Even if it were not something they should be expected to become more familiar with, it is worth teaching for the enjoyment it will bring to many children.

Four children's classics, philosophy included

Do philosophical questions really arise frequently in children's literature? We cannot attempt a comprehensive survey of the canon, identifying every single philosophical issue that arises. But we can run through four acknowledged classics, pointing out the philosophical components to illustrate our claim. We hope that readers find the readings plausible enough to attempt others of their own. The following books – *Where the Wild Things Are, Charlotte's Web, Alice in Wonderland* and *The Wizard of Oz* – each have at their core philosophical questions that are worthy of (and from professional philosophers, receive) the highest levels of adult contemplation. These books, loved by children much younger than 12 years old, have been fully accepted as part of the children's literature canon, but are replete with philosophical topics.

Where the Wild Things Are

In Maurice Sendak's *Where the Wild Things Are*, Max, a boy who has been misbehaving in his wolf costume, is sent to bed without dinner. While in his room, he goes on a journey to a land of Wild Things. After subjugating them with his stare, they name him king, and a wild rumpus ensues. Not satisfied with his new life, Max returns to his room where his dinner awaits him, and it is still hot.

In this brief illustrated book Maurice Sendak explores a variety of philosophical issues which are not lost on children. When children's minds are encouraged to range in considering this book, their abstract and philosophical questions bubble to the surface. Here are a few questions generated by a group of first and second grade students in England:

Does magic exist?
What is day dreaming and is it the same as night dreaming?
Are there real monsters in this world?
Why didn't the wild things have a wild rumpus on their own?
Why do people say that they love you so much that they will eat you up?
Would it be a good punishment to make Max not eat his supper?

(Winstanley, 2001)

Several of these questions are philosophical in kind, and they stem from ideas that are integral to the storyline itself, and are part of what makes this a fascinating story for children.

Does magic exist? Apparently something magical does happen in this story; a boy travels to a land of monsters and tames them. But because the story is book-ended by seeming concrete reality – the scold of a mother, and the warm dinner waiting on the bedside table – it calls into question what the intervening magical story was made of. If we take magic to mean occurrences that are not physically (but are logically) possible, such as the growing of a forest in a room, or the existence of large monsters, then it does seem there is magic in this book. But Sendak's narrative does not explain whether these things actually happened or were the invention of Max's mind, in a state of imaginative play (or daydreaming) or in a dream. Sendak's failure to explain makes the story intriguing. Even if the book makes no comment on whether magic actually exists or not, the things that happen to Max, or that Max creates in his mind, *are* magical; that is, we class them as magical. This raises the distinction between the concept of magic and the actuality of magic. Take unicorns. One would say they don't exist because they are invented, magical creatures. But in fact they are afforded a kind of existence because the concept of a unicorn as a magical creature exists. Therefore, at least the very real *idea* of magic exists in *Where the Wild Things Are.*

Three questions concern the monsters and their desire for dominance by Max. The first question – Are there real monsters in the world? – is less naïve than it seems. It all depends on how you define monsterhood. Clearly we have real examples in our world of beings with fantastical features and abilities. One only has to ponder the Venus Fly Trap or the deep-sea Angler Fish to summon up pictures of real-life monster-like beings. But there's a more important question, which has to do with behaviour. What is monster behaviour? Is it wild and irrational? Certainly we have real life examples of wild and irrational behaviour among the human race, in fact behaviour that is far more bloodthirsty and disturbing than that exhibited by these Wild Things. In some ways, the monsters in this story seem entirely rational: they know what they need – a leader – and they pursue it. For some reason, these creatures are begging for leadership – someone to lead their rumpus – which gets to the Hobbesian question about the human need for imposed order, and how our species behaves in the absence of such order. And what do we make of the paradoxical statement of the monsters: 'Oh please don't go – we'll eat you up – we love you so!' This gets at the core of the nature of love. Does love require domination or integration? Is love violent? Is it preferable to kill something rather than be rejected by it? Again, we have, unfortunately, examples of humans killing that which they can't have. But more likely children are referring to a commonly heard statement by loved-ones (and Sendak assumes familiarity with this saying): 'You're so cute, I could just eat you up!' What on earth does that mean? Does love drive people to desire complete assimilation of being? Does love necessarily entail domination?

Would it be a good punishment to make Max not eat his supper? The story on one level communicates the struggle for dominance between parent and child. Just as Max's mother subjugates him, Max subjugates the Wild Things, and having done so, desires to return to where 'someone loved him best of all.' In fact, the mother does not follow through on her threat about dinner, though it's implied that Max must now eat it in his room. The children's question really asks whether a parent should be able to withhold food as punishment and hints at a philosophical issue of what are or should be parents' children's rights? Should parents have such power of dominance over children, so much so that they could withhold a basic human need, food? Is this type of dominance beneficial, on the whole, for children? And does this story ultimately teach children that Max should accept this dominance?

Charlotte's Web

Another book canonical to American children's literature, *Charlotte's Web*, is similarly imbued with philosophy. E. B. White builds his beloved novel – again, its very storyline – around two core philosophical questions: What rights do all living beings have? And what is altruism? He takes as his subject a topic usually shied away from in children's literature: death. In fact, the novel opens with Fern's question, 'Where's Papa going with that ax?', and then lays out the basic arguments for and against animal rights, a current philosophical issue at the centre of debates on biotechnological developments which rely on animal experimentation. Also within this first, short chapter White raises a question about disability: should we treat those who are less physically capable with less regard than others? Wilbur is a runt; this is the reason Mr Arable plans to kill him. But Fern believes that Wilbur should not be treated differently. She shrieks at her father, 'You mean *kill* it? Just because it's smaller than the others? . . . If *I* had been very small at birth, would you have killed *me*?' As readers, we identify with Fern, but we can also see Mr Arable's point; he's running a farm, not a nature reserve, after all. While on the surface this dilemma seems not all that philosophically deep, the current debate in medical ethics about the status of embryos and about prenatal screening indicates how quickly this basic question seems vital. What *are* the rights of *any* being? Why do we tend to side with Fern, as White's narrative encourages us to?

Fern's intervention does save Wilbur temporarily, but it's Charlotte the spider's calm, logical, altruistic actions that ultimately secure his ability to live to old age. Why does Charlotte act altruistically? Is there something in it for her? Does true altruism require that one extracts no personal gain? Philosophers have struggled with this issue, examining in great depth whether or not there is an evolutionary reason for altruism. While one wouldn't expect a child reader, or even most adult readers, to have the experiential knowledge to connect the basic philosophical issues in the novel to those in the academic discipline of philosophy, it doesn't make the encouragement to ponder these questions any less immediate.

Alice's Adventures in Wonderland

Lewis Carroll's *Alice's Adventures in Wonderland* treats so many philosophical issues that it's difficult to choose one to focus on; nearly every page provides an intellectual adventure that playfully demands attention to ideas and the possibilities in, and oddities of, language. One of most pervasive philosophical topics in the book is that of identity, or what constitutes self. A child reader needn't be able to articulate the philosophical questions *Alice* raises; but to understand the thread of the narrative - which even young children generally do - one must follow this exploration of identity.

Take the chapter 'Advice from a Caterpillar.' Here Alice, who has just grown and shrunk a number of times, finding herself swimming in a puddle of tears and then wedged inside a house, meets the Caterpillar. He pointedly asks, more than once, 'Who are *you*?', in such a way that it's hard not to wonder how one might answer the question oneself. How does one explain who one is? And *why* should one answer this question? Alice can't answer why the Caterpillar should tell who *he* is before she tells who *she* is. Alice gives reasons why she can't explain who she is; they are that her body has changed so many times ('being so many different sizes in a day is so confusing'), and that she cannot remember things as she used to, such as the proper words to *You are old, Father William*, which the Caterpillar agrees are all wrong. After she leaves the Caterpillar and eats portions of the mushroom that make her hurtle up in size to tower over the treetops, Alice finds herself being accused of trying to steal pigeon eggs residing in nests below her. Even Alice has noted that her neck has grown so long that it bends like a serpent, but when the pigeon adamantly insists that she is a serpent, she finds it hard to argue with him, especially when she must admit that she, like a serpent, eats eggs. The pigeon retorts that if girls eat eggs, even if only cooked, then 'they're a kind of serpent'.

Throughout this episode, as in so much of the book, Alice's identity seems unstable. Carroll explores what determines our particular identity: Is it our particular physical being? Is it our memories? Is it how others perceive us?

The Wizard of Oz

Questions of identity also run throughout L. Frank Baum's *The Wizard of Oz*: what is it that makes us who we are, or, what is the nature of being? What parts are essential to us? Is where we live so important in determining who we are (as it seems to be for Dorothy)? The central characters in the story – Dorothy, the

Scarecrow, the Lion, the Tin Woodman, and the Wizard – all lack something (or believe they lack something) that would make their identity complete. The most intriguing case of these is that of the Tin Woodman who has no parts of his original self, as all of his parts were amputated by an enchanted axe, and replaced piece by piece with tin parts. If the Woodman no longer has any part of his original self, is he the same self? Is it important that what replaces the flesh and bones is now tin? And how can he long to love the Munchkin girl again without its (the longing for love) being love itself? On top of all of these puzzling questions about what constitutes being (and what love is), is layered the black humour of the Woodman doggedly regenerating himself with the help of a tinsmith. In the end, or even as made apparent from the beginning, the Tin Woodman does indeed have a heart. This of course raises further questions. Can a robot – a being not made of 'meat' as Dorothy inchoately refers to Toto's constitution – have emotions or think? Baum makes the point quite obvious that the Scarecrow, the Tin Woodman, and the Cowardly Lion do indeed have the parts they wish for; we see this in their actions. For example, the Tin Woodman cries over crushing a beetle; the Scarecrow thinks through and solves many of the group's problems; and the Cowardly Lion bravely positions himself to save the crew from the horrifying Kalidahs. It's only Dorothy who cannot herself solve her problem, for her identity – or maybe her very being – seems inextricably linked with Kansas and her people.

Like Carroll, Frank Baum has placed at the centre of his novel a philosophical question about what constitutes identity, a question that has puzzled philosophers for millennia. And he has raised these questions through the inclusion of quite violent but intriguing situations that his characters must overcome. How could he have thought this was material for children's contemplation? It seems that he did not consciously include the elements just discussed, for he states in the introduction to the book that he has written the book as a 'modernized fairy tale, in which the wonderment and joy are retained and the heartaches and nightmares are left out'. Nevertheless, these more 'adult' elements are there; Baum's unwitting inclusion of heartache and nightmare renders the novel, not only interesting, but philosophically deep.

Are children capable of philosophical thinking?

We think we have shown that each of the above-mentioned books contains strong philosophical themes near their core. But they are not, obviously, simply works of philosophy; there is much else to interest and entertain the child reader. The authors may have been overoptimistic about children's philosophical acumen, or may have included the philosophy simply for the sake of adult readers. Should adults eschew discussion of them? One influential reason for answering yes to that question is that children are simply regarded as incapable of philosophical thinking, or even of appreciating philosophical questions.

The most commonly understood theories of child development explain that children are quite different from adults in that they only develop the ability to think about abstract concepts after they have passed through a series of developmental stages. According to psychologist Jean Piaget, children develop in identifiable stages that occur in the same order and at approximately the same age. The child between the ages of two and seven is at the preoperational and egocentric stage, unable to understand any point of view but her own. Then, between ages six and eleven, the child enters the concrete operational stage where she has increased understanding of the world outside herself, but still can only manage very literal or concrete thought. Finally, the child of 12–15, at the formal operational stage, can understand abstractions. Piaget's work has been enormously influential on other theorists, such as Erik Erikson, who developed a parallel theory of psychological development, and Lawrence Kohlberg, whose theory of moral development largely follows the Piagetian stages (Nodelman and Reimer, 2003, p. 89).

There's now a wide body of literature that challenges not only assumptions of developmental psychologists, but also their scientific methods. As Charles Brainerd puts it, 'Empirical and conceptual objections to the theory have become so numerous that it can no longer be regarded as a positive force in mainstream cognitive-developmental research, though its influence remains profound in cognate fields such as education and sociology' (quoted in Nodelman and Reimer, 2003, p. 91). Nevertheless, the developmental stage model of cognitive and intellectual development persists in the fields that have most effect on the publication and sharing of children's literature.

One of the most convincing criticisms of the stage-theory of developmental psychology comes from Gareth Matthews. In his two books *Philosophy and the Young Child* (1980) and *The Philosophy of Childhood* (1994), he critiques with biting acuity the assumptions of Bruno Bettleheim and Jean Piaget, among others. We shall summarize Matthews' arguments, which we find compelling, and to which we have little to add. However, there is a rather obvious objection to his method of argumentation, which suggests a limit to how confident we should be in accepting his conclusions. Nevertheless, we think that the best response to this limitation is for teachers to attempt to address philosophical questions at least until they find that it does not work well.

Matthews recounts Bettleheim's 'ontogeny recapitulates phylogeny' theory of childhood (which he also has found in Dr Benjamin Spock's commentary on child development; and it is evident in Freud's work). The argument embedded in Bettleheim's work goes as such: child development mirrors the development of the human species itself over great spans of time; so just as we could only expect a lower level of sophistication in thought among Neanderthals, so we can only expect the same from children, whose development into adulthood will recapitulate these species-wide advancements (Matthews, 1980, p. 72). But, as Matthews points out, Western philosophy began in the sixth century BC, which is relatively recently. So when does a child begin to recapitulate philosophy? It seems from Bettleheim's work, not until puberty, when the children are, according to developmental theories, able to engage in abstract thought. Therefore, the purpose and importance of fantasy literature for Bettleheim is its psychological drama which goads children into self-discovery. Children are seen as primarily emotional beings, or 'pre-intellectual primitives' (ibid., p. 74). But as Matthews says, young children (at the age of 5 or 6) 'are, and have a right to be, thinking beings as well' (ibid., p. 82). He provides many examples of children engaging in deep philosophical thought that put to shame the framing of some of Bettleheim's questions (ibid., p. 73). In fact, Matthews has noted that children at young ages are *more* likely to think philosophically than older children, who have been socialized into thinking in more narrow and less creative terms. Overall, Matthews sees Bettleheim's work as demeaning the inner intellectual life of children. The question he poses and answer he gives sums up his assessment of Bettleheim's understanding of how literature can spark young minds to think: 'Has Bettleheim recognized the role that stories can play in stimulating philosophical thinking in young children? The answer is 'No'– a resounding 'No'" (ibid., p. 67).

Matthews' analysis of Jean Piaget and Lawrence Kohlberg's theories is important because although these scientists' work has been critiqued over the years, their models of development are still largely accepted. In reviewing Piaget's experiments with children concerning their development in understanding the concept of conservation of substance (for example, whether a clay ball, if flattened still contains the same amount of matter), Matthews exposes several flaws in the experimental design and many plausible explanations for why children's responses to the experiments are in fact quite intellectually sound and actually quite creative. While Piaget claims that children advance from stages of egocentrism and phenomenalism to a full understanding of the conservation of substance by the age of 12, Matthews suggests that 'this development cannot be viewed as a step-by-step victory of truth over falsehood' (Matthews, 1994, p. 53), as the axioms of this experiment are themselves false. That is, conservation of substance, weight and volume are all false principles since we now know that matter can be transformed into energy (ibid., p. 51). According to Matthews, that children seem to all arrive at the understanding by age 12 of the conservation of substance as Piaget defines it simply shows that they have been socialized successfully to accept basic and useful *working* principles of science. Matthews notes how 'arresting' Piaget's experiments are, that they are clever and do seem to explain something about how children develop, but that is all the more reason to examine the methods and results of these experiments thoroughly and question inherent assumptions about them. As Matthews explains, 'it is imperative that we not let the results of Piaget's genuinely remarkable experiments set our educational agenda or define for us the capacity for thought and reflection in our young children' (ibid., p. 40).

Similarly, Matthews examines basic flaws in Lawrence Kohlberg's work on the stages of moral development in children. Through a cogent examination of Kohlberg's assignation of stages to particular responses to hypothetical situations of moral complexity, Matthews comes to the assessment of the logical result of relying on Kohlberg's framework for determining moral development: 'What is both surprising and objectionable is the conclusion that the vast majority of *people* [our emphasis] do not have any real understanding of what morality consists in' (ibid., p. 60). This in and of itself is illuminating, but Matthews, whose focus is on children in particular, takes aim at Kohlbergian theories for being particularly condescending to children: 'Any developmental theory that rules out, on purely theoretical grounds, even the possibility that we adults may occasionally have something to learn, morally, from a child is, for that reason, defective; it is also morally offensive' (ibid., p. 67).

Matthews' work forces us to re-examine firmly held beliefs about the intellectual capacities of children because he comes from outside the disciplines of psychology and sociology; he gives us new reason to question these assumptions. He even puts it in moral terms. Seeing through the eyes of a philosopher, trained to examine arguments, one can more readily see the flaws in these theories. Matthews' work forces one to consider how popular acceptance of the stage theory of developmental psychology affects our assumptions of children's intellectual capacities: 'We must guard against letting [models of development] caricature our children and limit the possibilities we are willing to recognize in our dealings with them as human beings' (ibid., p. 29).

Instead of viewing children as deficient in the cognitive abilities of abstract thought, Matthews sees them as merely lacking a store of life experiences.[1] He quotes W. H. Auden's musings about children's literature as a good basis for thinking about how to define the genre: Auden said, 'There are good books which are only for adults, because their comprehension presupposes adult experiences, but there are no good books which are only for children' (quoted in Matthews, 1994, p. 103). As Matthews parses this: 'a good book for children will be one a reader need not have had adult experience to comprehend or appreciate' and it is also 'one a reader need not *lack* adult experience or sophistication to appreciate' (ibid., p. 103). He suggests through this definition that we should have a much expanded understanding about what is shared and sharable in children's literature.

We promised a cautionary note. Matthews has not offered an alternative, empirically based, account of child development. His strategy is to offer anecdotes that challenge the findings, while simultaneously critiquing both the experimental design and the interpretation of the results. We are convinced by his arguments, and by our own everyday observations that philosophical reasoning of a certain kind is available to even quite young children, while we accept that there might be a rational kernel to stage theory – children do develop as reasoners and thinkers, just not in the sharp way that stage theory claims. Furthermore, Matthews' method of criticism should lead us to be cautious about accepting more ambitious claims about children's capacities for philosophical thinking. He is, himself, a fine philosopher, and it is not inconceivable that his success with the children he discusses in the book turns on his own skills in drawing out the latent capacities of the children, in a way that could not be widely replicated by teachers in schools. So the integrity of philosophy to children's literature depends on children being able to engage at some non-trivial level with the philosophical ideas in the literature, not on a wholesale rejection of even the more modest claims associated with a modified version of stage theory. And our recommendation that teachers introduce their children to philosophical ideas through children's literature rests on what we take to be a reasonable hope, rather than the certain knowledge, that they will prove to be equal to this task.

Would teaching philosophy be wasteful or harmful?

Just because some subject or activity is valuable, and can be understood by most children, and is likely to be enjoyed by some children, that does not mean it ought to be taught in schools. There are too many potentially valuable, understandable, and enjoyable subjects for all of them to be taught. Teaching some of them would constitute a waste of time, not because nothing would be learned, but because more important or more valuable subjects would be crowded out. For example, Latin clearly falls in the category of subjects that are valuable, most can understand and some would enjoy. But the time it takes to teach Latin, many think, could be better used teaching a modern language, or some quite different subject like citizenship education, or an additional science subject. Would it be a waste, in this sense, to raise and discuss philosophical issues in the context of reading children's books? There are two reasons to doubt it. The first we have already hinted at in our initial argument: we believe that it is very important for children, eventually, to learn some philosophical skills; so introducing philosophical reflection to them in a gentle way at this early stage may have a later pay-off because the skills and reflection can be built on later. Second, we believe in common with Matthews (though we acknowledge that empirical research could prove us wrong), that many children are inclined to explore the philosophical ideas in the literature anyway; acknowledging these aspects openly and providing space to explore them can enhance children's intellectual experience and development rather than having them waste their time wondering what sort of questions they are raising and puzzling over why they are not being discussed openly.

Might teaching philosophy at this stage constitute a harm? Well, it might, and we should acknowledge that. Some religious traditions are particularly resistant to critical and philosophical thinking among non-adults, because of the fear that the activity will lead to a potentially damaging turn away from authority. We are not animated by that fear; but it is quite reasonable to fear that an activity which is not well-modelled in public life, and in which teachers rarely have much education themselves will frequently be taught in ways that are either off-putting or deeply misleading for children. Philosophical discussion can be especially difficult to manage, because it must be somewhat open-ended in order for it to elicit genuinely philosophical thinking, but it must not leave the impression that everyone's opinion is as valid as everyone else's or that there are no truths at stake, because if that were so the activity of critical reasoning would be pointless. So our proposal that teachers explore the philosophical aspects should not be taken up without careful thought about how teachers should be prepared, or should prepare themselves, for the experience.

Appreciating and sharing philosophy in children's literature

Children accumulate experience over time through what they do, but they also accumulate experience through what they read. Reading to children is perhaps the most important activity we can engage in with children in order to foster their intellectual capacities, and to give them new intellectual adventures or experiences.

But can it be any kind of book? Do all children's books engage the child's mind in a way that truly respects the capacities of the young child? Unfortunately, no. There are plenty of books published each year which 'dumb down' language, content and even image in order to appeal to what the author, publisher, book club, or parent believes will be appropriate for children. Think of Winnie-the-Pooh. An early lesson most parents learn is that one must refrain from buying any book featuring Winnie-the-Pooh which is not written by A. A. Milne. While the originals, with the Ernest Shepard illustrations, comprise perfect combinations of language, image, characterization, and philosophical whimsy, the various knock-offs, with their bright, cartoonish pictures and clunky prose simply do not provide the same experience for the child reader; they insult the child's cognitive capacities.

Beyond choosing *good* children's books, adults should be aware of how philosophical these books are. This is not to suggest that each reading should be laden with deep philosophical speculation, but to suggest that philosophy in children's literature is not something we should ignore so that we do not stanch the intellectual curiosity of those to whom we read. Part of this process involves questioning why we want to believe that children cannot understand these issues, why our culture persists in clinging to ideas about children that diminish our perception of their intellectual capacities. Is it due to desire for control?

Is it part of believing that childhood should be a time of simplicity? Is it conformity to the pace of capitalist society – that we haven't the time to contemplate philosophical questions fully in our rushed world? Or is reading, but not highlighting these issues, our way of gently introducing the overwhelmingness of the world to children? Perhaps it's due to the fact that many adults are themselves uncomfortable with addressing philosophical issues, as Matthews explains:

> Most adults aren't themselves interested in philosophical questions. They may be threatened by some of them. Moreover, it doesn't occur to most adults that there are questions that a child can ask that they can't provide a definitive answer to and that aren't answered in a standard dictionary or encyclopedia either. (Matthews, 1980, p. 73)

Conclusion

The last chapter of *The House at Pooh Corner*, 'The Enchanted Place,' is simultaneously melancholy, or wistful, and beautifully hopeful. The animals have all gathered, knowing intuitively that Christopher Robin will be leaving soon and that they want to say goodbye to him. They seem unconcerned with really understanding where he's going, or perhaps they're unable to understand. Christopher Robin too deflects the issue of why, but firmly concedes that he is indeed leaving. Although he tells Pooh that what he likes '*doing* best is Nothing,' he soon says, 'I'm not going to do Nothing any more' because, as he explains to Pooh, 'They don't let you'. Milne here implies that Christopher Robin is about to enter school – where you're concerned with Factors and Knights and Suction Pumps – and grow up.

Does our schooling encourage philosophical contemplation? Certainly pedagogy has advanced since Milne was writing. But perhaps there's still a disjuncture between the early years of children's lives, when they feel free to engage in philosophical questioning and engage in imaginative play (the inter-relationship of these two being another interesting topic), and the school years, which socialize and teach children not to think too deeply.

Note

[1] Matthews' contentions about children's cognitive abilities are supported by much recent scientific literature on the subject. For popular reviews of this literature see Gopnik et al. (2001) and Eliot, (1999).

Chapter Eleven

Philosophy in the Secondary School – A Deweyan Perspective

Judith Suissa

Many arguments for philosophy in schools are articulated with young children in mind. I do not wish to enter here into the debate about whether young children can do philosophy or what this means. Rather I want to focus on the important role philosophy can have in the school curriculum at secondary school level, particularly for the 14–18 age group. In this discussion, I draw on the work of John Dewey which, I argue, offers some rich ideas for thinking about philosophy and its educational role.

There is an intuitive argument to the effect that adolescent children would be good candidates for a course in philosophy. Adolescence is a time when children are notoriously preoccupied with questions of meaning, with the struggle to see the 'big picture', and with 'why' questions about every aspect of life. However, to say that children have a proclivity for a particular subject or activity does not, of course, amount to an argument as to why this subject or activity should be included in the curriculum. There has to be some independent argument to the effect that the particular subject is valuable, either intrinsically, or instrumentally, in terms of the values the curriculum is supposed to promote.

In the following discussion, I shall look at some of the ideas typically associated with the promotion of teaching philosophy to children, and shall critique these from a Deweyan perspective. My aim here is not so much to reject the reasons commonly given for doing philosophy with children, but to argue that the articulation of these reasons often leaves out an important aspect of what philosophy is, and one which offers, in my view, a particularly powerful justification for including it in the secondary school curriculum, as well as a compelling account of what it means to have it there and its relationship to other curricular subjects.

Philosophy and critical thinking

It is often pointed out that philosophy encourages critical thinking. I do not intend here to go into the arguments as to the value of critical thinking in education, nor to revisit the well-documented debate on the generalisability or modularity of critical thinking skills (see McPeck, 1981; Johnson, 2001; Bailin and Siegel, 2003).

However, emphasizing the fact that the study of philosophy involves developing critical thinking skills or dispositions does not seem to me a particularly powerful argument for its inclusion on the curriculum. For surely good teaching in any curricular subject is such that it encourages critical thinking, and there seems no reason, on the face of it, why history, literature or biology, for example, should not be perfectly conducive to the development of some type of critical thinking. If, in other words, one is arguing that philosophy develops critical thinking skills, one has, in order to justify its inclusion on the curriculum, also to offer an argument to the effect that it does so better, or differently, from the way in which such skills can be fostered in the context of other subjects.

Moreover, if the case for teaching philosophy in schools rests on its capacity to foster critical thinking skills, there will inevitably be an emphasis on the procedural aspects of philosophy rather than its substance.

And, in fact, much of the philosophy currently to be found in schools does have a primarily procedural focus. The guidelines on the UK's Philosophy A Level website, for example, intended to support teachers and students of philosophy, are typical of this approach (see www.alevelphilosophy.co.uk). A number of authors have remarked on the superficiality of many of the educational programmes and movements that have grown out of approaches linking philosophy with critical thinking, such as that of Matthew Lipman. Winstanley (2006), for example, provides a critical discussion of the way in which the 'area of Philosophy with Children has been somewhat subsumed into the thinking skills arena'. My concern here, however, is not to critique the pedagogical implications of associating philosophy primarily with critical thinking, but to explore the ways in which much of the dominant approach to the teaching of philosophy, whether by emphasizing procedural aspects such as thinking skills, or the classic concepts and questions posed by the traditional subject areas of philosophy, can be construed as placing an emphasis on truth rather than meaning, and to examine the implications of the pragmatist shift from truth to meaning for our thinking about the role of philosophy on the secondary school curriculum.

I do not wish to suggest that questions of truth are unimportant, or to downplay the importance of developing critical thinking skills, including the ability to recognize valid and invalid arguments. What I want to suggest is that questions of meaning are not only an equally important aspect of what philosophy is, but also an especially salient aspect of the experience of secondary-school-age children, thus making the study of philosophy particularly valuable at this age.

John Dewey and the pragmatist shift from truth to meaning

While John Dewey was sympathetic to the view that philosophy has a critical function, to construe critical thinking as the most central aspect of philosophical thinking and enquiry in an educational context would imply, he suggested, an undue prioritizing of questions of truth over questions of meaning.

In thinking about education, it is crucial constantly to remind ourselves that, as Dewey remarked,

> poetic meanings, moral meanings, a large part of the goods of life are matters of richness and freedom of meanings, rather than of truth; a large part of our life is carried on in a realm of meanings to which truth and falsity as such are irrelevant. (Dewey, in Hickman and Alexander, 1998, p. 91)

Yet in focusing on the realm of meaning and meanings, Dewey was not implying a shift to questions of the significance of experience, ideas or values for the individual agent, nor a detachment from the established shared pool of moral, cultural and social knowledge. He was deeply concerned that philosophy address, through asking the right kinds of questions, the significance and meaning of aspects of human life, in order continually to improve it.

In terms of the nature and role of philosophy, this emphasis on meaning reflected Dewey's concern to avoid a conception of philosophy that implied the existence of timeless, metaphysical truths. It is such a conception that seems to lie behind an approach to teaching philosophy that construes the subject as a list of 'the great philosophers' and introduces children, via a thematic or historical approach, to 'the problems of philosophy', or constructs a philosophy curriculum on the basis of the traditional areas of philosophy and the classic debates within them. Most versions of the A Level Philosophy syllabus, for example, are divided into three or four discrete units – generally: Ethics, Philosophy of Religion, Theory of Knowledge and Political Philosophy.

The idea that there is a predetermined body of philosophical knowledge and questions, with their own internal logic, obscures the point, so crucial for Dewey, that the essential function and significance of philosophy is as an intelligent, critical response to questions of meaning thrown up by human and cultural experience. Neglecting to emphasize this point would lead, in Dewey's view, to a static idea of philosophical subject matter, the educational consequences of which are, he suggests, nothing short of disastrous:

> a philosophy which exists largely as something to be taught rather than wholly as something to be reflected upon is conducive to discussion of views held by others rather than to immediate response. Philosophy when taught inevitably magnifies the history of past thought, and leads professional philosophers to approach their subject-matter through its formulation in received systems. (Dewey, in Hickman and Alexander, 1998, p. 46)

In rejecting this view and arguing for the necessity of establishing a richer alternative, Dewey argues that

Philosophy recovers itself when it ceases to be a device for dealing with the problems of philosophers and becomes a method, cultivated by philosophers, for dealing with the problems of men [*sic*]. (ibid., p. 68)

Yet it is important not to interpret this idea of Dewey's as a superficial call for 'relevance'.

In an attempt to try to make philosophy 'relevant', a great deal of literature on teaching philosophy to children has taken the approach of beginning from supposed problems and questions arising from the child's everyday experience, and drawing out their philosophical aspects, or the way in which they can be construed as philosophical problems.

The following extract, taken from the *Children Thinking* website, designed to support P4C in UK schools, is typical of this approach:

A skilled facilitator will endeavour to highlight the philosophical elements of the children's statements or questions and help them expand their thinking into that area.

Some examples of concepts that often arise:

Love, Hate, Revenge, Justice, Power, Reality, Consciousness, Freedom, Religion, Authority, Friendship, Morality, Death, Identity

These concepts might lead to questions such as:

Why are we born?
Should children be punished?
How do we know what is real?
Can life ever be fair?
Should we always do as we are told?
Would I still be me if I swapped brains with my friend?
Was there ever a first thing?
Is it ever right to hurt someone?
Why is it OK to eat meat but not our pets?
How do we know that life is not a dream?
Will I still be the same person when I am old?

(www.childrenthinking.co.uk/home.htm)

In programmes such as this, the questions themselves are supposed to be ones which arise from the children's spontaneous questioning and conversation. The 'philosophical elements' are then drawn out of them by a skilled facilitator.

This may be an appropriate approach with young children, and I do not wish to deny its educational value, or to enter into the debate as to whether such activities in fact constitute philosophy at all (see White, 1992; Wilson, 1992).

However, there are two main problems with using this approach across the curriculum for older children. These problems are interconnected and both, from a Deweyan point of view, have to do with the central notion of experience.

Firstly, such an approach tends to privilege the immediate experience of the individual. In fact, the conception of 'doing philosophy' in such a way as to draw philosophical problems and debates out of the everyday experience of children is often explicitly linked with the educational aim of promoting self-understanding.

Thus if one looks at the section of the Philosophy A Level website entitled *Why Philosophy?*, one finds that the connection between philosophy and self-understanding features prominently. Philosophy, it is claimed, can 'help you understand yourself' (www.alevelphilosophy.co.uk). Indeed, although other benefits of studying philosophy are mentioned, this is construed as the overriding gain: 'Taking all these ideas together – being able to think and think independently, thinking about deep questions but without resorting to what you already believe – philosophy can help you to understand yourself. It's what education is really about. What more could anybody want from an A level?' (ibid.).

A similar emphasis on self-understanding is evident in the work of some of the writers associated with the P4C movement:

> When I say philosophy I mean a quest for self-knowledge, or better yet, a love of wisdom. It entails good questioning, paying attention to the details of one's experience, dialogue with others, open enquiry, recognition of one's ignorance, and a willingness to follow the inquiry where it leads. (Sharp, 1992, p. 46)

However, from an educational point of view, there are obvious problems with an emphasis on self-understanding. I do not think that Dewey would be alone in rejecting the statement that self-understanding is 'what education is really about'. Surely one would not call someone 'educated' who had a very sophisticated degree of self-understanding, but not much knowledge or understanding of major aspects of human culture and society. Indeed, it is questionable whether one can make sense of the notion of 'self-understanding' independently of an account of the social and cultural context in which it takes place. The promotion of self-understanding as an independently valuable educational aim seems to me to be conceptually problematic. Furthermore, the above approach, as defended by Sharp, places great emphasis on 'listening to the lives of children doing philosophy' (ibid.) as an act of political empowerment. Yet in the context of the secondary school curriculum, focusing on the self and individual experience seems intuitively worrying when one stops to consider that most adolescents are already remarkably self-absorbed. If education is, apart from anything else, intended to help children become flourishing members of society, surely it should at least help them, at this age, not only to affirm their self-worth, but also to see themselves in relation to the wider world they inhabit, and in which they will, it is hoped, eventually take on active, participatory and constructive roles.

While the notion of experience features prominently in Dewey's work, it is important to note that he used it in a far richer sense than the kind of self-awareness often suggested by defenders of the educational value of philosophy.

This brings me to the second, connected problem with the way in which philosophy is often construed in an educational context. It is implied that there is a dichotomy between the world of philosophy, as metaphysical timeless truths, and the world of experience, as individual and immediate.

Advocates of philosophy in schools alert to the difficulties of associating philosophy primarily with critical thinking skills tend instead to emphasize the integrity of philosophy as an ancient discipline with its own traditional body of knowledge. The Philosophy A Level website, indeed, while emphasizing the value of independent and critical thinking, also notes the importance of 'subject matter', stating that 'the questions that philosophy investigates are the most profound questions that we can ask' (www.alevelphilosophy.co.uk). Yet while it seems a truism that philosophy, like any discipline, consists of both subject matter and procedure, from a pedagogical point of view it is important to gain some theoretical understanding of the way in which these two aspects are perceived and the implied relationship between them. It is here that Dewey's position offers some helpful critical insight.

Arguments for teaching philosophy such as those discussed above often seem to assume a dichotomy between the abstract world of philosophical knowledge or thought on the one hand, and the immediate experience of the individual on the other. The job of the philosophy instructor, it is implied, is to connect these two, as in the above passage taken from the philosophy for children website, where the instructor clearly has in mind some of the classic areas and questions of philosophy, and has designed a programme to map these on to children's articulation of their experience of everyday problems and dilemmas.

Yet for Dewey, experience is the ongoing, organic, active interaction between human beings and their natural and social environment, not an individual act of engagement with this world as something existing independently. As Ziniewicz remarks:

> For Dewey, human beings are not 'subjects' or 'isolated individuals' who have to 'build bridges' to go over to other human beings or the things of nature; human beings are originally and continually tied to their environment, organically related to it, changing it even as it changes them. Human beings are fundamentally attached to what surrounds them. (Ziniewicz, 2000)

It is in the context of this conception of human experience that the notion of meaning, and meaning-making, is to be understood. For once one rejects, as Dewey did, the dualism between human beings and the environment,

The significant distinction is no longer between the knower and the world; it is between different ways of being in and of the movement of things; between a brute physical way and a purposive, intelligent way. (Dewey, in Hickman and Alexander, 1998, p. 65)

Meaning, on this conception, is an intrinsic aspect of human beings' intelligent interaction with their environment.

This does not mean that human beings 'bestow' meanings upon natural events, as if meanings were entities somehow existing independently of actual experience (a priori), in some sort of isolated or detached consciousness, and merely 'added on' to the face of natural events. Meanings grow out of interactions and transactions of human beings with one another and with their natural environment.(Ziniewicz, 2000)

The Deweyan notion of experience thus captures the important sense in which humans and human thought are constantly changing, thus rejecting the dualistic view of nature as embodying static, timeless metaphysical truths. So although there is a personal, individual aspect to experience, it can never be just this as it encompasses not only the person doing the experiencing, but the way they experience and what they experience, in such a way as 'one cannot neatly determine where the individual ends and the natural environment or society begins' (ibid.). It is out of this intermingling that communal meanings are constructed and continually reassessed in an attempt to improve the conditions of life and society.

Dewey's philosophy of education is obviously a direct consequence of this approach; while education should ideally provide individual students with rich and valuable experience in the immediate short-term, it is also inescapably and importantly a crucial part of the project of improving society.

In light of this, we can begin to understand the way in which, while Dewey emphasizes the critical function of philosophy, he means this in a far wider sense than that implied by the suggestion that philosophy fosters critical thinking skills. This wider sense, so I want to argue, is particularly of value in the context of the secondary school curriculum, given the way this curriculum and life in secondary school generally is typically constructed. Criticism, for Dewey, forms part of the organic, meaning-making activity described above, rather than offering an abstract set of skills or an acquaintance with 'philosophical problems'. The Deweyan view, in short, rejects the privileging of individual experience in favour of a richer conception of experience rooted in the idea that humans are essentially concerned with a constant attempt to make and to improve shared meanings out of their active encounter with the natural, social and cultural worlds.

Adolescence and the search for meaning

This brings me to the main reason why a Deweyan perspective on the role and significance of philosophy is particularly valuable for adolescents.

Although it seems obvious that adolescents are concerned with questions of meaning, the sense in which this is true is very different from that in which the very young child, constantly living through new experiences and encountering new and puzzling aspects of the natural and social world, is filled with wonder. One could construe the questions prompted by young children's curiosity – Where do people go when they die? Do animals dream? Does God exist? – as philosophical questions. But the sense in which older children ask philosophical questions about the world they encounter is very different. Adolescents already share a wealth of cultural and social knowledge; what they are curious about is what it all *means*, what it is *for* (the refrain 'what's it all *for*?' will no doubt be familiar to parents of adolescents). Yet it is precisely during this stage in the school life of most children that the curriculum seems overwhelmingly fragmented into discrete units, each with its internal logic, in which there is not much space to ask why bits of knowledge are there, what they are for, what they mean, and how they are related to each other.

Furthermore, while it is possible to defend the view that children of a very young age have a natural tendency to ask philosophical questions, or at least questions about the world which we could correctly construe as philosophical questions, it would be inappropriate to suggest that they begin to comprehend the difference between philosophical questions and non-philosophical questions. To grasp what philosophy is, as a discipline, as distinct from other disciplines, surely requires a broader and deeper cultural knowledge than that of the primary school age child. And appreciating the ways in which the search for 'meaning' in human life involves the ability to ask questions from a range of different disciplinary perspectives, and grasping the difference between these, is an important educational goal.

In secondary school, children are already at a stage where they have been inducted into a vast world of cultural and social experience, knowledge and understanding. Their struggle to find meaning in the world is a struggle not just to understand the concrete aspects of experience with which they are confronted in their everyday lives, but to make sense of the human knowledge, ideas and concepts reflected in the social and cultural meanings that form part of their everyday life, whether in the media, in the context of interpersonal relationships, or in the subjects they encounter through the school curriculum.

I have argued that Dewey offers us a way of construing the problems of philosophy as not divorced from the real world, and yet not entirely subjective and drawn from the individual experience of students. Crucial to grasping this perspective is to accept Dewey's view of philosophy as, in essence, interpretation of culture. This approach reminds us that the problems of philosophy, like those of biology, sociology and history, are all parts of the problems of human culture. In the secondary school curriculum, this takes on particular significance as the curriculum is divided into subjects in a way which makes it easy to forget that these subjects were originally connected to and grew out of human attempts to make meaning out of the natural and the social world.

In *The Child and the Curriculum* (Dewey, 1902), Dewey describes how the child, before entering the world of school, inhabits his own world in which the various contents he encounters 'have the unity and completeness of his own life' (Dewey, in Hickman and Alexander, 1998, p. 237). Then, though, 'He goes to school and various studies divide and fractionalize the world for him. Geography selects, it abstracts and analyzes one set of facts, and from one particular point of view. Arithmetic is another division, grammar another department, and so on indefinitely' (ibid.). In each of the traditional school subjects, 'facts are torn away from their original place in experience and rearranged with reference to some general principle' (ibid.).

This fragmentation of subjects is especially acute in the secondary school curriculum, ever more dominated by the constrictions of the exam and assessment regime. Given this fact, and considering the natural search for meaning characteristic of adolescence, it seems inevitable that the question 'what is it all *for*?' will feature largely in adolescents' experience of schooling. The response suggested by a Deweyan approach is not to try and make the child feel connected to the predetermined subject matter of the curriculum by prioritizing and affirming the value of his or her own individual, immediate experience, and devising pedagogical ways of incorporating this into the teaching of the subject matter but to find ways to show how the very questions of biology, geography and literature represent part of the organic whole of human experience and attempt at meaning-making. Philosophy, I suggest, can offer a way to do this within the confines of the existing curriculum. The curriculum subjects themselves will be more meaningful (rather than just the inert data that Dewey so abhorred) if children are encouraged and given the tools to appreciate the sense in which they can be construed as questions of meaning.

The questions raised in philosophy, Dewey insists – and, thus, the questions which should be raised by the teaching of philosophy – come not from philosophy but from life. Yet life, by the time children have reached adolescence, is not just their direct experience of everyday existence, but the accumulated knowledge, culture and values learned from their ongoing social interaction and reflected in many aspects of their experience – among them the content of the school curriculum.

This approach suggests a sort of meta-meaning-seeking role for philosophy. I am not entering here into the debate about the nature and role of philosophy as a discipline, but merely using Dewey's ideas to suggest how, given the current structure and constraints of the typical secondary school curriculum, the introduction of philosophy could provide a valuable counter-balance.

In the final sections of this chapter, I suggest some possible ways in which this could work.

The philosophy classroom

To take an example of a topic covered by the secondary school curriculum: the biology syllabus requires students to study evolutionary theory and the notion of natural selection. A good biology teacher will hopefully not just aim at imparting the bare facts of evolutionary theory, but will try to encourage the students to ask, for example, what Darwin meant by arguing that natural selection is arbitrary and works on the principle of adaptability to the environment. There are obviously many questions, such as these, that constitute *biological* questions about meaning and that play a part in any serious attempt at biological thinking and research. Yet the extent to which these can be entered into given current curricular constraints is limited. It is here that philosophy classes could provide a valuable space in which students could articulate and discuss, in depth, related questions about, for example, the impact of Darwin's thought, and begin to appreciate the connections between these questions and aspects of their historical and cultural context that may arise in other areas of the curriculum, such as literature, RE, or history. A philosophy class could help children articulate *philosophical* questions about these ideas, such as whether evolutionary theory signifies a rejection of a teleological account of life, what this means, and its significance for how we think about human nature, responsibility and morality. Yet, equally importantly, it can also provide a space – perhaps the only space, within a discipline-led curriculum – for appreciating and understanding the difference between biological questions, historical questions and philosophical questions; for stepping back, in other words, and asking what each discipline *means* and what it is *for*.

Each curricular subject is defined and constrained by its own area of enquiry, and in a sense, of course, this is as it should be. Thus, if one looks at the official publications providing resources for the national curriculum subjects in the UK, one finds statements such as the following: 'Geography is a focus within the curriculum for understanding and resolving issues about the environment and sustainable development. It links the natural and the social sciences. Through geography pupils encounter different societies and cultures' (DfEE, 1999, p. 154).

Although this suggests a rich conception of geography, taking into account not just facts about the physical world, but ideas about the social and cultural context, there is no room from *within* geography classes to step back and ask philosophical questions about what a culture is, what society is, and why, as humans, we are interested in such enquiry, nor to articulate the ways in which questions such as these intersect with other questions and knowledge from different disciplines.

The approach to teaching philosophy suggested here emphasizes the point that the conceptual schemes used and the questions asked by scientists, historians and biologists, are themselves human questions framed and posed out and because of certain human understandings, desires, and needs. It is through understanding what these are, what they mean and how they interconnect that we can perhaps engage in the kind of philosophy that Dewey aspired to. I believe this approach is what Mary Midgley has in mind when she writes:

> The conceptual schemes used in every study are not private ponds; they are streams that are fed from our everyday thinking, are altered by the learned, and eventually flow back into it, influencing our lives. (Midgley, 2005, p. 150)

An important aspect of this conception of teaching and doing philosophy is not just the critical function, in the sense discussed above, but the role of imagination. In a school world largely dominated by curricular knowledge and facts to be understood and recalled for exams, philosophy can serve as a valuable supplement to adolescents' experience of school not just by asking the kind of meta-questions suggested above, but by encouraging the use of imaginative reflection on the ideas encountered. In his plea for a new kind of philosophy, Dewey lamented the fact, surely more pertinent than ever in the contemporary educational climate, that

> because we are afraid of speculative ideas, we do, and do over and over again, an immense amount of dead, specialized work in the region of 'facts'. We forget that such facts are only data; that is, are only fragmentary, uncompleted meanings, and unless they are rounded out into complete ideas – a work which can only be done by hypothesis, by a free imagination of intellectual possibilities – they are as helpless as are all maimed things and as repellent as are needlessly thwarted ones. (Dewey, in Hickman and Alexander, 1998, p. 83)

The philosophy syllabus?

The above considerations lead strongly to the conclusion that philosophy cannot be conceived of and structured like another curricular subject with its own 'bits of data'. If it is subject to the same kinds of curricular guidelines and assessment regime as other subjects, its contents will inevitably be turned into 'facts'. If philosophy classes are to truly enable children to engage in speculative, imaginative exercise, it would seem problematic to restrict them by means of exams and predetermined syllabi.

To compile a philosophy curriculum based on topics to be covered, questions to be asked and subjects to be addressed would undermine the approach suggested here. Rather, if philosophy is, as suggested, to be given the status of a sort of meta-subject on the curriculum, then the philosophy class should be loosely structured around the philosophical questions which arise from the aspects of human life, culture and meaning encountered through the rest of the curriculum.

In making this suggestion, I am not proposing that philosophy teachers abandon the encounter with philosophical texts as primary sources. Questions arising from a discussion of the implications of Darwin's theory of evolution, for example, could lead very well into a reading of some of the work of Aristotle, as well as the work of contemporary philosophers such as MacIntyre. The objection will no doubt be made that one cannot appreciate philosophers such as MacIntyre without a systematic training and understanding of the philosophical traditions that precede them. Yet arguably, the secondary school curriculum is not the place to provide a systematic, thorough training in philosophy, but to introduce children to philosophical ideas, to convince them of the value of philosophy, and to whet their appetite for further study.

What is important is to avoid the impression, often suggested by the Philosophy A Level syllabus, for instance, that the problems of philosophy are predetermined and exist independently of what Dewey termed 'the problems of men'.

Some thoughts on dumbing-down the curriculum

Given the common association of Dewey with the 'child-centred' movement in education, and the often misleadingly superficial perception of what this means, it is important to emphasize the importance Dewey attached to cultural knowledge and understanding:

> No just or pertinent criticism in its negative phase can possibly be made, however, except upon the basis of a heightened appreciation of the positive goods which human experience has achieved and offers. Positive concrete goods of science, art and social companionship are the basic subject-matter of philosophy as criticism; and only because such positive goods already exist is their emancipation and secured extension the defining aim of intelligence. (Dewey, in Hickman and Alexander, 1998, p. 91)

Yet at the same time, it is important to emphasize that Dewey's insistence that philosophy addresses the problems of life if not a superficial call for relevance. Richard Peters, in his essay on Dewey, noted that 'Dewey admitted the importance of making the child aware of his cultural heritage but only on the condition that he should be introduced to it in a way which stressed its relevance to present practical and social problems' (Peters, 1977, p. 113). Yet the approach defended here suggests that this implied distinction between the 'cultural heritage' offered to the school pupil and the 'present practical and social problems' of the child's experience misrepresents Dewey's epistemological position, especially with regard to the central notion of experience, as discussed above.

It often calls for 'relevance' which are behind curricular reforms that have in turn sparked fears of dumbing-down. Thus, for example, recent reforms to the UK GCSE science curriculum, proposing a notion of 'scientific literacy' built around topics such as global warming and mobile phone technology, provoked angry warnings of dumbing-down from leading scientists and academics. However, if relevance was interpreted in a Deweyan way, not by trying to make biology relevant to current issues such as teenage pregnancy or alcoholism, but by helping students to see how the central questions and concepts of biology themselves constitute a human attempt to construct meaning out of life – an attempt surely most teenagers can identify with – perhaps the curriculum would not seem so dumbed-down.

The insight of Dewey's approach to teaching philosophy is that it allows us to see the study of philosophy both as a resource for asking questions about meaning, and as itself a part of the ongoing human attempt to understand the world – not in any superficial or immediate sense of 'self-understanding', but in the sense of a shared endeavour to interpret, remake and improve human society and culture. Philosophy, on this view, is itself a part of culture, and indeed the problems of philosophy, for Dewey, must always be the problems of culture:

> philosophy, like politics, literature, and the plastic arts, is itself a phenomenon of human culture. Its connection with social history, with civilization, is intrinsic'. (Dewey, in Hickman and Alexander, 1998, p. 79)

An appreciation of this point will, I hope, help further our understanding of why philosophy is so important, why education is so important, and why both education and schools could do with a bit more philosophy.

Chapter Twelve

Philosophy, Wisdom and Reading Great Books

James C. Conroy

The Bookcase

Ashwood or oakwood? Planed to silkiness,
Mitred, much eyed-along, each vellum-pale
Board in the bookcase held and never sagged.
Virtue went forth from its very shipshapeness.
Bluey-white of the Chatto Selected
Elizabeth Bishop, Murex of Macmillan's
Collected Yeats. And their Collected Hardy.
Yeats of 'Memory'. Hardy of 'The Voice'.
Voices too of Frost and Wallace Stevens
Of a Caedmon double album, off different shelves.
Dylan at full volume, the Bushmills killed
'Do not go Gentle.' 'Don't be going yet.'

(Seamus Heaney)

Is it too much to suggest that education, or perhaps we should say schooling, has been reduced to, in Beatrix Potter's phrase, 'snippets and tippets'? Such a charge may be a little too extravagant. Might it not rather be argued that an explosion in information has precipitated a fragmentation of the school curriculum with shards of light and insight scattered amidst both sheer dross and myriad sources and resources? And with this radical dispersal has come a shift in the vision that underpins curriculum design, with an ever increasing dependence on frameworks desiccated by learning outcomes, instruments of assessment and depleted marking schemes.[1] Married to these infantilized structural conditions are a set of pedagogical practices that are equally dismissive of a claim that education might entail intellectual coherence sustained over time. So it is that pedagogical practices in the classroom are dominated by workbooks, discussion groups, circle time and sundry learning packs and strategies that break down learning into what are deemed to be manageable activities. What might underlie these practices? Perhaps it is that education-alists, having been persuaded that what is the case ought to be, have opted for a curriculum which reflects the contemporary penchant for accepting the proposition that children's attention spans are extremely limited. Because children's span of attention is deemed to be limited, pedagogical practices need to be adapted. Now it would be difficult to deny the need to construe education as an adaptive practice: otherwise no change in the world of affairs, from the advent of television to climate change, may have any claim on what is to be discussed in school. No new work of art or literature would make it onto the curriculum agenda however meritorious its claims. However, acknowledging this need is not to accept that what is the case ought always to determine what we ought to do. While the *is-ought* problem may well have fallen from grace in philosophical ethics and moral discourse, it may not be entirely redundant, even, or perhaps most especially, with respect to any number of prudential considerations. We are, after all, rather unlikely to accept that, because children not infrequently engage in fist fights in the playground, we should encourage rather more of them in the precincts of the school. Yet it would appear that when it comes to thinking about curricu-lum and pedagogy we are tempted to do just this. It is a temptation which has its roots in the thought of Spencer and certain readings of Dewey, and in particular Spencer's claim that 'children's understanding can expand only from things of which they have direct experience' (Egan, 2002, p. 17). Simi-larly, Dewey and Piaget's indebtedness to Spencer is most expressly revealed in their perception that the mind inexorably moves from the concrete to the abstract. One only knows that which one has done for oneself. Arendt puts this rather succinctly, observing that what we have done is to substitute 'doing for learning'. Consequently there is no imperative that the teacher 'master' her subject herself since this is likely to issue only in the passing on of inert material. Instead of inducting students into the world as encapsulated in such 'dead knowledge', teachers are required to 'constantly demonstrate the modes of its production':

> The conscious intention was not to teach knowledge but to inculcate a skill, and the result was a kind of transformation of institutes for learning into vocational institutions which have been successful in teaching how to drive a car or how to use a typewriter or, even more important for the 'art' of living, how to get along with other people and to be popular, as they have been una-ble to make the children acquire the normal prerequisites of a standard curriculum. (Arendt, 1954, p. 6)

Arendt suggests these developments have, beginning in the US, traversed the world as progressive education; a form of education which has overthrown both traditions and established pedagogic methods (Arendt, 1954).

Lest it be thought that relying on the observations of a mid-twentieth century political philosopher outside the mainstream of educational discourse is a precarious position from which to argue, it is worth reflecting on contemporary discursive practices and attitudes among educational theorists and teachers in Britain. Indeed, a cursory glance at a wide range of government documents on the curriculum betrays these tendencies. In 2004 the Scottish Education Department initiated the process of re-thinking the curriculum for 3- to 18- year-olds. In its document, *A Curriculum for Excellence* the Education Department claims that 'our aspiration is to enable all children to develop their capacities as successful learners, confident individuals, responsible citizens and effective contributors to society' (Scottish Executive Education Department, 2004). Moreover this process is claimed to enable 'us to anticipate changes and challenges which young people will face in the future, to take account of advances in education and to tackle the aspects of the current curriculum which must be improved' (ibid.). The document also extols the centrality of 'relevance' to student's present and future lives. Such public statements arouse little excitement because they are the commonplace language of education punditry and policy. All is relevance and capacity building. Nowhere is there any coherent or continuous sense of an historical polity. There are only the now and the future; no past and certainly no tradition.

It is in the midst of this that metacognition has emerged in recent years as a dominant theme in theories of teaching and learning. Students are increasingly subjected to a range of practices which focus attention not on the object to be studied but on the inner states and workings of the conscious and unconscious patterns of the subject doing the studying. By concentrating our energies on teaching students to learn how to learn we are in danger of losing sight of the critical centrality to education of ensuring that students become acquainted with the world in something akin to a coherent sense, or of ignoring substantial resources that may contribute to the cultivation of wisdom and discernment. In some important respects, this allows teachers off the hook of determining some kind of priority with respect to the choices to be made as to the content of the curriculum. If education is primarily concerned with the continual process of refinement whereby the student is increasingly conscious of, and knows how to employ, her 'learning style', then questions about what it is that one should learn are at best secondary and at worst irrelevant. After all, the argument goes, one only needs to know how to learn in order to be educated. If I know where and how I might access Pliny's *Letters* or Aristotle's *Ethics* or Homer's *Odyssey* then I don't actually need to read any of them – after all, I know they are there! At its most unpersuasive, the impulse to establish an education rooted in process is justified in terms of the displacement of tradition by novelty. The world is in constant and rapid flux. To deal with this Heraclitean fire we need to establish a curriculum and pedagogical practices which always face forward. Students must be induced to recognize the future as being substantially discontinuous with the past and, since the future is axiomatically unknown, they must be equipped to meet its challenges, whatever they may be. Such attitudes undergird the claim that education is increasingly, perhaps even primarily, concerned with competencies (OECD, 2001, 2006). It is no part of my argument, of course, that students should be anything other than competent: the issue is what constitutes competence. It may be that competence resides in learning that is not, at least in any simple way, reducible to skills, but rather rests on knowledge, insight and wisdom among other capacities and dispositions.

Allied to the drive for the new evidenced in such practices has been the emergence of the concept of equality. But as Arendt points out this surpasses the levelling of class distinction, or equality of opportunity, to be equality as a right (in this case a right of access). A negative concomitant of this move has been that others do not have rights to access those things which it is decided are not accessible to the masses. Better no access for anyone than restricted access for the few. In this way, and in public schools, the role of and access to certain cultural objects, such as music in the classical tradition and more especially philosophical and literary works, has been diminished. Ironically these cultural resources are not absent (or at least not entirely absent) from precisely those private educational institutions where social, political and cultural advantage remains pronounced. But they are, by and large, no longer to be found in mainstream state schools. An anecdote may serve to illustrate the point. Recently I was having a chat with a schoolteacher of my acquaintance who was berating a colleague for teaching a class of lower-attaining 16-year-olds Robert Bolt's play *A Man for All Seasons*. Bolt's play, a portrait of the turbulent relationship between Henry VIII and Thomas More, was, she opined, much too difficult. What, I enquired, might be too difficult in exploring a literary *tour de force* which dealt with fidelity and betrayal, self-denial and avarice, private conscience and public loyalty, love and hate, justice and injustice, ambition and self-abnegation? The teacher was to all intents a good, caring and professionally committed person, but she was, like many, seduced by the notion that high culture (if such this is) is not suitable fare for students who are not academically successful. It is indeed extraordinary that we not infrequently choose to deny those with least power access to a substantial range of cultural and, for that matter, emotional resources. But I shall return to this.

Whatever its provenance, the relevance-competence trajectory has come to offer theoretical bedrock to a range of educational and pedagogical projects, from *Philosophy for Children* and *Communities of Enquiry* to Feuerstein's *Instrumental Enrichment* programme. In the rather more prosaic pedagogies of mainstream schooling it gives rise to the propensity for conversational approaches to learning which move from the known to the unknown, the concrete to the abstract; pedagogies predicated on the self as arbiter. Indeed, with growing calls for an individualized, negotiated curriculum, not man but the individual is to be the measure of all things. Consequently, conversation is to be preferred to reading and argument appears more attractive than rumination. This is a course that makes little sense when cast in the light of the life of the imagination, wherein children can readily move well beyond the particularities of their own experience. Children's learning is not constrained by their experiences.

In reading A. A. Milne or Beatrix Potter to young children we do not assume that only those scenes that have some connection with the somewhat limited repertoire of their experiences are amenable to internalization and homologation. Where we do so it is only in the most marginal sense; that is, for example, where a child has been admonished by their parents for being naughty, they will recognize incidents where Peter Rabbit has been naughty. But what does even this entail? It requires that the child is capable of anthropomorphisms despite having no experience (one assumes) of talking, self-consciously reflective rabbits. Therefore the known to the unknown trajectory must be couched in terms of psychological states and not in terms of concrete particulars. But, as Joyce's *Ulysses* readily illustrates, minds are apt to roam over substantial territory in something rather less than a sequential manner. The imagination stretches out in front of our structured cognitions of the world, ever pressing us to new insights. The dominant view of developmentalism has issued in the delay or avoidance of educational engagements deemed inappropriate because the cognitive structures of the mind have not as yet reached a point where they are naturally receptive to particular kinds of ideas. But minds are not like bodies or brains and do not evolve in a linear fashion.

I now wish to turn directly to a consideration of teaching philosophy in schools. White (1992) and Murris (2000) provide two quite different perspectives on the appropriateness of teaching philosophy in schools. On the one side White suggests that philosophy as widely understood, is not amenable to children because they lack the requisite higher-order skills necessary to map a concept which they already know how to use. It is argued that children need to have internalized a substantial body of knowledge around particular concepts and their use, and indeed the implications of using such concepts in particular ways. Murris, in challenging this, suggests that White makes certain unsustainable neo-Aristotelian assumptions about children needing to build up their knowledge base and experience in order to make sensible or informed judgements about the ethical or epistemological provenance of particular concepts. Moreover, for White, a key distinguishing feature in determining the philosophical character of a question lies in the intentions of its author. The philosopher brings to bear a degree of intentionality not available to the child. Murris dismisses this line of reasoning, arguing that she has witnessed 'an enquiry starting off with the statement "Cows can't fly", which quickly turned into an enquiry about the moral implications of calling a group of molecules 'beef' rather than 'cow" (ibid., p. 269). These arguments are more recently taken up by Long who, with similarities to Murris' position and drawing on Thomas Reid's common sense philosophy, suggests that introducing children to philosophical modes of thought is not the kind of enterprise that requires the sort of precision desired by White. He opts rather for an approach that 'suggests that naïveté and vagueness are to be expected and indeed welcomed as part of the process . . . philosophy is more an art than a science [and] its work in the pursuit of wisdom begins anywhere within the interest and compass of the child's experience and not within questions familiar to adult thinkers' (Long, 2005, p. 608).

Now the argument between White on the one hand and Murris and Long on the other has some elements of a shadow boxing contest. Tilting at their respective windmills they miss, I suggest, the central issue and each other's points. White's windmill is the notion that philosophy begins with the naïve questions of children; Murris and Long's the idea that philosophy is a distinct, platonic form of thinking, requiring mastery of certain patterns of discourse and argumentation. What both miss is the complexity of the relationship between philosophical traditions and children's cognitive development. Philosophy is a way of thinking deeply rooted in particular historic literary traditions. The teaching of philosophy requires acquaintance with these traditions from the outset. The central pedagogical issue is not whether but how we relate the traditions of thought of the wider historical community to the development of children's thinking and the processes this entails. It is for this reason that, here, I am attempting to address the question of using philosophical and other literary texts in the development of philosophy in the classroom. I take it to be a self-evident truth that teachers want, in so far as they are motivated by educational considerations, to introduce their students to particular features of the world and the concomitant explanatory schemas and insights. Whether it is geography or history, physics or maths, literature or philosophy, the task is to nurture, expand and root children's understanding of how the world is. This entails engaging with and drawing on those traditions that have shaped the various ways in which we make sense of the world. I also presume that within the conspectus of education philosophers harbour a desire to induce wisdom and insight.

When Wittgenstein points us towards clearing up the confusions of language he does so, one may presume, in the hope that we might resist the temptation to travel up blind alleys, seduced by both over-determinations of meaning and surface misinterpretations. It is always something of a challenge to impute or indeed make sense of others' motives in directing our attention to particular pitfalls in the way we think about or, more importantly, use language. Nevertheless, if the object of Wittgenstein, and indeed other philosophers in the analytic tradition, is to help clarify our thinking, this must be in pursuit of some kind of goal. In this case might it not be reasonable to suggest that it is in the hope that we will not be ensnared and confused by our own use of words. To be so ensnared is arguably to make claims and decisions which rest on shaky, not to say shoddy, grounds. Where this is the case we are inclined to suggest that X has no grounds for believing Y and her willingness to do so, despite the evidence or argument to the contrary, makes her foolish. Surely education is concerned with the avoidance of foolishness among students. Philosophical education has to be concerned with the cultivation of wisdom and the avoidance of foolishness; indeed a central purpose of philosophy is wisdom. What else could it be? Are we not etymologically obliged to take philosophy to mean 'love of wisdom'? But wisdom does not emerge merely from the repetition of experience or its expansion. Something has to be added, and sometimes that additionality is introduced by the teacher pointing out to a child that thinking Y results in confusion, contradiction or indeed foolishness. The stumbling of the child on her philosophical journey, to which Long and Murris aver, is simply part and parcel of coming to know the world; this is no more or less the case in philosophy than in physics. There is no special kind of stumbling in philosophy. Moreover, the exercises in thought which Philosophy for Children (P4C) nurtures are precisely that, exercises in thought. Education should of course be predicated on cultivating the exercise of thoughtful questioning, but such thinking has, in much of the P4C literature, been transformed into a special kind of process which becomes its own end. Indeed, as Masschelein (2001) suggests, such a process model of education has no teleology beyond its own sustainability. 'Once there is no longer a distinction to be made between the processes of bare life and living the good life (between means and ends), living the good life may itself be measured by participation or non-participation in the processes themselves' (Conroy, 2004, p. 23). Understood here, 'bare life' suggests the condition of survival; that is, the wresting from the earth of what it is that we think we need. Initially this consisted in hunting and gathering, then husbandry and, more recently, the exchange of labour. Emerging alongside these necessities was an evolving conception of the good life. The Greeks, no less than subsequent generations, were able to distinguish the necessities of life from such notions of the good life. Most recently, the advent of the knowledge economy has displaced traditional forms of exchange in the acquisition of material goods. Learning, once seen, at least in significant part, as a means of understanding and progressing the good life, is now considered the means by which we survive. The process of learning as a means to cultivating the good life becomes indistinguishable from survival, and the good life itself becomes measured against participation in these processes. So it is that children are invited (though the invitation looks more like a command) into a world of lifelong learning which, with its rhetoric of 'learning how to learn' as the only means of living successfully in the world, condemns them always to defer learning about the substantive and/or normative claims to be made about the world.

The evolution of metacognitive processes as pedagogical ends, within which the domain of P4C resides, carries the danger of supplanting a key, if not the most important, end of education, the cultivation of wisdom. Of course, and here I agree with Murris and Long, wisdom is no more assured or complete in children than the capacity to map concepts and abstract principles. Wisdom has to be nurtured and cultivated; it may have humble beginnings but it is something for which we strive, knowing as we do so that many of our formulations are incomplete and partial. But wisdom cannot be cultivated by questioning and argument alone, however sophisticated the pedagogy may be. The problem with questioning is that it is perfectly possible to go through exercise after exercise in thinking about a particular issue and still remain bereft of the capacities of discernment and wisdom. Were this not the case many of our political, cultural, religious and educational leaders would offer evidence of rather more wisdom than is often the case. Of course teachers should always be seeking to improve the capacities of students to understand and manipulate abstract concepts, and we know that too often in the past such capacities have not been effectively nurtured (Kerry, 1980); but philosophical wisdom will not be gleaned from mere conversations in the classroom, which are too often solipsistic and self-referential. Even where students do develop sophisticated analytical skills as a consequence of the approach advocated by Murris and Long, this will not be a sufficient condition for the creation of a student body that is philosophically educated. Something else, I suggest, is required.

Here I wish to return to the lines of Heaney's poem with which I opened this essay. When the poet observes that 'Virtue went forth from its very shipshapeness', this is an exacting claim. In addition to those writers on whom he meditates, Heaney's bookcase is no doubt replete with vellum and morocco bound copies of Aristophanes and Cicero, Dante, Donne and Shakespeare, Beckett and Goethe. For Heaney the poet, the bookcase is no thing made out of wood, no ordinary piece of furniture; it is more than a depository, a somewhere to store things. Rather it is a repository of thought, reflection and insight. It contains his 'word hoard'; a place to call up rememberings and reminiscences (the Yeats of memory) as well as a resource to give voice and shape to his musings (the Hardy of the voice). The bookcase is no haphazard collection of inchoate cultural artefacts but is shipshape – that is, it embodies something akin to coherence. In this case it is the coherence of 'modern' poetry in the English language. There is connectedness in the volumes and in their being held together in that which enables and facilitates order; indeed, arguably it is order that enables or facilitates the browser to return to a particular spot in the row of books to remember and recollect what it was to which the volume brought one's attention. Access to the form and shape of a culture is contingent on knowing where to look. While the 'virtue' of serendipity must not be underestimated, neither must it be over-claimed. The issue at stake is quite simple. If philosophy is the capacity to create clarity and insight then it may be necessary to see through the muddle. It is not enough to get children to think analytically. That may be a necessary but it is certainly not a sufficient condition for the emergence of wisdom. In our anxiety to direct our attention to the future we have too readily turned our back on the cultural resources of the past. Novelty has too easily displaced rootedness.

Harold Bloom's *Where Shall Wisdom Be Found?* (2004) opens up the literature of great thinkers from across the ages, from the earliest wisdom literature through Goethe and Johnson, Freud and Proust and back again to St. Augustine. What Bloom attempts is the sketching of a topography of wisdom which issues out of the great literature of the ages as an antidote to those 'debasements of wisdom traditions [which] flood the marketplace [where] pop divas flaunt red strings that purport to be Kabbalistic, thus invoking the hidden lore of the Zohar, the masterwork of Jewish eroticism' (Bloom, 2004, p. 2). In all of this he argues that we learn to read from Augustine who first establishes the relationship between reading and memory, where life becomes text. Always, he suggests, 'we remain the progeny of Augustine, who first told us that the book alone could nourish thought, memory and their intricate interplay in the life of the mind. Reading alone will not save us or make us wise, but without it we will lapse into the death-in-life of the dumbing down in which America now leads the world, as in all other matters' (ibid., p. 278).

If children are to become adults they need some kind of enduring wisdom. In that future, novelty-oriented way we have been discussing there is a contemporary view that wisdom is mere transience, an ability to be part of the zeitgeist, to read the signs of the times, to understand fashions and trends whether these be in economics and politics or clothing and music. All we have to do is maintain and sustain what is relevant to the here and now. In this sense we are exhorted by educationalists and politicians, relying on those half-digested gobbets of Dewey and Piaget, or more recently Rorty, to accept and predicate our pedagogies on the pragmatic turn. Perhaps somewhat ironically, Rorty, the arch pragmatist, nonetheless wishes to retain some attachment to our cultural pillars manifest in the great books tradition in the school curriculum. He does so because he wishes to distinguish between socialization and individuation, with primary and secondary schools being the locus for the former and higher education the site for the latter. Time enough to discover one's individuality and exercise the capacity to overthrow established models of signification and explanation when one goes to university, since 'freedom cannot begin before some constraints have been imposed' (Rorty, 1999, p. 118). More importantly here he also recognizes that Dewey's imagined educational and political world suffered from his too quick rejection of a substantial curriculum content predicated on 'knowing stuff'. As Rorty has it:

> I doubt if it ever occurred to Dewey that a day would come when students could graduate from an American high school not knowing who came first, Plato or Shakespeare, Napoleon or Lincoln, Fredrick Douglass or Martin Luther King, Jr. Dewey too hastily assumed that nothing would ever stop the schools from piling on the information and that the only problem was to get them to do other things as well . . . (ibid., p. 121)

Rorty is hardly the only philosopher of a distinctly pragmatic bent to think that the substantial historical traditions of philosophical and cultural writing should be retained in school (Greene, 1995; Gingell and Brandon, 2000). There is however a weakness in his argument and one that is carefully exposed by Rosenow (1998). For Rorty, there is no absolute or essence, no final formulation or stipulative account of being. Everything is radically contingent and is subject to constant re-formulation, and as such great works of literature and philosophy offer no access to the kind of wisdom for which Bloom searches. Instead, as a liberal ironist, he constantly expands the number of possible vocabularies and cultural determinations of human being. Philosophy offers no real help here. It is merely another vocabulary, ideologically compromised and unable to offer any kind of Archimedean point. The only thing the ironist can do is cultivate their sensitivity to all the other possibilities in the hope that some kind of solidarity with others might be achieved. This gives rise to a conflict. How is Rorty to deal with the conflict in his thought between the needs for the socialization of school children and for the erotic encounter of college or university students with radical contingency? Rosenow suggests that he can only resolve this tension by holding fast to a distinction between the public and private domains. Socialization in school is a work in and for the public domain; irony is the task of the private person. Such a distinction simply can't work since, as Geuss (2001) and others have amply illustrated, there is no hermetically sealed public sphere immune to the predations of private irony. The attempt to distinguish public from private in education is doomed. Rorty can offer no persuasive case for suggesting that children should be exposed to the great thinkers of the cultural tradition within which one is nurtured. Better to admit defeat and return to the pragmatist's response of cultivating competence.

It is as a result of the deficiencies in Rorty's position that we need to look elsewhere if we are to make a case for the retention, nay introduction, of reading real books as a way of engaging in philosophical reflection in the context of the classroom. Education is both a public and a private activity and embodies public and private goals, and we may not easily disaggregate the ways in which it is so. We do, for example, want students to be wise on their own account, because this is likely to ensure that their lives are less troubled and more fulfilled. Equally, we want this for them because, as wise adults, they will contribute in a variety of ways to the common good. It would be difficult in practice to discriminate between these goals. Commenting on Oakeshott's aphorism that education is (or should be) a conversation between generations, Pring suggests that such a conversation should be 'embedded within literature, drama, oral traditions and narratives, [and] artefacts' (Pring, 2001, p. 109). All of these bear on the cultivation of wisdom, bringing together as they do insights from great philosophical, literary and poetical works. If classrooms are not sites of invitation into the lifeworlds and thought patterns of those who have contemplated some of the richest and most vital questions of being then they must always be condemned to be less than they might be. The task of the teacher, Pring reminds us, is to mediate to students the generalized insights of our cultural depository so that they may cultivate the dispositions of wisdom and discernment. But this is not just a private matter. Pring also recognizes that citizenship education aims at those very things that arise out of the considered study of the humanities. Clearly Pring does not subscribe to Rorty's claims that these cultural resources are contingent, seeing them rather as embodying certain insights into human being.

Of course there is an element of contingency in as much as great books are written in particular contexts and the language used and topics addressed are often subject to such particularities. But this is no reason to suggest, as Rorty might, that the insights articulated cannot transcend the contexts of their emergence. While it is fashionable to discount Kantian universalism, it should be remembered that his principle of the 'good will' finds much earlier expression in the Christian scriptures. Moreover, it is difficult to imagine an action one might justifiably wish to take that involved treating another in a way one was not prepared to be treated oneself. While the *Foundations of the Metaphysics of Morals* may not be suitable reading in the primary school, it should not be dismissed as a resource in the secondary school.

The choice of great books is not an arbitrary one. This does not mean that there is not a great deal from which to choose, nor does it mean that the canon is singular and fixed. But it does mean that the judgements we make about X or Y are considered. 'Every culture is characterized by a central stream or tradition of works that have not merely 'stood the test of time' but which continue to serve as models and inspirations for living practitioners' (Scruton, 2007, p. 4). Roger Scruton offers an interesting analysis of how we might understand judgement in this context. The habit of laughter is not, he suggests, immune from the exercise of judgement since one may deem a joke to be in poor taste or inappropriate. Indeed, he argues, to laugh at something is already to have made a judgement. So it is with those books to which children might or should be introduced. We make judgements which are not arbitrary but which are about appropriateness. Moreover, when new sources of insight from other, say migrant, cultures enter the western liberal democratic culture, these too are accommodated. Indeed, we are apt to think that those cultures which fail to allow other voices to appear in their public spaces are deficient in some important respects. In the domain of philosophical education, traditional texts (or at least, in the preliminary stages, parts of such texts) need to be made available to students so that they can begin the process of assessing their own reflections against those of the tradition.

I wish to return here to where I began this essay: the cult of relevance which infects so much educational discourse and practice. Scruton puts it thus:

It is one of the most deeply rooted superstitions of our age that the purpose of education is to benefit those who receive it. What we teach in school, what subjects we encourage in universities, and the methods of instruction, are all subject to the one overarching test: what do the kids get out of it? (Scruton, 2007, p. 28)

Against this common superstition he argues that the true teacher has a passion to pass on knowledge. The methods of the true teacher are not spuriously child-centred but follow the pattern of the things to be understood. Relevance is too facile a game and the consequences of playing it are serious not only for the individual but for the culture and polity as a whole. We need to introduce children to the ideas contained in great books, along with the particular expression of those ideas, because in so doing we do not leave them prey to their solipsism. However good the discussion in class, however dexterous the teacher in pushing the conceptual boundaries, should that be all there is then students are left perilously close to thinking that they understand concept X or Y, disposition P or Q. We need to teach students to measure their own thoughts against those great thinkers who have wrestled with the intellectual challenges of the ages. The tradition of important texts to which children should be introduced includes those properly designated as philosophical texts. The popularity of *Sophie's World* among children at the late primary/early secondary stage would suggest that, thoughtfully presented and taught, complex philosophical ideas are not beyond the intellectual reach of children. But the boundary between philosophical and literary texts should not be too sharply drawn. It is, after all, no accident that philosophers from Camus and Sartre to Murdoch have engaged simultaneously in philosophical and literary reflections. Indeed the aphoristic style of Nietzsche, the prophet of much thinking in late industrial and post-modern philosophical circles, is nothing if not literary. Both *Lord of the Flies* and *Lord of the Rings* open up important philosophical questions about good, and evil, power and authority; questions that are asked in more formal philosophical ways by Plato and Aristotle. Is the Prince of Denmark's confrontation with death any less philosophically compelling than Heidegger's treatment of it in *Being and Time*? Is not Aristophanes' excoriating treatment of corrupt politicians in the *Archanians* not the embodied reason and justification for Aristotle's concern to describe, analyse and prescribe a set of relations conducive to a workable and ethical politics?

If philosophy properly abstracts from our experience in order to make some generalizable claims about how we are to describe and make clear to ourselves our speaking and being, then literature re-engages the particular so that we can make such generalizations our own. Moreover, the particular to which we are directed points out the proximate relationship between our reflections and our feelings. Indeed, if we are to glean anything from Kierkegaard's entanglements with the German idealists it is that our philosophical and personal commitments are entwined. An introduction to philosophical texts can offer a transcendent structure to children's thinking; a correlative engagement with literature can promote comprehension of the implications of the philosophical generalizations. Arnold Weinstein offers an eloquent defence of literature as an intellectual, philosophic and affective resource upon which we should draw precisely because, like philosophy proper, it presses on the bounded space of personal limitation. 'The space of art', he suggests, 'yields a view of human reality as something networked, criss-crossed with ties and bonds, quite at odds with the individuated world we take to be real; our private body and mind as the fixed enclosure where we think we live as individuals' (Weinstein, 2003, XXIV–V). Teaching in the classroom demands attention to both the philosophic and the literary as necessary partners in the cultivation of wisdom.

In this way we teach children not only that wisdom requires time and space but that they are part of a tradition of thought which is not arbitrary but emerges out of shared conversation. It has been no part of the argument here that the cultivation of wisdom is the only purpose of education, or that great books should be the only concern of the teacher; but if the cultivation of wisdom is a central aim of education then it would be promiscuous to ignore the rich heritage of great philosophical and literary works. It is increasingly common to see in the philosophical literature references to 'boot strap rationality' (Bratman, 1981; Birrer, 1999), as a claim that we must start afresh each time with some contingent assumption and develop our particular social, cultural and ethical claim from there. How wasteful!

Note

[1] One anecdote, which might be repeated ad nauseam, will serve to illustrate the problem here. Recently an examination question asked students, 'What is a moon?' One student's written response was, 'A moon is a body of matter which circles around a planet.' The answer was deemed wrong and no marks awarded because the student had failed to use the word, 'satellite' and, since 'satellite' was in the marking scheme this was the only acceptable answer!

Bibliography

Abbs, P. (1993) 'On intellectual research as Socratic activity', in P. Abbs (ed), *Socratic Education*, Hull: University of Hull.

Alexander, R. (2006) *Towards Dialogic Teaching: Rethinking Classroom Talk* (Third Edition), Cambridge: Dialogos.

Arendt, H. (1954) 'The crisis in education', at http://www.eco.utexas.edu/facstaff/ Cleaver/350kPEEArendtCrisisInEdTable.pdf (retrieved September 2007).

Arizpe, E. and Styles, M. (2003) *Children Reading Pictures: Interpreting Visual Texts*, London: RoutledgeFalmer.

Asch, S. (1951) 'Effects of group pressure upon the modification and distortion of judgements', in H. Guetzkow (ed), *Groups, Leadership and Men*, Pittsburgh: Carnegie Press.

Augustine *Confessions*. Edition: trans. R. S. Pine-Coffin, London: Penguin, 1961.

Austin, J. L. (1952) 'How to talk', in J. L. Austin (1979) *Philosophical Papers* (Third Edition), Oxford: Oxford University Press.

Austin, J. L. (1956) 'A plea for excuses', in J. L. Austin (1979) *Philosophical Papers* (Third Edition), Oxford: Oxford University Press.

Ayer, A. J. (1956) *The Problem of Knowledge*, Harmondsworth: Penguin.

Baddeley, P. and Eddershaw, C. (1994) *Not So Simple Picturebooks: Developing Responses to Literature with 4–12 Year Olds*, Stoke-on-Trent: Trentham.

Baggini, J. (2007) 'What the clash of civilizations is really about', *The Guardian*, 14 April 2007.

Bailin, S. and Siegel, H. (2003) 'Critical thinking', in N. Blake, P. Smeyers, R. Smith and P. Standish (eds), *The Blackwell Guide to the Philosophy of Education*, Oxford: Blackwell.

Bambrough, R. (1969) *Reason, Truth and God*, London: Methuen.

Barrow, R. (1993) *Language, Intelligence and Thought*, Hants: Edward Elgar.

Baum, F. L. (1999) *The Wizard of Oz*, New York: HarperCollins.

Bettleheim, B. (1989) *The Uses of Enchantment: The Meaning and Importance of Fairy Tales*, New York: Vintage.

Birrer, F. A. J. (1999) 'Sustainability, democracy, and sociocybernetics', *Kybernetes* 28(6/7), 810–20.

Blackburn, S. (2005) *The Oxford Dictionary of Philosophy* (Second Edition), Oxford: Oxford University Press.

Bloom, A. (1987) *The Closing of the American Mind*, New York: Touchstone.

Bloom, H. (2004) *Where Shall Wisdom Be Found?*, New York: Riverhead Books.

Bonnett, M. (1995) 'Teaching thinking and the sanctity of content', *Journal of Philosophy of Education* 29(3), 295–309.

Bonnett, M. and Cuypers, S. (2003) 'Autonomy and authenticity in education', in N. Blake, P. Smeyers, R. Smith and P. Standish (eds), *The Blackwell Guide to the Philosophy of Education*, Oxford: Blackwell.

Bratman, M. (1981) 'Intention and means-end reasoning', *The Philosophical Review* 90(2), 252–65.

Bruner, J. (1960) *The Process of Education*, Cambridge: Harvard University Press.

Buckreis, S. (2005) 'Questioning with Derrida', paper presented at the Philosophy of Education Society of Great Britain Annual Conference, Oxford, April 2005.

Cam, P. (1995) *Thinking Together: Philosophical Inquiry for the Classroom*, Sydney: Hale and Iremonger/PETA.

Carroll, L. (1981) *Alice's Adventures in Wonderland and Through the Looking-Glass*, New York: Bantam.

Churchland, P. M. (1996) 'Folk psychology', in P. M. Churchland and P. S. Churchland (1998) *On the Contrary: Critical Essays 1987–1997*, Cambridge: MIT Press.

Conroy, J. (2004) *Betwixt and Between: the Liminal Imagination, Education and Democracy*, New York: Peter Lang.

Davidson, D. (1963) 'Actions, reasons and causes', *The Journal of Philosophy* 60(23), 685–700.

De Bono, E. (1969) *The Mechanism of Mind*, Middlesex: Penguin.

De Bono, E. (1970) *The Dog-Exercising Machine*, Middlesex: Penguin.

De Bono, E. (1976) *Teaching Thinking*, London: Maurice Temple Smith.

De Bono, E. (1992) *Teach Your Child How to Think*, London: Viking.

De Bono, E. (1995) *Teach Yourself to Think*, London: Viking.

Dennett, D. (2006) *Breaking the Spell: Religion as a Natural Phenomenon*, London: Viking.

DfEE (1999) *The National Curriculum Handbook for Secondary Teachers in England*, London: DfEE.

DfES (2004) *The National Curriculum Handbook for Secondary Teachers in England*, London: DfES.

DfES (2005) 'Thinking skills in primary classrooms', at www.standards.dfes.gov.uk/thinkingskills (retrieved December 2005).

Doonan, J. (1993) *Looking at Pictures in Picturebooks*, Stroud: Thimble Press.

Egan, K. (2002) *Getting It Wrong from the Beginning: Our Progressivist Inheritance from Herbert Spencer and Jean Piaget*, New Haven, CT: Yale University Press.

Eliot, L. (1999) *What's Going on in There?: How the Brain and Mind Develop in the First Five Years of Life*, New York: Bantam.

Ennis, R. H. (1962) 'A concept of critical thinking', *Harvard Educational Review* 32(1), 81–111.

Ennis, R. H. (2004) *Critical Thinking*, at www.criticalthinking.net. (Last accessed 4 October 2007).

Field, T. (1995) 'Philosophy for Children and the feminist critique of reason in critical and creative thinking', *Australasian Journal of Philosophy for Children* 3(1), 9–12.

Fisher, R. (1996) *Stories for Thinking*, Oxford: Nash Pollock.

Fisher, R. (2003a) *Teaching Thinking: Philosophical Enquiry in the Classroom* (Second Edition), London: Continuum.

Fisher, R. (2003b) 'Kid's stuff?', *The Philosopher's Magazine* 24(4), 33.

Fisher, R. (2005a) *Teaching Children to Think* (Second Edition), Cheltenham: Stanley Thornes.

Fisher, R. (2005b) *Teaching Children to Learn* (Second Edition), Cheltenham: Stanley Thornes.

Flew, A. (1989) *A Introduction to Western Philosophy* (Revised Edition), London: Thames and Hudson.

Gaarder, J. (1995) *Sophie's World*, London: Phoenix House.

Gardner, H. (1983) *Frames of Mind*, New York: Basic Books.

Gardner, H. (1999) *Intelligence Reframed*, New York: Basic Books.

Geschwindt, S. (2007) *Am I Right or Am I Right?*, Calgary: Trafford.

Geuss, R. (2001) *Public Goods, Private Goods*, Princeton: Princeton University Press.

Gingell, J. and Brandon, E. P. (2000) *In Defence of High Culture*, a special issue of *Journal of Philosophy of Education* 34(3).

Gopnik, A., Meltzoff, A. N. and Kuhl, P. K. (2001) *The Scientist in the Crib: What Early Learning Tells Us About the Mind*, New York: Perennial.

Greene, M. (1995) *Releasing the Imagination: Essays on Education, the Arts, and Social Change*, San Francisco: Jossey-Bass.

Hand, M. (2004) 'What is RE for?', in the IPPR Event Report *What Is Religious Education For? Getting the National Framework Right*, at http://www.ippr.org/uploadedFiles/research/events/Education/RE%20Event%20Report.pdf (retrieved June 2007).

Hare, R. M. (1964) *The Language of Morals*, Oxford: Oxford University Press.

Hare, R. M. (1973) 'Language and moral education', in G. Langford and D. J. O'Connor (eds), *New Essays in the Philosophy of Education*, London: Routledge and Kegan Paul.

Haynes, J. (2002) *Children as Philosophers*, London: Routledge.

Haynes, J. (2005) 'The costs of thinking', *Teaching Thinking and Creativity*, Issue 17, Autumn 2005.

Haynes, J. (2007) *'Listening as a Critical Practice: Learning from Philosophy with Children'*, (unpublished PhD thesis, University of Exeter).

Haynes, J. and Murris, K. (2006) 'The wrong message', paper presented at the Philosophy of Education Society of Great Britain Annual Conference, Oxford, April 2006.

Hextall, M. (2006) 'Leicester's youngest philosophers', in *SAPERE Newsletter May 2006*, Oxford: Westminster Institute of Education, 8–9.

Hickman, L. A. and Alexander, T. M. (1998) *The Essential Dewey* (Vol. 1), Bloomington: Indiana University Press.

Higgins, S. and Baumfield, V. (1998) 'A defence of teaching general thinking skills', *Journal of Philosophy of Education* 32(3), 391–398.

Holmes, E. (1911) *What Is and What Might Be*, London: Constable.

Honderich, T. (1995) *The Oxford Companion to Philosophy*, Oxford: Oxford University Press.

Hume, D. (1739) *A Treatise on Human Nature*. Edition: Harmondsworth: Penguin, 1985.

Hunt, P. (1999) *Understanding Children's Literature*, London: Routledge.

ICPIC (2006a) *ICPIC Newsletter Winter 2006*, at http://www.icpic.org/images/stories/skjol/newsletter2006.pdf (retrieved October 2007).

ICPIC (2006b) *ICPIC Newsletter Fall 2006*, at http://www.icpic.org/images/stories/skjol/newsletter%20fall%202006.pdf (retrieved October 2007).

Jackson, F. (1998) *From Metaphysics to Ethics: a Defence of Conceptual Analysis*, Oxford: Clarendon Press.

Johnson, S. (2001) *Teaching Thinking Skills* (Impact No. 8), Hants: PESGB.

Kant, I. (1781) *Critique of Pure Reason.* Edition: trans. N. Kemp Smith, London: Palgrave Macmillan, 2003.

Kelly, A. V. (1995) *Education and Democracy,* London: Paul Chapman.

Kerry, T. (1980) 'The demands made by RE on pupils' thinking', *British Journal of Religious Education* 3(2), 46–52.

Klein, P. R. (2003) 'Rethinking the multiplicity of cognitive resources and curricular representations: alternatives to learning styles and multiple intelligences', *Journal of Curriculum Studies* 35(1), 45–81.

Kohlberg, L. (1981) *Essays on Moral Development Vol. II: the Philosophy of Moral Development,* San Francisco: Harper and Row.

Law, S. (2006) *The War for Children's Minds,* London: Routledge.

Levinson, R., Douglas, A., Evans, J., Kirton, A., Koulouris, P., Turner, S. and Finegold, P. (2000) 'Constraints on teaching the social and ethical issues arising from developments in biomedical research', *Melbourne Studies in Education* 41(2), 107–120.

Lipman, M. (1988) *Philosophy Goes to School,* Philadephia: Temple University Press.

Lipman, M. (1991) *Thinking in Education,* New York: Cambridge University Press.

Lipman, M. (1997) 'Special Report to the APA Committee on Pre-College Instruction in Philosophy', *Proceedings and Addresses of the American Philosophical Association* 70(5).

Lipman, M. (2003) *Thinking in Education* (Second Edition), Cambridge: Cambridge University Press.

Lipman, M., Sharp, A. M. and Oscanyan, F. S. (1980) *Philosophy in the Classroom* (Second Edition), Philadelphia: Temple University Press.

Long, F. (2005) 'Thomas Reid and philosophy with children', *Journal of Philosophy of Education* 39 (4), 599–614.

Marquis, D. (1989) 'Why abortion is immoral', in *Journal of Philosophy* 86(4), 183–202.

Mason, M. (2005) 'Philosophy – can't live with it, can't live without it', *Think* 10, 35–41.

Masschelein, J. (2001) 'The discourse of the learning society and the loss of childhood', *Journal of Philosophy of Education* 35(1), 1–20.

Matthews, G. (1980) *Philosophy and the Young Child,* Cambridge: Harvard University Press.

Matthews, G. (1984) *Dialogues with Children,* Cambridge: Harvard University Press.

Matthews, G. (1994) *The Philosophy of Childhood,* Cambridge: Harvard University Press.

Matthews, G. (2003) *Socratic Perplexity and the Nature of Philosophy,* Oxford: Oxford University Press.

Mautner, T. (2005) 'Philosophy', in T. Mautner (ed), *The Penguin Dictionary of Philosophy* (Second Edition), London: Penguin.

McCall, C. (2007) 'Philosophical inquiry and lifelong learning: life, the universe and everything', *Proceedings of the International Conference on Dialogue, Culture and Philosophy, Graz, 2006,* Sankt Augustin: Academia Verlag.

McGuiness, C. (1999) *From Thinking Skills to Thinking Classrooms: a Review and Evaluation of Approaches for Developing Pupils' Thinking* (Research Report No. 115), London: DfES.

McPeck, J. E. (1981) *Critical Thinking and Education*, New York: St. Martin's Press.

Midgley, D. (ed) (2005) *The Essential Mary Midgley*, Abingdon: Routledge.

Midgley, M. (1992) 'Philosophical plumbing', in A. Phillips Griffiths (ed), *The Impulse to Philosophise*, Cambridge: Cambridge University Press.

Millett, S. (2006) 'Coming in from the margins: teaching philosophy in Australian schools', paper presented at the Philosophy in Schools: Developing a Community of Inquiry Conference, Singapore, April 2006.

Milne, A. A. (1992a) *The House at Pooh Corner*, New York: Puffin Books.

Milne, A. A. (1992b) *Winnie-the-Pooh*, New York: Puffin Books.

Murris, K. (1992) *Teaching Philosophy with Picturebooks*, London: Infonet Publications.

Murris, K. (1997) 'Metaphors of the Child's Mind: Teaching Philosophy to Young Children', (unpublished PhD thesis, University of Hull).

Murris, K. (2000) 'Can children do philosophy?', *Journal of Philosophy of Education* 34(2), 261–279.

Murris, K. and Haynes, J. (2000) *Storywise: Thinking through Stories*, Newport, Dialogue Works .

Nodelman, P. (1999) 'Decoding the images: illustration and picturebooks', in J. Stephens (ed), *Language and Ideology in Children's Fiction*, London: Longman.

Nodelman, P. and Reimer, M. (2003) *The Pleasures of Children's Literature* (Third Edition), Boston: Allyn and Bacon.

Nussbaum, M. (1990) *Love's Knowledge: Essays on Philosophy and Literature*, Oxford: Oxford University Press.

OECD (2001) *Investing in Competencies for All* (Report of meeting of OECD Education Ministers, Paris, April 2001), at http://www.olis.oecd.org/olis/2001doc.nsf/c707a7b4806fa95dc125685d005300b6/c1256985004c66e3c1256a2400438793/$FILE/JT00105480.PDF (retrieved August 2007).

OECD (2006) *Schooling for Tomorrow: Think Scenarios, Rethink Education*, Paris: OECD Publications.

Peters, R. S. (1977) 'John Dewey's philosophy of education', in R. S. Peters (ed.), *John Dewey Reconsidered*, London: Routledge.

Peters, R. S. (1966) 'The philosophy of education', in J. W. Tibble (ed), *The Study of Education*, London: Routledge and Kegan Paul.

Phillips, M. (1996) *All Must Have Prizes*, London: Warner Books.

Phillips, M. (2004) 'The subversion of religion and morals', at http://www.melaniephillips.com/diary/archives/000330.html (retrieved April 2007).

Plato, *Euthyphro*. Edition: trans. H. Tarrant, London: Penguin Classics, 1993.

Pring, R. (2001) 'Education as a moral practice', *Journal of Moral Education* 30(2), 101–112.

Ratzinger, J. (2005) 'Homily at the mass for the election of the Roman Pontiff', at http://insidethevatican.com/newsflash-apr18-05.htm (retrieved April 2007).

Rawls, J. (1972) *A Theory of Justice*, Oxford: Clarendon Press.

Reed, R. (1983) *Talking with Children*, Denver: Arden Press.

Rorty, R. (1999) *Philosophy and Social Hope*, Harmondsworth: Penguin.

Rosenow, E. (1998) 'Toward an aesthetic education: Rorty's conception of education', *Journal of Philosophy of Education* 32(2), 253–265.

Ryle, G. (1949) *The Concept of Mind.* Edition: London, Penguin, 1990.

Sacks, J. (1997) *The Politics of Hope,* London: Jonathan Cape.

Sandel, M. (2007) *The Case Against Perfection,* Cambridge: Harvard University Press.

Schaler J. A. (ed) (2006) *Gardner Under Fire: The Rebel Psychologist Faces His Critics,* Chicago: Open Court Publishing Co.

Scheffler, I. (1989) *Reason and Teaching,* Indianapolis: Hackett.

Scottish Executive Education Department (2004) *A Curriculum for Excellence: the Curriculum Review Group,* at http://www.scotland.gov.uk/Publications/2004/11/20178/45862 (retrieved August 2007).

Scruton, R. (2007) *Culture Counts: Faith and Feeling in a World Besieged,* New York: Encounter Books.

Sellars, W. (1956) 'Empiricism and the philosophy of mind', in H. Feigl and M. Scriven (eds), *The Foundations of Science and the Concepts of Psychology and Psychoanalysis, Vol. I,* Minneapolis: University of Minnesota Press.

Sendak, M. (1984) *Where the Wild Things Are,* New York: Harper and Row.

Sharp, A. M. (1992) 'Women, children and the evolution of Philosophy for Children', in A. M. Sharp and R. F. Reed (eds), *Studies in Philosophy for Children: Harry Stottlemeier's Discovery,* Philadelphia: Temple University Press.

Siegel, H. (1988) *Educating Reason: Rationality, Critical Thinking, and Education,* London: Routledge.

Siegel, H. (1992) 'On defining 'critical thinker' and justifying critical thinking', *Philosophy of Education Yearbook 1992,* 72–75.

Siegel, H. (1997) *Rationality Redeemed?: Further Dialogues on an Educational Ideal,* New York: Routledge.

Siegel, H. (2003) 'Cultivating reason', in R. Curren (ed), *A Companion to the Philosophy of Education,* Oxford: Blackwell.

Splitter, L. J. and Sharp, A. M. (1995) *Teaching for Better Thinking: the Classroom Community of Enquiry,* Melbourne: ACER.

Standish, P. (2005) 'The ownership of learning', paper presented at the Philosophy of Education Society of Great Britain Annual Conference, Oxford, April 2005.

Stanley, S. and Bowkett, S. (2004) *But Why? Developing Philosophical Thinking in the Classroom,* London: Network Educational Press.

Stephens, J. (ed) (1992) *Language and Ideology in Children's Fiction,* London: Longman.

Strawson, P. F. (1959) *Individuals: an Essay in Descriptive Metaphysics,* London: Routledge.

Styles, M., Bearne, E. and Watson, V. (eds) (1996) *Voices Off: Texts, Contexts and Readers,* London: Cassell.

Tate, N. (1996) Speech to the Schools Curriculum and Assessment Authority (SCAA), 15 January 1996.

Taylor, K. (2005) 'Thought Crime', *The Guardian,* 8 October 2005.

Thomson, J. J. (1971) 'A defence of abortion', *Philosophy and Public Affairs* 1(1).

Trickey, S. and Topping, K. J. (2004) 'Philosophy for children: a systematic review', *Research Papers in Education* 19(3), 365–380.

Velthuijs, M. (1989) *Frog in Love,* London: Andersen Press.

Wallen, M. (ed) (1990) *Every Picture Tells. . . . : Picture Books as a Resource for Learning in all Age Groups*, Exeter: NATE.

Warburton, N. (2000) *Thinking from A to Z* (Second Edition), London: Routledge.

Weinstein, A. (2003) *A Scream Goes Through the House: What Literature Teaches Us About Life*, New York: Random House.

White, E. B. (1980) *Charlotte's Web*, New York: Harper and Row.

White, J. P. (1992) 'The roots of philosophy', in A. Phillips Griffiths (ed), *The Impulse to Philosophise*, Cambridge: Cambridge University Press.

White, J. P. (2002) *The Child's Mind*, London: Routledge.

Whitehead, A. N. (1938) *Modes of Thought*, New York: Macmillan Free Press.

Wilson, J. (1963) *Thinking with Concepts*, Cambridge: Cambridge University Press.

Wilson, J. (1992) 'Philosophy for children: a note of warning', *Thinking* 10(1), 17–18.

Winstanley, C. (2001) 'Student teachers exploring Philosophy with Children', paper presented at ICPIC Conference, Winchester, July 2001.

Winstanley, C. (2006) 'I'm a philosopher – get me out of here! Philosophy for Children and thinking skills programmes', paper presented at the Philosophy of Education Society of Great Britain Annual Conference, Oxford, April 2006.

Wittgenstein, L. (1953) *Philosophical Investigations*, Oxford: Blackwell.

Ziniewicz, G. L. (2000) *Essays on the Philosophy of John Dewey*, at http://www.fred.net/ tzaka/democ.html (retrieved April 2007).

Index